Making Managers
Universities and (

SRHE and Open University Press Imprint
General Editor: Heather Eggins

Making Managers
in Universities
and Colleges

Craig Prichard

The Society for Research into Higher Education
& Open University Press

Published by SRHE and
Open University Press
Celtic Court
22 Ballmoor
Buckingham
MK18 1XW

email: enquiries@openup.co.uk
world wide web: http://www.openup.co.uk

and
325 Chestnut Street
Philadelphia, PA 19106, USA

First published 2000

A catalogue record of this book is available from the British Library

ISBN 0 335 20485 6 (pb)   0 335 20486 4 (hb)

Library of Congress Cataloging-in-Publication Data
   Prichard, Craig, 1962–
      Making managers in universities and colleges / Craig Prichard.
         p.   cm.
      Includes bibliographical references and index.
      ISBN 0-335-20486 4
      ISBN 0-335 20485-6 (pbk.)
      1. Management–Study and teaching.   2. Executives–Training of.   I. Title.
   HD30.4 .P753   2000
   658′.0071′1–dc21   99–41464
                                                                       CIP

Typeset by Graphicraft Limited, Hong Kong
Printed in Great Britain by St Edmundsbury Press, Bury St Edmunds, Suffolk

For my grandparents, Doreen and Bill Kerr,
Margaret and Percy Prichard; my parents, Marie
and Grahame and for Mary, Tasmin and Morgan

Contents

Preface

In writing this book two issues have arisen which I should like to address here. The first is a question of managerial levels, the second is the difference between further and higher education.

In relation to the first, the conceptual framework drawn on in this book *appears* not to recognize what some regard as a key point of *differentiation* between people in senior positions in colleges and universities – that is, the range of management 'levels', or put slightly differently, the differences in attitudes and behaviour of different levels of manager. This is a significant point. Yet the point both reflects a different approach to knowledge about managers, and strikes at the very basis of the conceptual framework which I have put forward. Let me be clear: 'management' in this framework is a general set of techniques of budget, audit and planning together with a range of discursive practices which disperse and reinforce these (e.g. meetings, interviews, etc.), and a whole raft of other interpersonal communicational practices. Of course the suffusion of these practices can be read as an effect of resource constraint (Williams, 1992). But *how* this is enacted and comes to be known is through these practices. The point is that rather than defining management as a set of levels in an organizational structure – management posts – the analysis is concerned with *positionings* which are an effect of management practices. Of course this general 'set' of management practices is distributed differentially and thus has the potential (but not necessarily actual) effect of producing an organizational structure with 'levels'. At the same time, the key 'innovation' of 'managerial practices' is the way in which the same kinds of practices are 'cascaded' or dispersed out across a domain, to a point where people's individual relations to themselves come to be mediated by these practices. The point is that rather than see organizations as islands of hierarchical stability and order in an environment of uncertainty – which is the common framework – the form of analysis advocated here turns this upside down. Forms of practice 'strain', as John Law (1994a) suggests, to produce 'levels' and hierarchies.

For example, the 1992 Further and Higher Education Act constructs a positioning which produces the vice-chancellor as responsible for the sound management of an institution. Devolved accounting practices and strategic management practices adopted by most universities (Williams, 1992; Berry, 1994; Thomas, 1997) and colleges have the effect of constructing academic or service heads as 'managers' of a cost/income centre. Meanwhile, contractual practices construct 'jobs', personnel practices attempt to codify sets of tasks which are said to make up such jobs, and research reports frequently use terms like 'first line', 'middle', and 'senior managers'. All these attempt to establish the solidity of these levels. Yet it would be wrong, I would argue, to accept this 'structure' as if it were 'real'. What we have are practices which have the potential to produce structure/hierarchy/levels. It would also be wrong to assume that other knowledge practices (academic or administrative disciplines, for example) do not mediate and seek also to govern sites in ways which might undermine a department as an 'income centre' or strategically-orientated, customer-focused, small- to medium-sized business.

So, rather than insisting on structures with levels and people with attitudes and behaviours, the aim here is to discuss the tension between conflicting and overlapping discursive practices. It is through this discussion that the complex pattern of continuity and change which makes up colleges and universities can be addressed in engaging ways. One effect of taking up this framework is that the world 'looks' a far less stable place than it does if we adopt a framework which insists on formal organization and the naming and distribution of tasks and responsibilities to particular people located at particular 'levels' in an 'organization'.

Turning to the second issue, the differences between further and higher education, I want to argue that there are important similarities between the sectors. These similarities flow particularly from the new regulatory, legislative and financial practices. Of course it would be foolhardy to attempt to argue that there are not significant differences between, for instance, the small further education college in rural Suffolk and the 'mighty' civic universities of the north of England. However this is a study of the construction of 'managers', and while the differences between institutions and across institutions do produce complex patterns of changes and continuity there are overarching similarities between the sectors.

Furthermore, I think we need to be aware of what a view of strong difference between the sectors is attempting to achieve. In part it is an effect of the logic of the 'market'. But also it is an effect of a more general logic of identity (academic identity, for instance) as it is expressed during insecure times. Both these logics have the effect of inducing us to read the 'other' as strongly different or in various hierarchies of difference. Peter Scott's (1995) typography of higher education shows not just difference across the sectors and within sectors, but the numerous ways in which differentiation can be constructed. This is potentially powerful identity work. Difference between sectors or within sectors is not simply based on substantive difference in size, resources or mode of conduct. It is socially significant as a means of producing institutional, managerial and academic identity.

Earlier versions of some of the chapters which follow have appeared elsewhere. All the work has been substantially revised. The publishers (Sage Publications Ltd and Walter de Gruyter) have granted permission for the publication of this material.[1]

The work that this book reports would have been impossible without the support, guidance and in some cases collaboration of a number of people. I should like to thank Graham Kelly, John Wallace and Hugh Willmott in particular, who in many different ways and at many different times have acted as guides and supporters. As with all supporters though, their influence informs rather than determines the work. Responsibility for this lies with 'me': the 'me', as the framework adopted in this book argues, which is of course an effect of the discursive practices of authorship.

Craig Prichard
Massey University

Note

1. A version of the material found in Chapter 5's section 'The coming of the manager in post-1992 higher education' is to be published in Hassard *et al.* (eds) (forthcoming) *The Body and Organization*, London: Sage. A version of the material found in Chapter 9 has been published in Collinson and Hearn (eds) (1996) *Men as Managers, Managers as Men*, London: Sage. A version of the material found in Chapter 6 has appeared in *Organization Studies*, 16(4) as 'Just how managed is the McUniversity?', co-written with Hugh Willmott, and a version of the material found at the end of Chapter 6 has been published in *Education Management and Administration*, 24(1) as 'Making managers accountable or making managers? The case of the code for management in a higher education institution'.

Introduction

In 1996 I shall be head of department for the first time in my career. The job has become a serious management post.

(Power, 1996: x)

There is a worry if universities become too centralised, employing too many administrators speaking the new management jargon of the age, seeking to overwhelm or isolate wayward professors and heads of department.

(Redwood, 1994: 12)

Senior staff [in universities] now have management responsibilities for the equivalent of large companies – hundreds of staff and millions of pounds – and yet, despite the growth in management development for others, many resist the need to train for their new profession.

(McNay, 1994: 12)

[Sir Colin] Campbell (of Nottingham University) clearly illustrates, among other entrepreneurial characteristics, that he has strong persuasive powers, risk-taking ability, creativity . . . Campbell's joint credibility as a manager and academic does seem to set him apart.

(Boyett, 1996: 44)

Among the old universities, Nottingham has led the field in the new managerialism. It hopes to improve the relationship between administration and academics. It needs to. Sir Colin Campbell describes his critics as a 'malevolent clique of malcontents' and they say privately that he is 'a vindictive bully'.

(Beckett, 1994: 5)

Personal leadership has its place, but any window of opportuntity for top down policy which can be created, generally does not last very long in a university. It is common experience that anything worth doing requires a number of people who want it to happen, and who often have to work at it for a number of years. And, there is a real problem in mixing academic values (as defined by the academic staff) with the organizational structure and the influence of the new kind of managerial values.

(Hammond, 1999)

There's far too much complaining that the funding isn't good enough, morale's low . . . let's get on with managing efficiently the resources that we now have. FE must become smaller, leaner and fitter.

(Ward, 1995a: 25)

In college after college it is possible to sense real frustration on the part of senior managers as they struggle to put their ideas and ideals into practice . . . they are becoming increasingly intolerant of any layer of the college hierarchy that delays or stands in the way of implementation of strategic decisions.

(Mansell, 1996: 13)

In July the lecturer's union NATFHE published a survey of the views of [Stoke-on-Trent] College academic staff. It said that no other survey had 'presented such a picture of arbitrary, bullying and tyrannical behaviour . . . Programme managers and above were frightened of senior management.

(Crequer, 1996: 29)

Management, as the above quotations show, has become a central feature of the flows of change across further and higher education (FHE). The term 'management', as the above quotations also show, is what Maile (1995: 86) calls a 'multi-accented signifer'. It is understood in a number of different ways, or made to mean a number of different things. At times 'management' means the colonizing source of much bullying and intimidation. At others, it is a largely autonomous, self-perpetuating and 'unreal' sphere separate from, yet challenging of, traditional normalized educational relations and practice. It is also known as an instrumental, necessary, even indispensable, component of sound educational practice in colleges and universities. This book is about the tensions between these ways of knowing 'management', and the people whose working lives have become enmeshed in this tension.

In the account of 'management' in universities and colleges which follows, 'management' is understood generally as forms of knowledge practices. These include those noted above, but more particularly the new knowledge practices or disciplines of audit, planning and budget control instituted across FHE and, in various forms, the public sector generally. These, it will be argued, are variably productive and colonizing. They reconstruct the ways in which educational practices of teaching and learning are done, talked about, thought about, even dreamed about in FHE. It is through these disciplines that the 'manager' is in part articulated and constituted. However, this articulation, this 'making of the manager' (and by necessity the *managed*) is by no means unproblematic and linear. While 'management' as a set of knowledge practices can be articulated, the 'managing' – the doing of managing to use Mangham and Pye's (1991) phrase, or the transforming of management labour into management labour power, to use Marx's term – is variably problematic, precarious and unstable. Particularly, it is at those nodal points among what the discourse describes as 'middle managers' or 'senior professionals' in colleges and universities that the problems of 'management's' colonizing trajectory are most intensely felt and elaborated. This is the central issue addressed here. The text is concerned with the nature of the problems surrounding the formation of the manager in FHE.

If, for the moment, I take up a geographical vocabulary, the book might be said to plot points where management's discourses and practices meet the flows and contours of the crumbled terrain of sedimented identities and practices. It is at these points that 'management's' efficacy as an ordering practice is tested. At some points it appears to inscribe new spaces and surfaces with ease. A head of department, a section manager, or programme coordinator, positioned by the documents of the managed college or university as a business manager responsible for delivering a certain level of activity against certain targets, speaks and enacts the disposition of the empowered educational entrepreneur (Boyett and Finlay, 1993; Gleeson and Shain, 1999). A head of department responds: 'I don't have the ability to move as fast as the manager of a small business, yet that is what I am'. At others, it appears to slide under and around existing inscriptions. A dean declares: 'I've told the executive, that if it comes to a "punch-up" I'm with the staff'. At others it becomes unhelpful and destructive: a section head recounts: 'I'm constantly caught between supporting the staff, thanking them, encouraging them, and then some thoughtless memo comes down from someone in SMT [senior management team], and it's like snakes and ladders – back to square one'.

But I have jumped the gun. It is hard to resist the appeal of these narratives. They want to be heard. Here, now, in the introduction and not deep in the text that follows. These are the voices of those who freely and in friendship gave time and space for my questions and my presence. The book draws together empirical materials from interviews, participant observation and observation in four universities and four further education (FE) colleges in the UK. I thank these people now. Inevitably they have been repositioned, not this time by the discourses of management, but by the discursive practice of a book which could not have been written without them.

I have also jumped the gun in another way. Before I can present a reading of talk and text which tells of the working lives of these people, I need to establish the framework for discussing the 'manager'. This issue forms the basis of the first two chapters. In Chapter 1 I discuss the recent literature on 'managers' in FHE. I set the scene through this discussion. In particular the scene is set between two poles of debate, between what might be regarded as the orthodox and the critical accounts. The orthodox 'manager' is regarded for instance as a necessary response to resource constraint, formalized through the detailed technologies of audits, reviews, budgets and controls. This is the Dearing Committee's 'manager' called upon to more efficiently and effectively manage higher education for the new millennium (National Committee of Inquiry into Higher Education, 1997).

The conceptualization of the 'manager' in this book begins from a different base. It challenges the smooth production and development assumed by the orthodox view. It draws on critical social science resources signalled by the terms 'dialogue and discourse', 'inscription', and 'subjectification', in order to explain how the 'manager' is not simply that which appears in organizational charts and job descriptions. The 'manager' of this 'contra' conceptualization is the carrier and connection in broader political programmes.

In the course of Chapter 2 I arrive at a focal framework which maintains some of the crucial tensions between the positions signified by such terms 'orthodox' and 'contra'.

In Chapter 3 I turn to discuss the historical, political and economic dimensions of what might be seen as the suffusion of management across FHE. I address particularly recent and current fiscal, regulatory and audit practices which have swept through these sectors.

In Chapters 4 to 9 I turn back to the narratives of the people with whom I talked and met, and the documents of 'managing'. In these six chapters I discuss in relation to further education colleges, and pre-1992 and post-1992 universities in Britain, the making of the manager, the problems surrounding this construction and the gendered dimensions of the development.

However, there are three caveats or conditions of which the reader should be aware. First, the discussion in Chapter 2 concerning 'language', the 'body' and 'subjectivity' is inevitably restricted. The literatures associated with, for example, language and subjectivity are enormous and perhaps inexhaustible sources of material. My discussion of language could have focused, for example, on any one of a large number of fields, including socio-lingistics, narratology or deconstruction. It might have dealt with, for example, post-Saussurrean linguistics, Heideggerean hermenuetics or neo-Marxian approaches to ideology. Within each of these fields the work of particular authors might have been addressed in detail – for example, Barthes' semiotics, Ricoeur's narrativity, Habermas' theory of communicative action. I do touch on some of this work, but within a restricted and limited range. The key reasons are space and the need to address the topic to which this book refers, namely the making of managers in colleges and universities.

The same point should be noted in relation to the more substantive literature presented in Chapters 3 and 4. This book could have been written in innumerable ways in relation to this literature. These chapters discuss the historical, political and economic dimensions of the suffusion of management across the terrain of FHE. The education manager – entrepreneurial, customer focused, consultative yet decisive, a first among equals (in the role's more positive gloss) – must be understood as co-dependent with an era of cuts, growth, financial deficits and intensified auditing of the public sector. Co-dependent also with the attempt by the state to reduce the costs and increase its control of public sector post-compulsory education is the enrolment and reconstruction of FHE as a service industry. Within this are numerous issues which legitimately could have been addressed. I am conscious particularly that a number of relevant chapters could have been written concerning, for instance, links between post-compulsory education and the state and the economy, or charting the professionalization of academics, administrators and managerial workers.

In general terms, however, the conceptual literature in Chapters 1 and 2 should be read as located broadly within the sociologically informed literature in management and organization studies. In terms of the substantive literature found in Chapter 1, the approach taken is to discuss, in the main, only explanatory works around 'work, organization and management' in FHE management, particularly work informed by critical, or what I have termed 'contra', perspectives.

The epistemological approach that underpins this book has within it a potential paradox. Pushed to its logical extreme, the poststructuralist approach to knowledge advanced in this book could be said to cancel itself out. There is little basis from which research can be justified or defended as producing knowledge about some entity, if one is at the same time arguing that knowledge inevitably constructs particular entities including the 'researcher'. Given this, one can hardly claim to be outside such conditions. My approach is thus a 'tempered poststructuralism'. By drawing on Fiske's (1993) work in particular, I am signalling that while I am aware of these problems I do not consider that they should simply silence the writer – or knowledge producer. I am signalling my belief and commitment to the possibility that knowledge, while constantly constitutive and political, also opens up spaces for reflexivity, distancing and difference. Through such spaces we may construct political and innovative identities other than those defined and constituted by dominant social alliances.

These issues set out the basis upon which this book has been written and, I hope, will be read. With these points in hand, I now turn to Chapter 1.

1

Making Sense of 'Managers' in Colleges and Universities

This chapter discusses and reviews the conceptual frameworks adopted by recent authors engaged in providing critically informed accounts of the reconstruction of colleges and universites in Britain. Before embarking on this however it is important to note the significant divide in the education literature. On the one hand are works that can be seen to be seeking to 'help' managers better manage difficult problems and situations. On the other are those that seek to explain, challenge or critically illuminate the problems, situations and managerial/administrative responses to these. Marsden and Townley (1996) usefully call these two strands in management and organization studies 'normal' and 'contra' approaches.

The 'normal' literature tends to provide prescriptive accounts for the 'development' of managers. It draws conceptually from contingency or systems theories of organization, or economic theories of organizational behaviour. In the education literature on colleges and universities such works include those by Davies (1989), Middlehurst (1993, 1995, 1997), Gray and Hoy (1989), Thody (1989), Warner and Crosthwaite (1995), Brodie and Partington (1992), Burton (1994), Lawrence (1995), Harper (1997) and Gorringe *et al.* (1994). The tone of this literature varies but one major criticism is that these accounts tend to ignore critical discussion of the conditions and processes which give rise to the problems to which management is considered to be a response. Another major contention is the lack of critical discussion of the problems that 'management' as the solution to such problems then presents. To take an example (an extreme example perhaps): Harriett Harper begins her 1997 book entitled *Management in Further Education: Theory and Practice* with the statement: 'Being a manager in a college is, in most respects, no different from being a manager in any other organization. The fundamental requirement for the job remains the same: to manage people, tasks and information, to allocate scarce resources, and to ensure the continual monitoring of services or products' (p. 1). Compare this with John Smyth's introduction to his 1989 article: 'Organizationally speaking, we have AIDS! The new disease that is sweeping through higher education in this country [Australia] takes the form of corporate management, a particularly nasty virus which has the potential to slowly but surely cripple and destroy the fabric of the social relationships of our organizations' (p. 143).

While the 'contra' literature might be accused of failing to provide answers to the question 'What is to be done?', its focus instead is the exploration and critique of processes that constitute, for instance, the problems for which 'management' is the taken-for-granted solution in the 'normal' literature. It is with the 'contra' literature that this chapter primarily engages. It arguably provides a far superior account of the processes, forces or 'drivers' that produce 'management' and thus the 'manager' as a solution. However, in what follows I critically review this literature on FHE. I shall also draw examples from the former 'normal' literature to highlight the contested nature of the debate over the changing character of work in FHE. I begin with an account of the small critical literature on work, organization and management in FE and then move to a review of the critical higher education (HE) literature.

Approaching further education critically

Hughes *et al.* (1996: 13), in a review of the FE literature, suggest that 'there has been relatively little critical analysis of policy and practices within further education, in the sense of trying to explain and understand these experiences from outside'. They suggest that the mainstream or 'insider' literature tends to be involved in either describing, or arguing in favour of, particular policies or practices. These works tend to adopt open system theory assumptions in their accounts of the sector. Canter and Roberts' (1986; Canter *et al.*, 1995) series of texts on FE are perhaps the best examples here (others include Burton, 1994; Fook, 1994; Gorringe and Toogood, 1994; Hall, 1994; Lawrence, 1994; Whyte, 1994; Smith *et al.*, 1995; Todd, 1995; Drodge and Cooper, 1996). Despite the subtitle to Canter and Roberts' 1986 edition – *A Critical Review* – the book is more a chronicle of events related to FE. It positions colleges in a changing system funded by the state but administered by local authorities. However, such assumptions of a 'system' obscure other forms of analysis. Ainley and Bailey (1997: 6) suggest that Canter and his co-authors give 'a misleading impression that the system is in fact systematic. This is certainly not how it is experienced by many of the students, teachers and managers working within it'.

There is little attempt in Canter and Roberts publications to explore, as Hughes *et al.* (1996) suggest, the events and relationships that surround FE in a broader explanatory framework. For example, in the final chapter of their 1986 text, Canter and Roberts seem particularly unwilling to ask *why* a 'more stringent climate' was currently being applied to FE, and why 'national planning has increasingly become the order of the day' – in the form of the National Advisory Body (NAB) (1986: 254). Equally they are unwilling to address some of the gendered assumptions present in their discussion. They point out that at the time of writing there had been 'a small flood of new appointments at director and deputy director level [of polytechnics]'. They suggest that 'this new generation of *relatively young men* will undoubtedly make an impact during the next decade' (1986: 255, my emphasis). On the last page of the text they note the 'very slow progress being made to . . . entice more women and girls into further education' (p. 259). They then applaud the former Further Education Unit's initiative to examine the role of women at all levels in FE. Far from being a critical review, the text is simply a reportage of events that fit a broadly functionalist and systems-based understanding of FE. There is little sense, for example, that the text might be reproducing unreflectively the gendered character of FE, or that FE is more than simply an administrative system, but a social terrain where relations of power that reproduce social effects such as gender are worked out. Canter *et al.* (1995) continue this tradition, but seem even *less* willing to address the profound changes in the sector from within an adequate explanatory framework. This is compounded when the authors unreflectively draw on the commercial vocabulary which has swept through the sector to introduce their account of the management of FE colleges:

> Further education colleges have become increasingly complex institutions to manage. In terms of 'product lines', the largest of them resemble the variety offered by a medium-sized supermarket, but one which produces, markets, finances and tests its own products. Among the smallest, however, are sixth-form colleges which may run a relatively narrow range of courses for mainly full-time students and would probably reject any such comparison with commercial or industrial management models.
>
> (Canter *et al.*, 1995: 96)

There is, however, a small critical FE literature which in the last few years has attempted to explain and critically investigate issues surrounding the reconstruction of the sector. It addresses the conflict between managerial and professional cultures in FE colleges, the gender, ethnicity and class axes embedded in FE colleges and the increased commodification and control of the sector by the 'managerial' or 'contract' state. Some of this can be linked to work undertaken either by the major FE academic staff union, the National Association of Teachers in Further and Higher Education (NATFHE), or by academics with strong union affiliations. Of course it is no surprise that the expanding 'normal' science literature tends to be written or published by government departments and agencies, particularly the Further Education Development Agency (McNay, 1988; Brownlow, 1997), or by senior college post-holders (Frain, 1993; Burton, 1994; Gorringe and Toogood, 1994; Clark, 1996). As mentioned, this literature generally aims to provide examples of management practice and advice on critical issues across the sector. For example, it addresses the application of strategic management, marketing, quality, cost saving and human resource management practices in FE colleges.

The critical literature meanwhile aims to position such practices within a broad account of the changing nature of the FE sector and also to support resistance to particular practices. A key issue has been to explore the shift from an FE sector imbued with the ethos of an educational public service to one engaged in market-orientated business operations. In general terms these critical works are informed by conceptual frameworks drawn mainly from sociology, particularly labour process theory. But a small number also draw on feminist and poststructuralist literatures. In this review I shall identify each study's conceptual basis, its analysis of the changing character of work in FE and its understanding of the construction of the manager across the sector.

Commodifying and controlling colleges

At odds with the dominant managerial literature produced by senior post-holders in FE (Burton, 1994; Flint and Austin, 1994; Gorringe and Toogood, 1994; Lawrence, 1994; Todd, 1995; Bradley, 1996; Drodge and Cooper, 1996; Harper, 1997) Frank Reeves (1995), the former deputy principal of Bilston Community College in Wolverhampton, offers a broadly Marxist critique of the reconstruction of FE colleges. While he locates this as an outcome of the processes of modernity (using Giddens' 1990 discussion as a guide), he also draws on elements of labour process theory (Braverman, 1974; Thompson, 1983; Knights and Willmott, 1985), particularly Braverman's account of Taylorism and elements of the Fordist/post-Fordist debate. Through these conceptual devices Reeves provides a spirited attack on the changed legislative, funding, regulatory, curriculum and auditing process that is reorganizing FE.

While Reeves leaves open the question of whether these changes should be attributed to a more general 'pattern of modernity' or are the 'practical manifestations of the ideological quirks of a right-of-centre party in power for 15 years' (1995: 94), he nevertheless challenges the reconstruction on three main grounds. First, the narrow, nationalized utilitarianism of the new FE which he sees as being at the expense of a broad educational programme relevant to the specifics of the local communities in which colleges operate. Second, and relatedly, the intensifed commodification and degradation of teaching and learning in FE induced by new organizational practices, funding structures and qualification frameworks. In relation to this, Reeves argues that colleges have been subject to both Fordist and post-Fordist processes. In highly evocative terms he argues that colleges have been forced to become 'knowledge factories' where 'student carcasses have to be kept moving along the line' (1995: 79), and also post-Fordist 'knowledge retail outfits' (1995: 83–91). Teachers, in this reading, come to be either knowledge process workers or knowledge 'shop assistants'. In relation to the knowledge factory, Reeves argues that increasingly 'the individual senior professional lecturer with an exclusive curriculum expertise, will disappear to be replaced by a depersonalised system for curriculum delivery' (1995: 40). Third, and again relatedly, the rationalization of the college as an organization, through the adoption of what Giddens calls 'expert' systems', (i.e. management systems), leads to the reconstruction of the senior professional as a 'manager': 'The model of the business organization replaces collegiate ideals and transforms former professionals into managers and workers' (Reeves, 1995: 34).

These three aspects, Reeves argues, lead to an increased alienation of teachers and students from their labours and colleges from their communities as the traditional community-based FE is consumed by rationalizing and modernizing processes. In summary Reeves argues that:

> Further education has chosen to draw its inspiration from the tedium of the work routine. It is easier to explain this economically motivated, industrially driven aberration than it is to forgive its educationally destructive consequences, particularly its obliviousness to all aspects of creative teaching and instruction. With greater professional and community control of education, such a costly exercise might have been avoided.
> (Reeves, 1995: 103)

In a similar, but much more explicitly labour process vein is the work of Randle and Brady (1997), and Longhurst (1996). The core thesis of the latter is that the introduction of a unitized, learning activity based funding methodology, introduced by the state via the Further Education Funding Council (FEFC), and the simultaneous 'independence' of colleges on 1 April 1993 under the Further and Higher Education Act 1992, transformed further education into a commodity. This, Longhurst argues, means that: 'a complete inversion of the aim of colleges has occurred . . . the new system means that the dominant preoccupation of college senior management must be to maximise income and minimise costs' (1996: 55).

The funding methodology, which directly links teaching work to college income, means that its exchange value comes to dominate its use value which, according to Longhurst, is the historical basis of funding FE. While these claims are difficult to support empirically given the diversity of the sector's provision and the funding formulas used by local education authorities (LEAs), particularly after the 1988 Education Reform Act (which required LEAs to devolve greater financial decision making to colleges), the argument nevertheless provides a useful basis for Longhurst's broader analysis of the changing nature of work in FE. He argues that commodification has the inevitable effect of producing the new 'breed' of FE managers who have had to become agents of the funding councils as monopoly purchasers of educational labour. As a result antagonism is inevitable between these managers and the educational labour force – the teachers. Longhurst then moves on to outline how the commodification of FE and 'independence' inevitably leads to moves to intensify, substitute or deskill teachers' work. This is attempted:

- through new teaching contracts that increase teaching time;
- through increased class sizes;
- through reduced class contact time;
- through the substitution of teaching labour with 'cheaper' part-time teachers and 'instructor' grades who supervise workshop projects;
- through resource and computer-based learning programmes for class-room sessions.

However, technological substitution, Longhurst argues, is unlikely to significantly increase the 'amount of surplus value [managers] extract from teaching staff' (1996: 61). Managerial interest will, as a result, he predicts, be largely confined to the intensification of teaching labour or its substitution with cheaper forms (1996: 61). This will be particularly important, Longhurst argues, if senior management continue to increase the level of their own salaries and the number of non-teaching administrative workers, both of which rely on 'the surplus value obtained from paying teachers less than the value of the educational commodity that they produce' (1996: 62).

Thus for Longhurst the managerialization of FE has its material basis in the commodification of FE as units of activity now 'produced' for a managed market and 'sold' to a monopolistic purchaser. For Longhurst, senior post-holders are positioned in these new relations as the agents of the purchaser. While they 'do not want to see themselves as exploiters', Longhurst notes, 'to be able to carry out their oppressive and exploitative role adequately then their ideological outlook has to undergo some transformation' (1996: 63).

Like most other authors who address this issue of the transformation of FE 'managers', the actual mechanisms and extent of this 'ideological' transformation are left unclear. Senior managers are for Longhurst simply 'under pressure to oppress and exploit their staff' (1996: 65) and are motivated by their own survival. If they do not oppress and exploit they risk bankrupting the college and/or their own dismissal. The extent to which teaching staff will be oppressed and exploited will be decided, however, through industrial and political struggle. A struggle whose lines, according to Longhurst, must be drawn between staff and senior management because of the commodification of FE. In addressing this position three key problems are evident:

- an over-reliance on a structuralist ontology;
- the problems of a realist epistemology;
- a lack of empirical elaboration.

In recent years this 'strong' Marxian analysis has been 'unravelled' by challenges on grounds of empirical validation, structuralism, and realism (Teulings, 1986; Cooper and Burrell, 1988; Knights and Willmott, 1989; Thompson, 1989). In short this kind of analysis is overly reductionist, lacks a convincing understanding of human agency, and has been undermined by what Curt (1994) terms the 'climate of problematization' of knowledge – particularly in relation to the 'post-critiques' of poststructuralism and post-modernism (Williams and May, 1996). An account such as Longhurst's relies on the objectifiable 'reality' of a strong division between teachers and managers in particular. Questioning such a claim to knowledge about such a 'real' relation is one issue. Another is that such a claim negates or obscures the effect of other divisions and 'struggles': between for instance managers themselves (embedded in competing 'expert systems', to use Giddens' (1990) phrase), between men and women across the college, between senior and junior staff and between core, full-time staff and peripheral temporary or part-time teaching staff. The reductionism in Longhurst's account means that other embedded relations of power, alongside the contradictions and problems of actually managing others and becoming a 'manager' in FE, cannot be adequately addressed within this framework.

Three further studies (Elliott, 1996a; Ainley and Bailey, 1997; Randle and Brady, 1997), all in a critical vein, also in my view do not adequately address this issue of the problems surrounding the construction of the 'manager'. While all these works are admirable and much needed in this field, in themselves their narratives rely to varying extents on the assumption that the sector's reconstruction *unproblematically* positions some staff as managers and others as teachers. And yet, trade journalism on this topic (Mansell, 1996), the accounts given by the respondents in the study reported in this book, and some more recent research (Gleeson and Shain, 1999) suggest this is of major concern.

Writing in the sector's trade management magazine *FE Now!*, former FE college administrator turned trade journalist Phil Mansell (1996: 13) suggests that:

> In college after college it is possible to sense real frustration on the part of senior managers as they struggle to put their ideas and ideals into practice . . . they are becoming increasingly intolerant of any layer of the college hierarchy that either delays or stands in the way of the implementation of strategic decisions by those who really matter – the members of staff who are in contact with the college's clients.

While both the Ainley and Bailey (1997) and Randle and Brady (1997) studies note this issue, it is left largely undeveloped. Ainley and Bailey draw attention to the problems of being a manager. They suggest that the 'schizophrenic manager' has appeared who 'gets carried along in two tracks': one being a financial survival 'track' and other the educationalist's 'track'.

Randle and Brady (1997) in their survey- and interview-based study of 'Cityshire' college note that across the FE sector 'The erstwhile "administrative manager" from head of department upwards is now being replaced by a new type of manager primarily concerned with resource management, particularly financial resources' (p. 232). Yet this 'replacement' has been less than smooth. Senior managers put this down to 'teething problems' which they claimed were the result of rapid change and a lack of expertise among academics now occupying management positions. Randle and Brady, however, argue that this 'pays too little attention to the fundamental causes of resistance, which are associated we argue with the impact of the new management upon professional autonomy' (1997: 231).

Randle and Brady then leave this issue and go on to discuss the conflict between managerial and professional 'paradigms'. They argue, like Longhurst to some degree, that this conflict is induced by the proletarianization of academic labour across FE through the 'imposition of market relations by the bureaucracy of the FEFCE [Further Education Funding Council of England]' (1997: 235). While they do not address in detail the commodifying form applied to education, as discussed by Longhurst, they argue, as does Longhurst, that proletarianization involves deskilling, substitution and intensification of teaching labour. These processes, and the bitter struggle of lecturers against these changes have served to underline the limitations of traditional professional practices, and the 'degree to which lecturers are coming to terms with their changing position' (Randle and Brady, 1997: 239) – proletarianized labour and not professional artisan, in other words.

Meanwhile Ainley and Bailey's (1997) work, based on research at two colleges ('Inner City' and 'Home Counties'), gives an account of 'the experience' of FE in the 1990s from the perspectives of managers, staff and students. Yet by relying to a large extent on the frameworks embedded in the accounts given to the researchers by the college respondents themselves (that is, taking a 'grounded theory' approach), issues of commodification, control and proletarianization of labour are not addressed directly. Their approach arises out of concern that research on FE be written *for* FE and not 'by [HE] academics for academics' (1997: 3). Ainley and Bailey hope, through this approach, to both contribute to the political debate surrounding FE, and to provide material through which FE can be theorized in its own right.

In relation to the construction of the manager, Ainley and Bailey broadly underline the tension between the new manager and the teaching staff, induced by the funding methodology. Yet they suggest that the incorporation of colleges, through the 1992 Further and Higher Education Act and the changed funding practices, have *modernized* what were considered to be the largely feudal processes of FE management. According to their account, FE before incorporation was managed by small collections of 'baron' heads of department who relied on face-to-face, hierarchical semi-feudal relations (what one of the respondents described as a 'drawbridge and defences' management style). This is contrasted with the new centralized, finance-driven, spreadsheet to spreadsheet, memo to memo, managerial regime composed of hierarchically-ordered teams.

However, one underlying problem with this account is a lack of distance from the accounts of some of the managers Ainley and Bailey interviewed. While this reading of the seeming 'modernization' of FE is seductive, particularly for those who have found favourable positions with the new regime, it lacks links to the broader analysis discussed above in relation to commodification, proletarianization and autonomy and control. By not making these connections directly in this text Ainley and Bailey have tended to reply unproblematiclly to the discourse they have retrieved from their respondents. They discuss for instance changing managerial regimes in terms of the changing 'organizational structures' or changing 'chain of command'. The account unproblematically reproduces the system-based functionalism of the managerial approach, discussing for instance 'matrix' organizational structures. The account fails to ask why such stories and accounts of the 'organization' are being told, and what such narratives reveal.

There are a number of interrelated issues here. One is that in an effort to tell a story of 'what it is like' (Ainley and Bailey, 1997: 6) in contemporary FE the authors have been unable to give sufficient space to developing their conceptual analysis around terms like 'experience' 'language' and 'practice', and the agency of the actors involved. For example, organizational structure charts and accounts of changing structure are, it could be argued, important symbolic resources for the construction of managerial identities in sectors where corporate business discourse is relatively new and unfamiliar. Such devices, which help construct at a micro level the state-demanded 'corporate college', are also ways of dealing with the uncertainty of the new managerial positionings. This is supported by, and supports, new funding and auditing processes which work to increase the sense of exposure, and possibility of failure, that can be attributed to particular post-holders. One of the FE college principals I spoke with highlighted the extent to which fear and uncertainty pervaded the sector, induced by the funding methodology: 'at every level there is a climate of fear in the sector at the moment because of the exposure and accountability at every level. It is through the inspection process, the audit process, the accountabilities to the public accounts process. It is extremely exposed'.

Thus the receptiveness of senior post-holders to taking up managerial practices and language, reproduced in Ainley and Bailey's account, needs to be unravelled further. Whitehead's work, discussed below, argues that these insecurities, which underwrite receptiveness, managerial practices and language, also fuel a re-masculinization of FE management. The search for control and the displacement of insecurities thus helps draw in devices like organizational charts, business language and 'managerial' physical and social spaces (elaborately decorated offices, boardrooms and front entrance ways). Thus 'origin' and 'structure' stories and artefacts (such as 'matrix' organizational charts) found in Ainley and Bailey's account, framed as they are in the dominant functionalist language, must also be considered as ways of dealing with fear and uncertainty. However, Ainley and Bailey, I suggest, miss the opportunity to address these issues because of a commitment to foreground the 'experience' of 'what it is like' (1997: 6) in FE.

Lecturers strike back: two cultures in FE?

Geoffrey Elliott's work (1996a, 1996b; Elliott and Hall, 1994; Elliott and Crossley, 1994, 1997), I think, can also be challenged on similar grounds. It was undertaken as part of his studies in the University of Bristol's Ed.D programme and is based on a participant observation study among lecturers in one department in a case study college. It takes up a 'grounded theory' approach to knowledge (Elliott, 1996a: 37). In the book-length account of the work, the views of staff are assembled along with secondary material into an account of themes, issues and practices through which lecturers make sense of their circumstances. Elliott's approach is constructivist and humanist in orientation which, he admits, causes problems as the account moves from what the lecturers told him to making broader linkages (1996a: 50). In making this move, Elliott draws on a number of potentially conflicting frameworks and concepts. At one point he discusses ideology and the state (1996a: 11). Later there is a discussion of open and closed systems theory (1996a: 22–3). There are also discussions of values in relation to managerial and pedagogical cultures. In the conclusion the author introduces the term 'discourse' to describe the various orientations to the topic. Throughout, however, the texts maintain a commitment to the pedagogical values of the occupational group studied. In essence it appears as if the 'grounded theory' approach used in the account, which largely eschews a discussion of issues of the status of practitioner knowledge, agency and the subject, induces an eclecticism in conceptual materials and a lack of sufficient conceptual distance between the researcher and the research.

Broadly, however, Elliott argues that the government's FE 'reforms' have created contradictory and oppositional forces in FE, particularly between a managerialist culture embraced by senior post-holders and a democratic ideology based around pedagogic practices. However, Elliott argues that while market and inspection mechanisms have been imposed by an 'ill-prepared and compliant college management' (1996a: 9), lecturers draw on a 'repertoire of strategies to thwart attempts to impose external systemic and specific changes that [lecturers] perceived to be at variance from their core [educational] values' (1996a: 7):

> There were a large number of management decisions that impacted upon the day-to-day working practices of staff in an irksome and unpleasant manner. Resentment built resistance, which served to feed a counter-culture, sustained and supported by the activity of undermining initiatives which were designed to build a unified corporate culture.
>
> (Elliott and Crossley, 1997: 87)

In an earlier paper (1994), Elliott argues that one of these responses was the creative *re-naming of practices* in FE without substantial change to actual teaching and managing practices themselves. While in the later publications (1996a,b) Elliott drops the suggestion that new management ideas and practices had not changed actual college management practices, the text continues to argue that teachers maintain a critical, tactical and broadly resistive approach to managerial demands.

In the study, one of the major battlegrounds between lecturers and managers was the college's 'quality' programmes. Resistance to such programmes took a number of forms, particularly the removal of cooperation (e.g. not responding to information requests and form-filling exercises). As well as non-cooperation, 'lecturers engaged in what one called "subversive, rather than overt confrontation"; creative timetabling and post hoc completion of registers are common practices of this kind' (1996a: 73). Elliott asserts that such resistance was grounded in the 'firm belief in the lecturer's responsibility to meet the needs of the student, rather than institutional or systemic needs' (1996a: 74). He goes on to argue that the lecturers offered, through their own practices, a 'viable, alternative model of management derived from the lecturers' perspective and grounded in pedagogical culture' (1996a: 96). Here the emphasis would be on educational rather than business values, which the lecturers considered had become, for managers, an 'end in themselves' (1996a: 96). In essence Elliott's argument is that the lecturers' tactical response to the managerialism which senior post-holders had little option but to implement (1996a: 106) can be seen as a pragmatic strategy of working within the conditions:

> By asserting the centrality of a pedagogical orientation which centres upon students' needs, lecturers present a powerful alliance for managing change. Educational policy and managerialist strategies which are regarded by them as subversive of critical pedagogy are resisted. On the other hand opportunities to underline their pedagogical orientation, through adoption of other strategies, are seldom missed in order to buttress their position within the institution and safeguard the arena of their expertise.
>
> (Elliott, 1996a, 105)

Yet while Elliott does address this issue in relation to lecturers, the same analysis is not offered to 'managers'. Elliott does discuss at turns the development of managers across the sector, and his work suggests that while incorporation has come to symbolize the imposition of managerial relations, the introduction of managers was a more subtle and consensual process than Longhurst (1996) and Randle and Brady (1997) suggest, for instance:

> For practitioners at least the development of a market-led conception of FE was evolutionary, and its antecedents can be found in the broad collectivity of reforms across all educational sectors brought about by government legislation, associated government-sponsored reports and the increasing inclination within the sector itself to provide a responsive service to a wide range of customers and clients.
>
> (Elliott, 1996a: 7)

However, viewed from the perspective of the lecturer, senior post-holders have been largely complicit in articulating a 'hard', uncompromising top-down managerialism that has invariably turned colleges into a battleground. Elliott's second point, in relation to the making of managers, is that 'middle managers' were largely 'caught' in the midst of this: 'There was a clear undertone to the effect that middle managers were under scrutiny, were perceived to be failing in their duty, and that increasing pressure would be exerted upon them to include formal disciplinary procedures to deal with instances of non-compliance' (Elliott and Crossley, 1997: 83). Rather than discuss the contradictory and problematic position of 'middle managers', and their 'failures', Elliott and Crossley go on in this paper to discuss the 'rise and rise of managerialist culture' in FE. They conclude by suggesting that managers should take the 'needs and orientations of practitioners into account' (1997: 90) and adopt a more 'adaptive and consensual approach' between differing 'work cultures' (1997: 90). While some might see this as a naive statement, given the kind of approach taken above, it nevertheless flows, I would argue, from the 'grounded theory' approach, from a lack of discussion of power, knowledge and disposition/identity, from the use of a contradictory array of conceptual resources to illuminate the 'forces' at work in FE colleges and lastly from a humanist and perhaps managerial response to the question 'What is to be done?'.

Two major issues are missing in the texts so far discussed: the gendered character of the reconstruction of both FE and management in FE, and the inclusion of conceptual approaches that challenge the strongly dualistic theorizing embedded in the texts so far discussed.

Gendering management in FE

Stephen Whitehead's exploration of gender in FE management, and his explicit use of a poststructural account of knowledge, represents a major break from the works discussed in the previous sections (see Whitehead, 1995, 1996a, 1996b, 1997a, 1997b; Kerfoot and Whitehead, 1995). Three key elements are found in Whitehead's papers and thesis. First, drawing on feminist literature, his work aims to 'break the silence' surrounding the interrelations between becoming managers and being men in FE. Second, drawing on Foucault's notion of discourse and feminist reworkings of this (Butler, 1990b; McNay, 1992), Whitehead's aim is to read gender identity and management as particular ways of being or 'doing' working life which are not in general terms specific to particular people. A discourse is understood as a privileged network of statements, knowledges and practices – particularly discursive practices of the self – which provide ways in which people engage with social life. For Whitehead, social power is embedded in particular discourses (e.g. managerial formations), and particular discursive practices of being a man or men: 'Any power that men or women may exert is only made possible through the taking up of, and being in, dominant discourses' (1997a: 10). He argues that it is the interrelations between new management discourses and the discourse of a competitive masculinity which underscore and produce the new manager in FE.

Third, Whitehead argues that the links between competitive masculinity and management practices are dependent on a new work culture in FE induced by both post-industrial/post-Fordist economic changes, and a 'New Right' government agenda. This aims to increase FE's contribution to workforce training, but to reduce the relative cost of that contribution. As a way of grounding this debate, Whitehead argues that prior to the incorporation of colleges FE was 'undisturbed by the consequences of post industrialism and its attendant associate post-fordism. The chaotic consequences of, for example globalisation, new technology, international competition and rapid, unpredictable flows of capital' (1997a: 7). He suggests that the period between 1987 and 92 was a twilight period. The 1992 Further and Higher Education Act made the reconstruction of FE explicit.

Whitehead's central argument concerns the interdependence of the practices and vocabularies of being a man, and becoming a manager in the reconstructed quasi-business environment of FE. Generally, Whitehead suggests that being a manager in FE 'fits comfortably with the dominant discourses of masculinity; competition, control, rationality; task orientation, leadership and instrumentality' (1997b). The managerialization of FE, Whitehead argues, has reconstituted the sector from one based on a sleepy paternalistic masculinity to one based around an aggressive, competitive masculinity (Collinson and Hearn, 1994):

> The paternalistic, gentlemanly amateur of yesteryear has made way for the more hurried, aggressive, detached and functional individual, a person who acquires the label 'professional' through their ability to be competitive and to measure up to externally dictated, normative consequences. Their reward is to be located in an environment which privileges their 'natural masculine traits' and within which they, as men, can make explicit statements about their (gendered) potency and power.
>
> (Whitehead, 1997a: 20)

Whitehead is a former manager in a Yorkshire college. His study is based around interviews with 22 FE managers in 13 colleges between 1994 and 1995. In his PhD thesis (1996a) he draws in part on his own experience of work to discuss the suffusion of managerial discourse – what he terms the 'discourse of performativity', from Lyotard (1984) – and how this changed the gendered structure of the college. For Whitehead (1997a: 18), this new discourse of performativity 'materialized' in a number of ways: staff appraisal, new job descriptions and contracts, targets for an increasing number of staff, encouragement of income-generating work, reduction in class contact time by 50 per cent over two years, increased class sizes, cost-centred management, audit processes, the redesignation of students as customers and increased emphasis on marketing. In the midst of this managers were 'required to provide two, three and five year plans for their departments, informed by statements of objectives and action and performance targets for every individual and programme area' (1997a: 18). Underlying this was the increasingly fragile financial situation: 'As FE institutions felt, for the first time, real insecurity, financial fragility and the wider effects of market forces, management's response was to present itself as ambitious, competent and with a vision' (1997a: 16). Whitehead argues that this discourse of performativity is 'particularly seductive for most men/managers as it privileges instrumental achievement, competition and aggression and the functionality of performance measurement' (1997a: 16). Whitehead's case is that these measures induce a new work identity embedded in practices of the self which develop a 'symbiotic relation to the new masculinisation' (1997a: 16).

However, this relation is not always unproblematic. Whitehead also suggests that the existence of unique histories of particular managers, as well as particular practices and histories embedded in the locales of colleges, meant that at various points and times disruption and subversion of the dominant discourse occurred. The strength of a poststructuralist approach is that rather than seeing the construction of two blocks of activity embedded in two groups of people (lecturers and managers), disruptions occur in both groups and are understood as largely ubiquitous and ongoing. As Whitehead notes: 'the aspect of the subject's resistance to dominant discourses, described in this paper, is not undertaken as a strategic, rational act, but in the moments wherein subjects reconstitute and become reconstituted in discourse, a process reinforced by the very fragility and unpredictability of being' (1997b: 22).

Whitehead argues that moments, spaces and gaps exist between those practices demanded by managerial discourses. These potentially threaten the continuity and directionality of such practices. Such disruption is induced on the one hand by the historically unique subjectivities of those engaged as 'managers'. On the other it is fuelled by the sheer ambivalence, unpredictability and fragility of our ontological being. This uncertainty is a direct challenge to the identity of the 'manager'. In the discourse the 'manager' is required to be constantly ambitious, competent and competitive.

One issue left open by Whitehead is the position of women in this remasculinized FE. What effect has the expansion of managerialism in FE had on the employment of women in senior positions, and has the new work culture and discourses of performativity required women, perhaps more than men, to relate to it in a masculine fashion? Whitehead suggests that research among women managers in FE would, given these assertions, provide important insights into the changing character of the sector, and particularly the nature of management (1997b: 20). This is precisely the issue I shall return to in Chapter 8. One issue needs to be raised here however. It seems important that in the development of a poststructural account of management in FE, which brings together issues of ontological security as well as the colonizing and seductive discourses of management, issues raised at the beginning of this section concerning the intensification of work and its performance by less expensive workers are not lost. Women's recruitment to management work needs to be read against this framework, as well as that which addresses the problems of the construction of managerial subjectivities.

In summary, Whitehead's work presents an engaging and thorough account of the gendered aspects of the development of managers in FE. The poststructural and feminist approaches are a direct challenge to other works in the critical FE literature which, as I suggested above, suffers from debilitating dualisms, determinism and a lack of engagement with issues of power, knowledge and agency. Much of the work in this book, which focuses on the construction of the managerial 'station' (Fiske, 1993), and the resistances (including the gendered resistances) to this should be read as complementary to Whitehead's work – elaborating and filling in elements not addressed. From the FE literature I now want to turn to the critical literature on work in HE. Unsurprisingly, this literature is both enormous and diverse by comparison to the small, but worthy, critical FE literature. However, many of the same approaches and concerns are voiced.

Approaching higher education

Studies of the changing character of work in HE approach the topic from a number of differing, but at times overlapping, orientations. As with FE, 'contra' or 'critical' literatures can be distinguished from a broad 'normal' literature that provides and underpins advice and prescriptions to practitioners and managers across the sector. Below I discuss this as a 'functionalist' orientation to work in HE. Contra or critical work meanwhile can be seen to draw on Marxist, Weberian/Foucauldian, poststructuralist and feminist strands. In this section I overview these particular 'orientations', note the characteristics of each through the work of particular authors and also address briefly how each approaches the question of the construction of the manager.

We're all labouring for capital now

A Marxist-derived analysis of the changing character of work in HE is embedded in a broad political economic analysis (Wilson, 1991; Ainley, 1994; Miller, 1995a, 1995b, 1996; Miller and Edwards, 1995; Smyth, 1995; Willmott, 1995; Winter, 1995; Miller and Higson 1996; Shumar 1997; Noble, 1998). The key feature is addressing and linking the changing conditions of work in HE to the changing conditions of capitalist accumulation, and the changing responses of the state, as the main public sector employer of labour, to these conditions (e.g. by reducing the 'load' that public sector legitimation and reproduction processes place on private accumulation – see for example Salter and Tapper, 1994). As Willmott (1995: 12) argues in relation to academic work:

> the key to understanding change in the organization and control of academic work lies in an analysis of the trajectory of the distinctive organization and dynamics of the capitalist society in which it is embedded and not in the impersonal force of rationalization or the capacity of individuals to collaborate in, or resist, its seemingly relentless advance.

The core line of argument is that pressures applied by the state in response to the current conditions of capitalist accumulation are engaged in attempts to either reduce the costs of labour in HE or maintain or enhance its contribution to processes of accumulation and legitimation (e.g. intensifying the state education's contribution to the production of a skilled workforce, the costs of which capitalist enterprises are unwilling to bear themselves). This is manifest in pressure and control from the state in attempts to force down wages and salaries, to replace relatively expensive labour with cheaper forms or to substitute labour with less labour-intensive or technologically-based processes. This can be illustrated in the introduction of, for example, early retirement schemes, the replacement of lecturers and professors with cheaper graduate assistants, short-contract staff and computer-aided learning. Alongside this, efforts are made to intensify the contribution of that labour, particularly by increasing the numbers of students enrolling and being taught for the same cost, or institutions attempting to generate surplus through entering fully capitalist market relations (e.g. industrial research, conferences, fees from consultancy and full-cost programmes).

Yet these multiple processes, or potential processes, do not occur mechanically of themselves. They require the development of a managerial, or a second-order, labour process across the sector which proves in varying degrees to be both complicit and resistant to the full elaboration of such strategic directionalities. Thus as HE becomes increasingly commodified through its intensified engagement with quasi or managed market processes (and thus treats itself as if it were a capitalist enterprise) the head of department/service or the dean or director of university services becomes increasingly enrolled as a representative of capitalist production and consumption relations, rather than as a representative of academic faculty or administrative professionals (Shumar, 1997).

Ideal types and panoptical gazes

A Weberian/Foucauldian analysis of work in HE (e.g. Halsey, 1992; Ezzamel, 1994; Parker and Jary, 1995; Shore and Roberts, 1995; Ritzer, 1996; Grant, 1997; Shore and Selwyn, 1998) is concerned less with political economy and more with *how* these dynamics are played out. In general the processes are labelled and characterized as 'rationalizations' or 'modernizations'. The core line of argument, for instance in Scott's work (1995: 10), is that universities are both producers of and subject to the 'restless synergies of plural modernisations – of the academy, polity, economy, society and culture' (Scott, 1995: 10). As can be appreciated, Marxist-informed political economic analysis tends to be broadly suspicious of such pluralism, arguing that such an approach fails to grasp the key dynamics. Parker and Jary (1995), in defence of a Weberian approach, accept that the analysis of work should be concerned with a political economic analysis at a broad level and agree that 'the driving principle would seem to be ensuring that HE played its part in state capitalism', but they suggest that Ritzer's neo-Weberian 'McDonaldization' thesis,[1] and Foucault's analysis of changes to the regime of power relations are required to explore *how* the elaboration of such changes at the levels of the organization of work and subjectivity are more or less successfully carried out. For example, in relation to academic work, and drawing on Weber and Ritzer, they argue that: 'The NHE [new higher education] is in danger of becoming a fast-food outlet that sells only those ideas that its managers believe will sell, that treats its employees as if they were too devious or stupid to be trusted, and that values the formal rationality of the process over the substantive rationality of the ends' (Parker and Jary, 1995: 335–6). And from Foucault (1991), in relation to the production of new forms of academic subjectivity, they argue that:

> it is less convincing to talk about a university as a community of scholars; perhaps instead it is a legally constituted web of corporate surveillance mechanisms. The search for excellence, for a corporate culture, for total quality management is the search for a way to regulate the labour of academics and other employees.
>
> (Parker and Jary, 1995: 327)

Parker and Jary argue that in response to the worsening conditions of their labour, and increased surveillance (Henson, 1995), academics change the way they come to know themselves and their role. Careerism, ritualism and retreatism are the core responses. The new academic is 'more instrumental and rationalized', being concerned less with their academic discipline and more with career, quality ratings and rewards. Senior academics and administrators meanwhile have been reconstructed in parallel ways. Enhanced salaries, new contracts, less teaching and the introduction of new practices of accountability have repositioned them as 'academic managers' (Williams, 1992; Townley, 1993a) or 'charismatic leader-managers' (Parker and Jary, 1995) in the new higher education (NHE).

There are a number of problems with both the Marxist and Weberian/Foucauldian analyses. First, each could be said to adopt an over-determined or over-socialized understanding of the social subject and down-play the problems, disorder and unintended consequences of either instituting or achieving the desired outcomes from the methods adopted (Game, 1994; Dearlove, 1995; Ryder, 1996). Second, and relatedly, there is a lack of engagement with the problems of actually achieving these new relations and configurations. To take Parker and Jary's paper for example, these authors argue that their ideal type of 1990s UK university exhibits among other things 'greater managerial power' (1995: 320). Management discourse has been imported, they argue, to enhance the 'importance of management as a process and to legitimate the activities of particular members – executives, directors and so on – as key decision makers' (1995: 324). Parker and Jary stress that the 'language of "line managers", "customers" and "products" *begins to displace* the academic language of deans, students and courses' (1995: 324, emphasis added). One objection to this claim is that just because a language is to be found in a particular social terrain, it does not necessarily mean that existing languages and practices have been reconstructed to mirror the 'new' discourse. Parker and Jary, it seems, are attempting to read the effects directly *off* a discourse without addressing the extent to which the 'new' managerial discourse leaves unchallenged those practices they attempt to narrate in new ways. They also ignore the ways in which passive or active resistance is directed at and rebuffs this 'greater managerial power' (e.g. see Ezzamel, 1994). Only in two brief sentences do Parker and Jary touch upon these resistant practices. They argue (against their own thesis perhaps) that:

> the professional academic does not necessarily want to please their management because they gain status from their relationships with their students and other academics inside and outside their organisation. It is a powerful argument, and as noted it probably begins to explain why universities still function at all when their resource base has been cut so badly.
>
> (1995: 328)

If then, as Parker and Jary suggest, an academic identity is likely to be somewhat ambivalent in its relationship to the new discourse and practices of managerialism, surely this forms the basis on which to argue that 'greater managerial control' is also likely to be a somewhat ambivalent endeavour. Yet nowhere do Parker and Jary give effective voice to this issue. Nowhere, paradoxically, do they place themselves as resistant voices, despite the fact that their experience of working in their own institution (namely Staffordshire University) is an important motivation for their paper.

These problems are in part a result of the authors' selective application of ideas from Weber and Foucault. Much is made of Weber's 'iron cage of rationalization' thesis: 'The institution becomes an effective iron cage populated by Weber's cogs in the machine, specialists without vision and sensualists without heart' (Parker and Jary, 1995: 329). Little is said about the residues of affective and value-rational action or about the paradox of consequences. Likewise, much is made of Foucault's notion of the construction of subjectivity via panoptical practices (1995: 329): 'greater managerial control and an increasingly restricted sphere of academic professional autonomy will result in new forms of subjectivity amongst academics' (1995: 331). Virtually nothing is said about the central importance of transgression in Foucault's work (see Knights and Vurdusakis, 1994).

Finally, these authors tend to shy away from empirical analysis (see Buchbinder and Newson, 1988; Miller, 1995a, 1996b; Prichard and Willmott, 1997; Trowler, 1998). However, that said, such accounts do form a useful antidote to the dominant instrumentalist open systems analysis of the changes to work in HE.

Dancing to the system's tune?

In this approach (Becker and Kogan, 1992; Middlehurst, 1993; Schuller, 1995; Warner and Crosthwaite, 1995) (what I've termed the orthodox or 'normal science' reading of HE), the university is understood to be made up of various functioning parts, each contributing to the general 'equilibrium' of the institution. Meanwhile this whole is itself part of a broader HE system which undergoes various instabilities to which it attempts to respond and adjust. In this reading each institution is considered to have various functional capacities and characteristics, whose work is managed by managers responsible for responding to the changing conditions of the system, and realigning or 'managing change' in relation to their own function areas. When problems occur they are often blamed on poor communication or inappropriate structures which have failed to empower people to change their own environments. As House and Watson (1995: 19) advise:

> People being managed through periods of significant change, especially when the implications are on the face of things distressing and in that sense at least not chosen, appreciate and are more likely to respond positively to clear information on what is happening and why. They are also more likely to accept changes if they understand them and respect the motives of those driving the changes.

Of course this systemic functionalism does not simply assume that systems function in and of themselves. In this analysis systems and functions are staffed by people who carry out particular roles. A 'role' is understood to comprise various tasks which, in turn, require particular skills or knowledge appropriate to each particular functional element in the whole (Brodie and Partington, 1992; Middlehurst, 1993). While there has been a general move to introduce the notion of culture, values and language (e.g. McNay, 1995; Thomas, 1996) to the approach, this often overlays 'roles', 'structures' and 'functions'.

Systemic functionalism is however the dominant 'code' used by managers and senior post-holders to understand and speak, in public at least, about their work and organizations. Occasionally senior post-holders take up other approaches (Bull, 1994), and are regularly critical of such formalism (Price, 1994), preferring to understand themselves as leaders engaged in creating the 'right atmosphere'. However, functionalism continues to underlie the approach. Such functionalism is often challenged by other approaches for its blindness and complicity, most recently by poststructuralism, beginning most directly perhaps with Lyotard (1984).

Language gaming, textual tactics and making spaces

Lyotard's (1984) analysis could be said to be strongly inlaid with Marxist and Weberian threads. Lyotard entertains the notion of commodification of knowledge and has a view of the 'system' as a 'vanguard machine dragging humanity after it, dehumanising it in order to rehumanise it at a different level of normative capacity' (1984: 63). However, the importance he gives to the pluralism of language games as constitutive of a fragmented social subject, together with a distrust of *prefigured* metanarratives, renders his work poststructural. Broadly, his assertion is that 'events' (Auschwitz, the 1968 Paris uprisings and the prolonged recession of the 1970s) have produced a widespread de-legitimation of the modernist grand narratives (scientific reason and emancipatory humanism) upon which the contemporary university is founded. In their place, performativity becomes the dominant criterion of judgement. In response 'management', the ideology of the performative whose target is simply the most efficient input/output ratio, steps forward convinced that it can take control. As Peters notes in his empirical work in relation to UK HE, which draws on Lyotard's approach, 'each of us lives at the intersection of many [language games], the technocratic decision makers proceed on the assumption that there is commensurability and common ground among them and that the whole is determinable' (1992: 134) (see also Peters, 1996a).

Thus, HE is understood as a mass of language games or *petit recits* (small narratives). The plurality and heterogeneity of these are denied by technocratic managerialism which works to subordinate and position other narratives in relation to its constructions of efficiency and accountability.

Such a framework, while not always referenced to Lyotard directly, but drawn from the general trajectory of a poststructural analysis, forms the basis of a number of recent studies of work in HE (Fairclough, 1993; Weil, 1994; Bloland, 1995; Holmer-Nadesan, 1996; Ibarra-Colado, 1996; Lander, 1996; Peters, 1996a, 1996b; Selway, 1995). All, in different ways, are concerned with exploring work in relation to its textuality, which might be understood as the point at which language and practice intersect. Weil (1994), for instance, using an approach reminiscent of Becher's (1989) discussion of tribes and territories in academic life, notes that

> Story telling lies at the heart of any institution and any significant change process . . . Managers may communicate policies, report decisions, assert what is right and what is misunderstood, but what is spoken about in a myriad of ways [are] the dramas, the feelings, the passions, the power, the pain, the values, the celebrated, the despised.
>
> (Weil, 1994: 153)

And yet,

> What has gone very wrong in many institutions is that, for example, the funding council story, or the manager's story, is 'living the people'. The story becomes one of being 'done to', rather than making sense and 'doing with'. The spect-actors who have been required to carry through changes are reduced to spectators.
>
> (1994: 161)

While it could be argued that Weil's advocacy of narrativity or 'storied-ness' is ultimately subordinated to developing managers adept at using stories to extend their control, the approach does stress the ontological importance of textuality, storied-ness or narrativity in the constitution of work in HE.

This emphasis on the colonization of the textuality of work in HE is given much firmer treatment in Fairclough's (1993) critical discourse analysis of the marketization of universities. Broadly, Fairclough is concerned with the constitutive effects of colonizing discourses, particularly those of marketing and management in HE. While Weil's approach tends to take a more interpretativist line, understanding people as meaning-makers, Fairclough's draws on structuralism and questions the extent of the control (or presence) we have over how meaning is made. Broadly, Fairclough's analysis shows how the identity of HE institutions and the nature of the identities that make them up are being reconstructed through changing discursive practices. His analysis suggests that our ability to reflexively engage with and challenge these is somewhat limited. Fairclough argues for instance that the professional identities of academics are being moved to a more entrepreneurial (self-promotional) basis, which includes a foregrounding of personal qualities (1993: 157).

While Fairclough's textual approach focuses on the reconstruction of institutional and professional identities, Holmer-Nadesen's (1996) post-structural analysis of relations between university managers and service workers supports and extends the work. It addresses particularly the way that the ubiquitous discourses (structuring social practices) of gender and class make-up work in HE, first by analysing the largely neglected 'service' work of universities (Delmont, 1996; Miller and Higson, 1996), and second by exploring resistance to managerial discourse, through the concept of 'space of action'. In relation to resistance, Holmer-Nadesen argues that managerial discourse is but one of many forms of knowledge and practice through which workers position and reproduce themselves. It is this 'surplus of meaning' that produces space for contingency and choice, and thus resistance. However, this is tempered by the way in which discourses overlap and support others. Holmer-Nadesen shows how women workers in a university hall of residence resist their positioning in managerial discourse as 'service workers' by engaging in attempts to extend their control over their space and time at work. One way in which this is done is by drawing on a maternal discourse and positively articulating themselves as 'mother', 'sister' or 'housewife' in relation to 'their' students. However, Holmer-Nadesen argues, this ultimately leads back to and reinforces administrative and managerial discourse, and thus reduces their space of action and scope for collective action:

> Most institutionalized understandings of mother, sister and housewife are articulated within the discourse of patriarchy where women are positioned in relation to dominant males. Reproduction of traditional familial relations within a male dominated bureaucracy, such as that

found in this university, has the effect of over-determining authoritarian, male power. Consequently, that service workers articulate self as mother need not be incommensurable with formal organizational discourse.

(Holmer-Nadesen, 1996: 77–8)

Gendering the HE worker

Holmer-Nadesen's work is among a growing number of works that broadly engage in a feminist critique of HE, while at the same time drawing on elements of a poststructuralist orientation (Mumby and Stohl, 1991: 325–9; Game, 1994; Heward, 1994; Morley, 1994; Farish *et al.*, 1995; Yeatman, 1995; Lander, 1996; Prichard, 1996b; Brooks, 1997, 1998; Walker, 1997; Blackmore and Sachs, 1998). Broadly, such analyses illustrate and challenge the various ways in which work in HE is gendered. In general terms they seek to illustrate how, as in the case of Holmer-Nadesen's paper, ubiquitous patriarchal discourses reproduce HE, and how this militates against equitable distribution of rewards and status and the limitations of formalized efforts like equal opportunities initiatives (Farish *et al.*, 1995), or schemes such as Opportunity 2000. Adrian Webb (1994: 42), vice-chancellor of the University of Glamorgan, shows how this operates in account of his 'first step' up from head of department:

> as head of department at Loughborough I inherited a very skilled and experienced departmental secretary. She transformed the administrative incompetence which I effortlessly generated into a standard of efficiency and dependability which impressed my superiors. They subsequently promoted the wrong person – me not her – and the rest is history.

Feminist accounts of work in HE seek to explicate the processes which produce gender oppression and gendered divisions of labour (as Webb's account illustrates). Morley (1994: 197–8), for instance, argues in relation to her study of women working in academic posts that 'within academia there is a weave of criss-crossing threads or matrices of discursive practices and a complexity of social identities. Women . . . are in the interstices. Subordination is systematic, structured, extensive, stable, with the ability to constantly reproduce itself'. Such analyses have, unlike those discussed, also attempted to bring the 'body in', showing particularly the culturally mediated nature of embodiment (Morley, 1994; Lander, 1996; Roper, 1996). As Morley again notes, 'women's "emotionality" and "physicality" are placed in binary opposition to men's "rationality"' (1994: 201). Some authors have addressed how particular positionings are literally inscribed on the bodies of workers in HE. Holmer-Nadesen in her study notes how the programme director, who ran a staff development session for the service workers, entitled 'Working Together', aimed at reducing the workers' 'space of action' 'was trim, dressed in professional attire made of natural fabrics while the service workers were almost uniformly plump, dressed in polyester uniforms or casual polyester slacks and blouses. Their very bodies were inscribed with differences of class' (1996: 67).

Game (1994) and Lander (1996) meanwhile throw their nets much wider. Drawing on the structuralist notion that meaning is produced negatively through difference between dominant and subordinate terms, they show how the very notion of 'work' in relation to HE relies on an interdependent series of oppositions between dominant and subordinate signifiers: knowledge work over service work, head/mind work over body/hand work, men's work over women's work, clean work over dirty work. Thus work is organized in HE through material structures of meaning that conflate 'knowledge-head-men-clean' and position it over 'service-body-women-dirty'. Women in HE management positions are, in this analysis, and as Game (1994) notes, 'matter out of place' and thus a challenge to dominant meaning practices.

Of course the *post*structuralist move is to argue that language is inherently unstable. Multiple readings are constantly being produced while power relations are engaged in seeking to stabilize the meaning produced through these pairings. Game describes how, by taking up the post of head of department, she became aware of the attempts to position her as 'secretary' who 'manages the dirt, cleans up the academics' mess' (1994: 48). Being a woman head of department compounded attempts to position her as secretary. She notes that refusing these 'comfortable' feminine positionings which 'go quite smoothly in management is unsettling: for many men and, I suspect, for some women' (1994: 49).

Lander (1996: 4) meanwhile addresses the gradations of clean and dirty in the distribution of work in HE:

> Bodily service work is hermetically sealed in deference to hygienic considerations and truth considerations. This is consonant with the social and cultural distinctions of head work and hand work. It renders the service worker as different, as dirty, as *Other*. Within the service identity of the university there are subcultures each bound by subtle gradations in the social ranking of the unclean . . . the ranking of the unclean is proportionate to services most closely associated with bodily functions, appetitive and eliminative.

This form of analysis suggests that becoming a 'manager' in HE involves reproducing or disrupting particular meaning practices. In Game's case she sought to disrupt those which would position her as secretary or mother. Similarly for men, such implicit and unsaid meaning practices work to produce the interdependence of particular masculinities (e.g. father) and management. The advantage of a poststructuralist approach is that it allows a non-subjective and non-subject-specific account of the agency of management and how it is reproduced through the unsaid practices of masculinity in particular sites and locations.

Summary: a critical literature going poststructural?

The above discussion illustrates the strands that make up the critical literature on work in FHE. As is clear, the move to a poststructural analysis in the feminist and feminist-inspired work in both FE and HE (e.g. Game, 1994, and Holmer-Nadesen, 1996, in HE and Whitehead, 1996, in FE) avoids a strongly dualist and realist epistemology. However, this does not deny the importance of a political–economic reading of the reconstruction of FHE. It simply asserts the need to read it in a different way from that presented in the Marxist approaches discussed above. Workers in FHE *are* involved in a fundamental reconstruction of the sector from public service to public enterprise. Attempts *are* being made to intensify the effectiveness of labour, to reduce costs and increase non-state income. Yet this is not simply a mechanical programme that can be 'read-off' from the prescriptions found in the managerial texts or from a set of college or university management financial statements, or from assumptions about the commodification of learning in units of activity. It involves the reconstruction of identities and relations and thus must be thought of as embedded in the tensions and conflicts between particular knowledges and discursive practices. The epistemological commitment of such a reading is to the manager an effect of the tensions *between* and among differing modes of discursive practice.

In Chapter 2 I shall attempt to provide an account of the development of managers which complements this developing literature. These modes of discursive practice are in dynamic and changing relations to each other. They may be understood to be qualitatively different in scope, variably conflicting and enacting of variably divergent identities, relations and forms of knowledge. Drawing on the framework advanced by Fiske (1993), I will argue that a key difference between these modes is their strategic and tactical orientations. Localized forms seek control over immediate forms of life, while strategic modes attempt to control generalized ways of living/being/acting. The key aspect in the constitution of the 'manager' is tension surrounding the changing character of the relation to 'oneself', understood as a subject position found within these differing modes of discursive practice. To give an example drawn from the research to follow, these competing forms of knowledge potentially constitute college or university departments in conflicting ways. Management knowledges seek to constitute the department as strategically focused, customer-orientated, excellent in and teaching research, and effectively managed. Professional knowledges constitute departments as student-centred, teaching or research focused, collegially organized and possibly politically active. The discursive practices of devolved budgeting, department-based teaching, research assessment and audit processes, funding bids, promotions and contracts, however, position senior post-holders in FHE as more directly responsible for the performance of others, thus challenging and potentially undermining the identities produced by collegial discursive practices. Thus one can argue that through the intensified use of managerial discursive practices one comes to know oneself as directly engaged in managing others' time, space and effort. This is in contrast to the discursive practices of academic colleagues where one's relation to oneself is mediated by the discursive practices of peer review, peer-based promotions and group-based forms of organizing often highly individualized work.

Note

1. Parker and Jary use the term 'McUniversity' which is derived from Ritzer's discussion of 'McDonaldization' (1992), a process where Fordist standardization and rationalization of production methods replace craft skills.

2

Reading the 'Manager': A Critical Conceptual Framework

It is one of the great modern mysteries that although so much is owed by our times to the organising and production genius of management, the world must constantly be reminded of this fact which it seems so obstinately reluctant to learn and believe.

(Levitt, 1976: 73–4)

This palpable ambivalence and doubt, where you pretend to be the commercial business that you cannot be, has led to the present, near fatal crisis where it seems to be thought that the wounds (often self-inflicted) can be stanched by shuffling about word-processed words about a new 'management culture' . . . Management, management, management, the word sticks in one's interface. Please excuse me if I dare to laugh but I know that every age has its little cant word coiled up inside real discourse like a tiny grub in the middle of an apple.

(Potter, 1993: 1)

These two quotations from management theorist Theodore Levitt and playwright Dennis Potter highlight in their own ways the effectiveness of management in contemporary society. While 'management' as an occupational category and economic function has been massively elaborated during the twentieth century (Chandler, 1977; Whitley, 1989), just how 'management' is understood is the question at hand here.

This chapter discusses the various priorities and commitments this book takes up in relation to the study of 'managers' in FHE. It sketches a more detailed picture of the framework presented briefly in the last few pages of the previous chapter. In this chapter I address such priorities and commitments as language, power relations, subjectivity, embodiment and desire. It may, at first, seem strange to discuss managers/managing/management, particularly of universities, in such terms. However it is impossible, I suggest, to fully appreciate the way management has permeated FHE, and the public sector generally, without addressing language, which includes managerial language practices, the embodiment of managerial positions, and the development of managerial identity/subjectivity. Of course 'normal' science and conventional accounts might frame such issues in terms of changing employment relations, changing organizational cultures, economic development or rationalization.

The quotations from Levitt and Potter neatly illustrate the tension between normal and contra, or critical, ways of addressing managers and management. Potter's comment, written as part of a critique of managerial changes at the BBC, points particularly to the way management operates *discursively.* Language is crucial to management's effectiveness, in other words. Potter identifies 'management' as the 'little cant word' of the age which is chanted ('management, management, management') in order to address ('often self-inflicted') crises and problems. By comparing 'management' to a grub 'coiled up inside real discourse', Potter suggests that 'management' works to create a pretence ('where you pretend to be the commercial business that you cannot be'), to which people subscribe. This allows issues to be conceptualized in particular ways, and thus to be amenable to particular kinds of action. Through this Potter highlights how management can be understood not just as a set of production techniques which increase the efficiency of labour, as Levitt suggests, but more as a set of *knowledge practices* which reconstruct problems and crises in such a way as to make 'management', in various competing approaches, the necessary response.

In the case of the BBC, the need to renegotiate its broadcasting licence with a hostile neo-liberal Conservative government in part prompted attempts to introduce 'management reforms' such as the introduction of an internal market for services, staffed by managers. In the case of FHE, the simultaneous decentralization of responsibility for education 'performance', centralization of control and reduction of state funding relative to student numbers drew in and greatly increased the plausibility and effectiveness of managerial knowledges and practices.

It would not be an exaggeration to suggest that *the manager* did not exist in FHE before 1970 (Baron, 1978; Scott, 1995). Tertiary education prior to the 1970s was administered rather than managed. From this critical perspective however the shift in terminology to the 'manager' and 'management' is not simply evocative of the issues at stake here. Nor does it illustrate a newly-enlightened approach to the problems of work and organization. It is actively engaged in the repositioning of FE from public service institutions to public enterprises (Hoggett, 1996). The political nature of management knowledge is a fundamental priority in the study that follows.

A second priority, again suggested by Dennis Potter's point, relates to the broad question of how we might conceptualize the difference between 'management' as a set of structuring practices, and 'managers' as agents. While studies of management and managers approach their objects in numerous ways, most conventional accounts assume the existence of the individualized actor, the manager, who is set within an organization hierarchy, and involved in and responsible for planning, controlling and evaluating the work of others (e.g. see Hales, 1993 for discussion).

Yet if we shift our priority to management, the discussion changes direction with the emphasis then on the organization of work and those tasks and skills (Whitley, 1989) required to produce, distribute and consume goods and services. The manager, as an actor, 'disappears' to some extent in this approach, or is construed as the embodiment of a regime or strategy attempting to efficiently achieve the production, distribution and consumption of goods and services in response to changing conditions. While the commitment to the nature of knowing is retained, the priority as to what can be known, the nature of (human) being, is towards the 'manager' as constituted by and reproductive of broad systemic forces – for example the market, capitalism, or patriarchy.

In this more structuralist kind of account, the 'public' sector education manager of the 1990s is understood less as an actor and more as a node within systems of monitoring, performance management and competitive relations with other decentralized small- to medium-sized public enterprises (SMPEs) (Hoggett, 1996). For instance, output-based funding, audit processes and competitive practices attempt to constitute the process of education management *as if* it were engaged in full capitalist market relations. Management is thus bound by these forces to reduce costs, increase efficiency and maintain control over education work. While public sector education management might be understood as forming part of the state's commitment to enhancing and reproducing, through various means, capitalist relations of production and consumption, how this is done is through knowledges and practices that mirror the private sector. Yet while this kind of systemic or structuralist understanding of management challenges an emphasis on the 'actor', it tends to retain a commitment to a particular way of knowing: the assumption that language can produce accurate *representations* of reality remains intact.

Recent social theory, labelled poststructural, postdualist or postmodernist, has, however, challenged the epistemological commitments which produce such dualist accounts of human societies (structure or agency/actors). While Anthony Giddens (1979) for instance has opted for the analytic of the duality where both structure and agency are interdependent and Pierre Bourdieu (1990) emphasizes tension between different forms of practice, others have turned to language, or more precisely *knowledge*, and argue that such dualistic distinctions are themselves constituted through power-invested linguistic systems and practices. The analytical trajectory thus turns to producing accounts of how these establish themselves and maintain their salience.

This is not linguistics in its traditional sense. It might be understood as the point of intersection where social pragmatics meet social–cultural–economic practices in the midst of psychological processes. This to some extent is the 'new', post-1960s, terrain which authors from the humanities, such as linguistics, through the social and human sciences in the western academic milieu, have sought to excavate. This postdualist social theory adopts a radicalized understanding of the way language operates. Rather than assume an epistemology where language reflects reality, language is understood as actively engaged in materializing reality, or alternatively that reality is neither structurally produced nor derived from social action, but is textually constituted. The nature of material reality is radically undecidable, it is assumed, and must be materialized textually or, in other words, must be realized in discourse in some way.

A poststructural approach requires that we understand reality as 'realized' through language or knowledge practices. The shift is away from an analysis which suggests that power relations, for instance, are found in economic relations *per se*, and towards approaches that understand discourse as that mode by which economic relations and individual workers or consumers are mutually produced. In this approach relations of power, identities, even bodies, are textually or discursively constituted through the ordering and organizing practices of particular discourses. Knowledge about some entity, such as the 'manager', can be said to be involved in actively strengthening the 'presence' or bringing into existence of that entity.

Language, knowledge, discourse

But how does 'language' accomplish this? What it is about *language* that makes this possible? There are, in the midst of this broad epistemological commitment to the importance or materiality of language numerous ways of exploring language in relation to management and organization studies (Putnam *et al.*, 1996). Two approaches might be highlighted. One priority might be with the performance of managing through language practices of, for example, storytelling (Boje, 1995; Linstead *et al.*, 1996; Sosteric, 1996; Barry and Elmes, 1997; Downing, 1998). Here managing, as Shotter argues, involves 'arguing persuasively for a "landscape" of new possible actions upon which the positions of all those who must take part are clear' (1993: 156).

A second priority might be with the way language allows the ordering, organizing and structuring of conduct or practices (Townley, 1994). Here managing, as Miller and Rose (1990: 8) suggest, involves 'techniques of notation, computation and calculation; procedures of examination and assessment . . . the standardisation of systems of training and the inculcation of habits'.

In relation to the first priority, managerial work might be understood as *dialogical*. The emphasis is placed on the 'conversations' which organize work. In this vein Gower and Legge (1996) refer to managing as an oral tradition. Yet even this commitment to analysis of the practices of dialogue, stories and narratives (rather than to 'dialoguing' human beings), seems to fall short of the claims of a postdualist social science (Reed, 1997; O'Doherty and Willmott, 1998). Clearly 'dialogue', no matter how structured it may be by various genres of discursive practice, struggles to contribute to an account of the relative permanence of particular power relations, inequitable distribution of scarce resources and the ascendancy and relative permanence of capitalist wage-labour relations.

To address these issues, emphasis needs to be shifted away from language *per se* (e.g. narrating, uttering, conversing), towards *discourse*. This might be understood here as politically active knowledge practices and formations.

Discourses are not simply the discursive practices of talk and text, but are, rather, modes of ordering or organizing which recursively realize and constitute the 'real', which of course includes particular discursive practices.

To give a 'concrete' example, in one of the four colleges included in the study on which this book is based ('Tower College'), one of the first moves the new principal made on arrival was to turn four heads of department out of a room they shared together. He repositioned them with their colleagues in the shared departmental staff workroom. Placing of the head of department's desk in the middle of the department teaching staff can be read as a *discursive statement*. But its significance with regard to the organization of work, power relations and the development of the manager is more productively addressed by seeing it as part of a new *discourse of managing* in the college; that which attempts to increase the control and supervision of teaching work and reduce possible sources of opposition to itself by, in this case, a group of heads of department.

To summarize, what is being suggested is that the priority is with 'discourse'. This reads discourse as having folded within it power relations, discursive or communicational practices and actual embodied effects. In this way, discourses provide ways of being (identities), ways of relating to others (relations) and ways of understanding the world (knowledges) (Fairclough, 1992). The epistemological commitment in this is away from attempts to define the contours and features of a real organizational world, of production and organization, and towards an exploration of the way knowledge practices are constantly engaged moment by moment in constituting the 'real'. In Game's (1991) terms the commitment is towards putting the power-laden practices of mapping the 'real' into the making of such maps (Game, 1991).

Identity and subjectivity

'The politics of identity and identity representation may be the deepest and most suppressed struggle in the work place and hence the "site" where domination and responsive agency are most difficult to unravel' (Deetz, 1992: 59).

In the previous section I suggested that identities are embedded in, and effects of, particular discourses. Yet they cannot be simply 'read off' from such discourses for, as the Stan Deetz's quotation suggests, this would deny the importance of 'struggle' and tension between identities. It would also tend to close off the issue of agency which is at the core of discussion of managerial work (Chandler, 1977; Whitley, 1989; Hales, 1993). The question becomes how to conceptualize agency, in the context of this shift to a postdualist way of knowing managerial work within 'critical' or contra management studies.

To reiterate, most accounts of managing tend to speak of management as either a role or positioning in a structure, or of the manager as agentic actor. Of course 'management' is linked to the historical development of paid-work organizations (Chandler, 1977). A structuralist reading of such developments suggests that management either functions in a system of relations, or 'stands in for' the forces of capital or the state in the commodification and realization of efficient relations between the potential of labour and actual labour.

In an agentic reading, management is anthropomorphized as the manager or managers who are motivated by various incentives or rewards, and who learn to become and act as managers through interaction with others. Organizations are negotiated orders, more or less, and managers are made responsible for, more or less, achieving this negotiation. In an agentic reading *identity* or *subjectivity* is assumed to pre-exist and be reconstituted through social interaction with others. In a structuralist reading human subjectivity is broadly the canvas upon which structural processes work. A commitment to a poststructural or postdualist epistemology meanwhile 'annoys' both such accounts of identity or subjectivity.

The 'agentic manager' suggests that the 'self' is composed of various techniques of, for example, reflection, remembering, assessment and discussion, which give us a sense of being. However this 'sense' is not an ontological given, but an *effect of*, for instance, management knowledges and practices. These practices of *reflexivity* are not inherent in 'the individual', but are learned techniques engaged in producing and refining a particular individual identity or self. While some postdualist or poststructuralist writers give ground to an assumption of a fundamental separation within ourselves as both potentially subject and object, self and other ('I's', and 'me's') others (Deleuze, 1988; Law, 1994a) prefer to read subjectivity as an 'infolding' of the outside. So for instance the supposed agency of say a 'manager' is read as an effect of the infolding of exteriorized relations into strategies of reflexivity.

In relation to a structuralist account, where the identity or subjectivity of management is derived from its functional role in a social system, or the structure of capitalist or patriarchal relations, the challenge is around issues of determinism, realism and positivism. Knights and Willmott, for example (1985, 1989; Willmott, 1994, 1998; Knights, 1997) are among the authors who have sought to establish such a postdualist position in relation to a structuralist account of management. In relation to determinism, they argue that managerial identities cannot be derived *directly* from capitalist or patriarchal structures. In a series of papers they have argued that conditions of 'world-openness', or our generalized ontological insecurity, together with the underdetermination of identity by capitalist labour relations and modern forms of power, all work to reinforce particular identities. In short, subjects are constructed as 'free', but the conditions and practices by which this 'freedom' can be enacted are tightly circumscribed. For example, in relation to public sector FHE the manager is said to be 'free to manage' resources, but this is constructed through the knowledges and practices of inspections, performance management, income targets and budgets. Such practices also 'worry' our generalized anxiety over how one is meant to be/ act in the world, and by providing 'solutions' to these 'worries' their plausibility and legitimacy is boosted. Managerial knowledges and practices are thus embraced precisely because they offer positive ways of articulating and securing a sense of managerial identity.

In relation to realism and positivism, Knights (1992: 530) argues that management knowledges often unreflectively privilege representational strategies to the point where 'distinctions are transformed from heuristic devices into reified ontological realities' (Knights 1997: 4). Thus representations of the manager as functioning in a social system or as masculine hero or as paternalistic benefactor are engaged not simply in representing management, but in actively constituting managerial subjectivity. Thus supposedly scientific accounts of management are politically engaged in 'knowledging' the manager into place, so to speak. The seeming objectivity and certainty of such accounts is a device for attempting to shore up legitimacy.

While Knights and Willmott (1989) have drawn on a range of resources, more recent work (Knights, 1992) derives in part from Foucault's analysis of modern forms of power. Foucault (1972, 1983, 1991) argued that contemporary society is premised not so much on relations of exploitation or domination, but of *subjectification*. That is, modern power works at creating particular 'individuals' with particular relations to their bodies and themselves (conscience). Thus while the 'manager' might be understood from a structuralist position as attempting to cohere productive economic relations of production or patriarchal relations of dominance over women and other men in work organizations, these relations do not in themselves produce the 'manager'. The 'manager' is an effect of particular knowledge practices, which could also be said to simultaneously produce capitalist or patriarchal structures. Another way to put this would be to suggest that contemporary public and private sector corporations are as much interested in producing the right kind of individual worker or consumer as in producing the right kind of service or product.

In the case of the manager, modern power works through various devices (e.g. tactics of reflexivity) to attach a particular self to, or inscribe a particular self upon, a particular body – a self that is responsible and accountable for particular areas of activity. Managerial subjectivity or identity is a relation to a self produced, as Knights and Willmott note, through 'disciplinary mechanisms, techniques of surveillance and power–knowledge strategies' (1989: 554).

Yet this conceptualization would seem to have again eschewed the question of agency, which might be translated as resistance to imperializing power, or as our sense of being aware of our status as objects of knowledge, or as our awareness of being actors in a field of potential actions. I want to explore this issue briefly by drawing on debate between the sociologists Stuart Hall and Nikolas Rose. This debate centres on the issue of identity in relation to agency within the poststructuralist 'turn'. Broadly the debate 'runs' in two directions. Hall, worried that resistance is being overlooked, suggests in relation to agency that identity be read as linking psychoanalytic depth to discursive practices. What is required, he argues, is a 'theory of what the mechanisms are by which individuals as subjects identify (or do not identify) with the 'positions' to which they are summoned; as well as how they fashion, stylise, produce and "perform" these positionings' (Hall, 1996: 14). Such a theory requires an account of the processes of articulation, understood as the contingent and non-intentional suturing of the unconscious and discursive positionings. Hall asserts that Foucault's 'flat' or 'thin' ontology (his rejection of interiority or the unconscious) leaves little space upon which to address this relation without recourse to some notion of intentionality.

Rose meanwhile moves in the other direction arguing that agency be read as an outcome of the heterogeneity of discursive practices (1996a). Following Foucault he thus rejects any approach that might assume some 'interiority':

> The human being, here, is not an entity with a history, but the target of a multiplicity of types of work, more like a latitude and longitude at which different vectors of different speeds intersect. The interiority which some may feel compelled to diagnose is not that of a psychological system, but of a discontinuous surface, a kind of infolding of exteriority.
>
> (Rose, 1996a: 143)

The fundamental point for Rose and other governmentalists (a term used by Hall) is that the way in which human beings give meaning to experience has its own history. For Deleuze 'thought thinks its own history' (1988: 119). More specifically, as Rose argues, giving meaning to experience involves practical, technical devices of meaning production. This include grids of visualization, vocabularies, norms and systems of judgement. For Rose *these* produce experience; experience does not produce *them* (1996a: 130). Such devices, with their embedded power relations, can be described as making up the means by which 'human beings come to relate to themselves and others as subjects of a certain type' (1996a: 130–1). Yet Rose later suggests that 'in any one site or locale, *humans turn programmes* intended for one end to the service of others' (1996a: 141, emphasis added). Rose is suggesting a 'theory' of agency that assumes human beings have the ability to translate the practices or part practices of one locale/site and apply these to others.

The key point is that in this latter position the ontological commitment is to a human being whose 'interior' is formed through discursive processes of *subjectification*. The earlier position, on the other hand, talks of processes of *identification* which assume a dynamic desiring interior or unconscious which engages dynamically with discursive processes. Yet Rose does assume some minimal 'theory' of agency where actual 'human being' exceeds systems of thought. Rose's work admits, perhaps reluctantly, that 'human being' involves turning programmes intended for one end to the service of others. This involves inventing, refining and stabilizing particular practices. It involves occupying spaces, challenging practices, and potentially founding, in the terms used here, new alliances and power blocs. While Rose rejects romantic agency, the agency he accepts is more technical and pragmatic. When 'forced', as Hall predicted, he takes up a limited explanation of human intentionality. For his part, Hall accepts that 'selves' are potentially regulatory ideals, but that this does not diminish the potency of political and psychodynamic struggle over our insertion into particular subject positions.

Despite these differences, there is no need to choose between these explanations. The broad argument is that each of these processes is engaged in forming human subjectivity as a dynamic, multilayered, biographically infused 'depth' from which various 'I's' can be spoken/articulated and that the suffusion of new discourses (e.g. of 'management' in post-compulsory education institutions) is formed through the interdependence of discourses as they connect and overlap with biographically located and gendered subjectivity.

Identities and subjectivities in organizational contexts: reading the tensions vertically and horizontally as locales and stations

Fiske's work is intertextually linked to the approach to subjectivity suggested by both Rose and Hall. For Fiske, use of the terms 'power bloc' and 'people' provides a means of retaining elements of Hall's debate over resistance and 'vertical' relations of power, alongside Rose's discussion of a 'flat' ontology of the subject. Fiske's form of analysis thus provides a powerful means of using the insights of the debate concerning agency and the construction of the subject.

For example, in relation to Hall's approach, Fiske agrees that 'the people versus the power-bloc: this rather than class against class, is the central line of contradiction around which the terrain of culture is polarised' (Hall, 1981, cited in Fiske, 1993: 9). Yet for Fiske the 'power bloc' is not a class or a state but a precarious alliance of dominant interests articulated through various imperializing knowledges and practices. The 'people' meanwhile maintain localized and tactical forms of knowledge practices which themselves provide particular valued identities and dispositions. These sets of dispositions, identities and relations carry within them various social interests. Thus while dominant social alliances could be said to exist in what Wetherell and Potter (1992) describe as established economic and social resources, the social interests themselves are dispersed through mobile forms of knowledges and practices which have the effect of attempting to extend or maintain such strategic interests.

A crucial element in Fiske's conceptualization, and what further distinguishes his work from that of Rose, is the qualitative distinction he makes between the ordering practices/forms of subjectification produced by the 'power bloc' and the 'people'. Broadly, Fiske overlays a Gramscian or de Certeauian understanding of tactical politics (1989) on a Foucauldian understanding of how modern power operates, thus taking up the wide criticism of Foucault's work that power fails effectively to deal with resistance. The result is an understanding of identity as a tension between *individuated* identities produced by top-down processes of assessment, evaluation and control, and 'horizontal' or 'bottom-up' *individualized* identities, embedded in localized relations and practices. To provide some analytical purchase Fiske introduces the terms 'station' and 'locale'. Locales are established and maintained at the 'grass roots' by those concerned about their immediate conditions of life. They are often made up of 'hard won' individualized identities. As Fiske (1993: 12) puts it, 'Constructing a locale involves confronting, resisting or evading imperialization, for imperializing power wishes to control the members of its own society as strongly as it wishes to control the physical world'.

Stations, in contrast, are imposed from 'above' in an effort to incorporate or colonize 'the people' into a system designed by the power bloc. These exhibit individuated identities. Those who seek to establish and maintain stations, Fiske (1993: 12) continues, 'must control the places where people live, the behaviours by which they live and the consciousness by which they make sense of their identities and experiences. It [the power bloc] attempts to stop people producing their own locales by providing them with stations'.

Thus for Fiske a *station* is: 'both a physical place where the *social order is imposed upon the individual* and the social positioning of that individual in the system of social relations' (1993: 12, emphasis added). In opposition to the top-down power of 'power blocs', the subordinated formations of 'the people' comprise and articulate localized knowledges and practices.

So, for example, the position of the manager in work organizations has been established through a succession of expert knowledges underpinned by a separation of ownership of property and control of resources. These knowledges position managers as experts at controlling organizations and, in particular, the profitable organization of human labour. In UK colleges and universities the presence and legitimacy of managerial knowledges have been boosted by the introduction of particular funding formulas, performance measures and auditing practices. Practices such as the research assessment exercise seek to station academics by individuating them in relation to their work. The strategic aim is to enjoin them to constantly assess and evaluate themselves, using particular norms and measurements, as productive individual researchers responsible for their own productivity. These measures simultaneously evaluate the productive organization of academic labour within departments and across institutions. They thereby increase pressures upon senior post-holders to assess and improve performance according to the criteria established by these measures and their associated league tables of performance. In this way, institutions, departments and individuals are stationed as objects of power bloc knowledges (e.g. measures of research output and assessment of teaching quality) that increasingly become a major focus of interaction and mutual surveillance within and between institutions (Thomas, 1994; Willmott, 1995).

However, each 'individuated subject', each stationed department and its 'manager', is also crucially embedded in localized cultures of practices which produce other relations to the self – that is, individualized identities, which variably resist and subvert managerially individuated identities (stationings). Examples of this abound in discussion with staff and senior professionals in colleges and universities. While senior post-holders spend time developing and implementing performance review processes, staff members engage in counter moves to resist the intrusion of such reporting and surveillance by ignoring requests and advice, by failing to attend meetings, or by 'losing' memoranda and proforma.

From a Fiskean perspective, those who 'lubricate the mechanisms' of subordination (such as top-down performance measures) are understood to be participants in the reproduction of a 'power bloc'. 'The people', in contrast, are distinguished by 'their comparative lack of privilege, [and] their comparative deprivation of economic and political resources' (Fiske, 1993: 11). That said, the conflict between such formations means that the imperializing ambitions of a particular power bloc are constantly falling short of their objectives as they are variably resisted and challenged by the ubiquitous micro-organizings of locales. Also the same 'individuals', on different occasions, act to support or challenge a power bloc's legitimacy and extension. There are then multiple dimensions of polarization between 'the people' and 'the power bloc'. Fiske (1993: 11) offers the following example:

> A blue-collar white man may form a social allegiance with Black men who share his skills and conditions of subordination at work, but may, in his leisure, ally himself with other white men in relations of social dominance. The first allegiance would be with the social force of the people, the second with that of the power-bloc.

Recurrent struggles between 'power blocs' and 'the people' occur within groups but more importantly 'within' people whose allegiances shift depending upon their positioning within diverse sets of discursive social relations. In other words, we all move in and out of relations which maintain and extend the power bloc into and across our lives and the lives of others.

The upshot of shifting allegiances is that there is no guarantee that the imperializing knowledges and techniques will overturn existing localized practices and identities. In the case of performance measures within universities and colleges, there is no certainty that the *spirit* of procedures will be observed, although there may be a dramaturgical management of appearances to simulate conformity. For example, in one of the universities discussed in a later section of this book, the common 'story' about top-down appraisal processes was that they became a chat between colleagues over a cup of coffee. The practices of the locale filled the space made available by the imposition of appraisal. In this we can see the crucial difference between imperializing and localizing knowledges and practices. The *station* and the *locale* are different ways of representing and enacting the same physical and social space. Whereas the imperializing knowledges and practices of the power bloc are strategic in their colonizing intent, the concern of localizing power is not to expand its terrain but, rather, to strengthen its (tactical) control and defences over the immediate conditions of life.

The locale might appear in these descriptions as essentially defensive in orientation. Yet it seems likely that during particular periods and moments the discourses of the locale could be taken up to serve the imperializing processes of an ascending power bloc. It may be that the practices of a locale replace those of the stations of the older power bloc. As Fiske (1993: 81) notes, 'Localising power is not fixed in its relations with imperialising, top-down power: indeed, it is impossible to specify in advance what forms these relations will take'. Fiske's conceptual framework, which puts identity at the centre of links between broad socio-economic alliance and the micro-politics of locales, forms the basis of this exploration of the manager in FHE.

However, it is worth emphasizing here that the 'station' and 'locale' *do not* ontologically exist. What exists are various imperializing and localizing knowledges and practices which produce variably individuated or individualized identities and relations. The notion of 'station' and 'locale' are sensitizing devices, or 'analytics' (Curt, 1994), which allow particular readings of empirical material. Ontologically the priority is, as with Law's work (1994a), to address the effectiveness of qualitatively different ordering practices within the broad epistemological commitment to a postdualist social science. Where Fiske's approach differs from Law's is that by drawing in Gramsci's notion of the power bloc as a precarious alliance of socially dominant interests, a sense of a broader and embedded picture of advantage and disadvantage can be drawn. More importantly there is a political commitment embedded in Fiske's approach. The tensions between stations and locales, produced by historically contingent socially dominant imperializing practices and socially marginalized, defensive or subordinate localizing practices restores to a postdualist approach a sense of what Harvey described as the ability to distinguish between 'significant and insignificant differences' (1993: 63). However, this aside, the key point is that the approach is not attempting to reintroduce dualistic entities (e.g. the agentic individual and the structuring organization) but to create an analytical device that maintains the tensions between differing modes of ordering which produce both 'individuals' and 'organizations'. The aim is to maintain a commitment to the potentiality of the tension of dualistic analysis without recourse to dualisms. The critical difference is not to be party to the transformation of heuristic devices (stations/locales) into ontological realities.

Having said this however, it is also necessary to offer a small number of clarifications and extensions to Fiske's approach. While the contention is that imperializing practices, such as those of management, seek to continuously extend control over space and time, and localized practices are concerned primarily with control which provides a relatively secure and pleasurable existence, Fiske (1973: 78) is *not* assuming that these forms of power are in strict opposition or that they maintain their control. Fiske (1993: 81) suggests for instance that:

> workers are constantly developing practices which enlarge their terrain of control within the work place. These are not always resistant or disruptive, but may at times be complicit with the aims of the corporation, and may make its operations more efficient. Localising power is not fixed in its relations with imperialising power.

Equally, Fiske is not assuming opposition between actual people and actual corporations or organizations. While he suggests that 'people are agents' (1993: 82), the emphasis is on the variable histories of identities, competencies and interests that are brought to disciplinary systems. These histories provide, for Fiske, the tactics by which disciplinary practices are sometimes inverted, disrupted, opposed and evaded. They provide the 'sand that [people] put into the gearbox [of disciplinary practices] from outside' (1993: 82). In common with Rose, Fiske assumes no centred conscious human being, but emphasizes politically potent ways of being and relating to oneself and others, with differing strategic objectives.

Embodying stations and locales: some additions

The analytical framework just presented provides, in my view, the best possible vehicle for elaborating the problematic terrain of the 'development' of the post-compulsory education manager, given the ontological priorities and epistemological commitments taken up so far. Yet I want to briefly outline an extension to the conceptual framework.

Fiske (1993: 17) argues that the two concepts, 'locale' and 'station', provide a way of incorporating aspects of social experience which are frequently separated: the interior elements of consciousness, the physical dimensions of bodies and socio-political relations. For Fiske the body is fundamental to the reproduction of both imperializing and localizing forms of power: 'Social agency, both of the power-bloc and the people, is put to work on the body, for the body is the primary site of social experience. It is where social life is turned into lived experience . . . the change in the regime of power must occur at all levels, and finally, must occur at the most micro level, that of the body' (1993: 57).

Yet Fiske's account of the body lacks a means of discussing this 'micro level' which includes not just how bodies are positioned in space, how they are covered and spoken about (what might be termed 'body surface'), but more importantly the affective, sensuous, desirous dimension, which might be termed 'body depth'. Fiske's framework lacks, in my view, a way of addressing the inscription and enactment of body 'surface' and 'depth' by tactically and strategically orientated discursive practices (Prichard, forthcoming). To reiterate, such terms as station and locale, depth and surface, do not describe the ontological reality. They are terms through which empirical material can be organized. The spatial, physical and verbal aspects (Halford *et al.*, 1997) which could be said to make up 'body surface' are ways of analysing and discussing those knowledges and practices which construct and reconstruct the body in social relations.

These two axes, 'surface' and 'depth', provide a means of reading the body's physical, verbal and spatial placement, and its unstable sensual, desiring and emotional inscription. The first axis, body 'surface', involves the mapping of the spatial, verbal and physical materiality of embodiment. Body depth, meanwhile, understands the body as political matter which is inscribed, folded and reworked through the dynamic interplay of desire (physical energy), signification and practices (Prichard, forthcoming). The point at issue is that we do not experience our bodies in terms of their biological organization, but as patterns of sensation and intensities. These patterns seem to be 'natural', but in the framework presented here they are understood as 'organized' in the interplay of social practices, knowledges and the desiring body.

To take an example: being made redundant from one's job often leads to strong emotions and grief as well as abrupt changes to health and fitness. By relying on a conventional self–body dualism we might say that a sacking challenges and threatens a particular self. From a body depth perspective however, the loss of a job severs many of the routinized mappings (or assemblages) through which desire flows. One of the key mappings for men particularly is how work organizations overlay *familial patternings* of desire. For instance, a person's patternings of desire might be invested (projected) positively in trusting his or her head of department, professor, manager, college or university (Roper, 1996). This in turn overlays powerful family and father/mother mappings. To be made redundant, sacked or not to have one's contract renewed is to sever these inscriptions which tap deeper mappings of rejection by father and family. The severing of these markings or foldings (through redundancy or sacking) might 'present' or be expressed as grief, pain, illness and a loss of health and fitness. The key point is that identities and relations are often deeply embodied. From a 'surface' perspective redundancy means the removal of the body from particular spaces, its recovering in different fabrics and the calling up or speaking about that body in new ways – as an unemployed body.

Summary

The two dimensions of body topography are used here to complement and extend Fiske's notions of station and locale. I shall therefore, at various points in this book, draw on surface and depth as dimensions of locales and stations. This addition to Fiske's approach allows a reading of body depth as dynamic and capable of creating new patternings, not simply as inscribed and ordered by the patternings of locales and stations. Again there is no determined relation between localizing and imperializing forms, and 'desire/anxiety' is engaged in maintaining locales and extending stations. As noted, the difference between these is that the locale is a product of the subordinate social formation which is typically held defensively and tactically against the stationing power of the dominant which is applied strategically. Thus the managerial body is likely to move through and embody various locales and stations. The spatiality of the desk, the physicality of the suit and the team briefing can be read as stations, for example. Likewise, the physicality of the lunchtime 'pint' (Watson, 1994), the different spatiality of pre- and post-meeting discussions, even the training event are sites where potential new orderings, different ways of embodying the manager, and the investment in other bodies and knowledges can be produced. The managerial station may also be reconstructed by other practices and knowledges which challenge the spatial, physical, verbal and desiring aspects of the embedded managerial station.

To take one example, the new female, and feminist, pro vice-chancellor at Southern University[1] brought 'sticky buns' to university committee meetings when she started work. The dominant knowledges and practices of the university's senior post-holder meetings, which produce the station, had, prior to this, tended to operate through a series of differences or separations: between men and women, between food work and knowledge work, and between clean and dirty (Lander, 1996). The sticky buns challenged these oppositions and forced the introduction of different body practices into the meeting space – the desiring, eating and consuming body. This challenged, in a seemingly small but potent way, the practices of the existing stations of the university, which were understood by the pro vice-chancellor and other senior women post-holders to work against women. The sticky buns came to symbolize among a group of senior women administrators the beginning of a concerted challenged to the established station. This involved attempts to introduce more 'women-friendly' practices into the masculine orderings of university meetings. As one of the pro vice-chancellor's supporters said later: 'She has a very open way of chairing meetings and a very different kind of way. The first meeting she had she ordered sticky buns and things like that, you know [laughs], like people were just taken aback, didn't know what to do with it'.

The sticky buns are part of a challenge to the way the university is/was managed and as Fiske notes any change to the regime of power requires ultimately the reconstruction of the intimate micro practices of the body in these sites. Sticky buns introduce different spatial, physical, verbal and desiring micro practices into these managerial sites, and thus challenge the existing embodied practices and knowledges of the managerial station.

Note

1. Names of institutions have been changed in line with anonymity agreements.

3

Further and Higher Education's Turbulent Years

The truth is that this neo-Stalinist shift to centralisation, and policing flies in the face of not only centuries of history – during which British universities, curiously, contrived to become world-class long before the QAA was ever dreamed up – but of genuinely forward-looking management thinking.

(Taylor, 1998a: 60)

The years 1997–2000 may in retrospect mark the beginning of a major reconstruction for FE colleges and universities in the UK. Under steerage from a Labour government which comprehensively disposed of its rival in 1997, both sectors are at the time of writing now confronting the first policy moves which address Blairite, rather than Thatcherite, priorities.

For instance, moves are afoot to slow down and offset the increasingly desperate financial circumstances faced by most universities and colleges between 1995 and 1998 in both sectors. This has been welcomed by college and university representative groups. At the same time the Blairite rhetoric of 'partnership', 'collaboration' and 'investment' is beginning to be translated, across both sectors, from ministerial speeches to policy statements, funding directives and programmes (HEFCE, 1998; FEFC, 1999).

Among these are, for instance, moves to curb college franchising of courses to private training providers, to stimulate college-based recruitment, particularly of 16–18-year-olds, and to reduce the speed by which the sector's average funding level (AFL) is being driven to a particular value. David Melville, the FEFC chief executive, enthusiastically welcomed these initiatives telling college principals in 1999 that 'we are extremely pleased that FE has, at last, taken its place in the Government's spotlight' (Melville, 1999). He said that the government's project is about investment in learning and modernization and 'we are, as a sector, inextricably bound into the Government's project' (Melville, 1999).

Of course the development and extension of what might be termed a Blairite power bloc in relation to colleges and universities confronts the knowledge, practices, languages and dispositions of what I shall term the Thatcherite power bloc (whose party won five consecutive general election victories), which is strongly inscribed across both sectors. For example, resistance to the Blairite expectation that colleges and universities will cooperate and form partnerships seems inevitable following years of direct competition for students and funding between decentralized, corporately-focused colleges and universities. The managerial station in colleges and universities is, I shall argue, largely an effect of the Thatcherite power bloc. Current and future reconstruction will be mediated against this formation.

The aim of this chapter is to sketch briefly the development of the Thatcherite power bloc and to trace its lines of impact across the FHE sectors. Addressing the impact of the new regime is outside the scope of this account. The chapter overviews the legislative, regulatory and fiscal elements that bear down on and elaborate the construction of the 'manager' in FHE. Yet to make sense of these an account of the wider processes of political–economic reconstruction is also required. The aim here is not to read these changes sequentially and neutrally. They have been constitutive of an ascendant managerial station, to use Fiske's (1993) term, or to use Law's (1994a) term, a 'mode of ordering' in colleges and universities.

Positioning the 'power bloc': changing political–economic alliances, and education as a service industry

Drawing on the notion of the 'power bloc' presented in the previous chapter, the reconstruction of FHE in the last 15 years can be read as an effect of attempts by an ascendant neo-liberal (Thatcherite) power bloc to radically rewrite the terms by which post compulsory education is organized and governed (Ryan, 1998). The Thatcherite power bloc in general though can be said to comprise a distinctive set of alliances between private capital, a radical conservatism propagated by, for example, Sir Keith Joseph, and heterogeneous sections of the electorate. This power bloc encompassed diverse shades of political opinion, notably in relation to the meaning of nationalism and the European question. As moves towards European federalism were made or projected, the Thatcherite alliance became progressively split and disorganized as a populist ideology as well as a political force. The last Thatcherite government was dramatically swept from office in April 1997. However, this was not before it had won five consecutive general elections and, it can be argued, significantly reconstructed the UK's political and economic landscape (MacInnes, 1987; Jenkins, 1995; Clarke and Newman, 1997).

In terms of the public sector, the key elements of the Thatcherite power bloc's 'common sense' was that the state sector was a 'drain' on the UK economy, was inefficient and unresponsive to taxpayer 'needs' and largely controlled by élite professional groupings. Such a construction of the public sector was set early on in the Thatcher government's term in office. Mrs Thatcher wrote in the 1979 Conservative Party manifesto: 'No one who has lived in this country for the last five years can fail to be aware of how the balance of our society has been increasingly tilted in favour of the State at the expense of *individual freedom* . . . the state takes too much of the nation's income; its share must be steadily reduced' (quoted in Pollitt, 1993: 44, emphasis added).

The neo-liberal emphasis on 'individual freedom' provided the basis for a reconstruction of the 'public' as consumers, and the public sector as public enterprises engaged in providing services to meet individual consumer/customer/client needs (the emphasis was away from notions of collective social provision). Through this, public sector organizations were re-imagined and reconstructed as 'businesses' by new funding and regulatory practices which positioned them as having to bid or contract to provide a certain level of 'output' to a certain specification (Hoggett, 1996). Hoggett identifies three key strategic elements to this: creation of operationally decentralized units with increased centralized control (principally through funding and output targeting), competition between units, and intensified auditing of these units.

Thus public sector organizations were re-imagined as contractors and service providers and managerial knowledges and practices came to suffuse the terrain previously occupied by professional and administrative knowledge and practices. Public sector organizations were said to be without 'effective management'. The classic anecdote of this is found in the 1983 Griffiths Report (DHSS, 1983) on the NHS which recommended the introduction of general managers to hospitals. The report suggested that if Florence Nightingale was carrying her lamp through the corridors of the NHS today, she would almost certainly be looking for the people in charge (DHSS, 1983: 12). The 'manager' thus becomes a central figure in public sector reconstruction, charged initially with being responsible and accountable for service provision against centrally controlled 'contract' levels of work (Willocks and Harrow, 1992). As Clarke and Newman (1997: 36) note: 'Managerialism intersects with the New Right project in several ways. Decentralisation, contracting, the creation of "quasi-markets", privatisation and other processes integral to state restructuring have all placed a new emphasis on managerial and business skills'.

Generally, these practices have been variably productive in reconstituting the public sector as an extension of the service economy. While large segments have been turned over to corporate capitalism, the 'core' areas of education, health, social services and defence remain broadly taxpayer funded and publicly accountable to Parliament. Yet in these areas, the aim has been to transform the sector *as if* it had been privatized. As Hall (1993: 15) notes, 'The right . . . wanted [the public sector] to be submitted to the institutional logic of the market. It is only to be worked, operated, regulated and disciplined in ways that markets do'. Hall's general point, and that of other writers (du Gay, 1996; Rose, 1996a), is that the public sector does not need to be privatized as such, but the way in which it is organized and governed 'should' mirror private sector practices.

Critical analysts of public sector reconstruction note that the key point of this infusion of 'managerial skills' is that such restructuring is not simply the application of progressive and 'necessary' business skills, but politically and culturally significant ones. Broadly, the stationing of the 'manager' is an attempt by an ascendant power bloc to cement in place a particular disposition which reinscribes the relations between state and public, between public sector employees and those they serve and, most importantly, between, for example, the way we as a public understand and enact ourselves as a group with needs, rights or demands. This re-mapping engages a broad cultural reconstruction of notions of the public, citizenship, professionalism and conceptions of education generally. Education is progressively constructed as an individual economic 'good' provided by post-compulsory sector colleges and universities who compete to meet the needs of various customers/consumers. Management and business skills, while often presented as such, are neither neutral, apolitical nor disinterested. Despite powerful and mystifying claims to the contrary, management is a *social* practice, not a scientific/technological one. The 'manager', as Reed (1990: 81) notes, can be said to be a social category positioned in an attempt to finesse a way between structural demands and constraints and human objections. The theoretical content of management is not derived directly from science and experimentation, but from the various practices borne from crises and elisions in the historical and cultural relations of power (particularly of capitalism and patriarchy) which have enabled and impeded, at turns, management's emergence (Alvesson and Willmott, 1996: 38). Responses to such crises and elisions have then claimed or been glossed with the legitimating, neutralizing and objectifying force of scientific discourse. Management in this light might be more adequately considered a problematic and precarious process of political manoeuvre, which draws on and progressively exhausts particular 'innovations' as they fail to secure the effects promised (Eccles and Nohria, 1992). As a result there is, as Thompson and McHugh (1990, 1995) assert, no 'one-best-way' to manage, only different routes to partial failure.

If we read management as politically engaged (but with a tendency to deny this engagement), we will not be surprised by the fact that there were a number of varieties and variations to this 'managerial logic' during the Thatcher/Major years, and variable degrees and configurations by which particular state sectors were subject to each variation (Hood, 1991; Stewart and Walsh, 1992; Willocks and Harrow, 1992; Farnham and Horton, 1993; Pollitt, 1993; Clarke *et al.*, 1994; Jenkins, 1995; Clarke and Newman, 1997). There is in other words no 'management station', but various seemingly contradictory practices and knowledges, which work to produce management 'stationings'. As one is 'exhausted' the potential of another proves alluring and is engaged. As Eccles and Nohria (1992: 31) so neatly write, 'New vocabularies cycle quickly through the elaborate social system of management discourse – adopted under the promise of change and innovation, discarded when they are no longer able to inspire and mobilize action'.

Broadly, the legislative, regulatory and organizational 'reforms' which swept through the public sector during the 1980s and 1990s approached the 'problems' of the public sector (articulated by the Thatcherite power bloc in relation to its cost, relative efficiency and producer 'capture') by moving initially, as Pollitt (1993) suggests, from Taylorite specification and control of costs, to more consumerist and culture/human relations-based approaches in the later years of the Conservative era.

Constructing the 'accountable manager'

The public sector management literature amply illustrates the move from what I shall term the 'accountable manager' to the 'enterprising manager'. The 'accountable manager', to some, is the line manager and to others the 'hard' Taylorite managerialist dispatched to cut costs across the public sector. The 'accountable manager' can be seen as Griffiths' general manager (DHSS, 1983), Hood's (1991) 'new public management' and Pollitt's (1993) 'implementor of new disciplines of measurement and rationalisation'. The opposition upon which this positioning is built is that the public sector has been or is controlled by unaccountable professions or consensualist management. As Pollitt (1993: 85) notes: 'Everywhere the hierarchy of "line management" is said to need strengthening – presumably against the forces of organisational pluralism and professional autonomy'.

Conservative ministers constantly reproduced this opposition and positioning during the 1980s and 1990s. Kenneth Clarke (1993), who held a number of significant cabinet posts during the Thatcher and Major years, including education, declared that the Conservative-driven changes involved 'taking on powerful vested producer interests' and the 'acceptance of modern thinking and modern management in the public services where virtually none existed before'.

Yet the 'accountable manager' as a source for inspiration was limited. As Common *et al.* (1992) noted, in the early 1990s disillusionment among public sector managers arose as they confronted seemingly intractable barriers between the way managers were 'meant' to operate (possibly as the 'accountable manager'), and the 'realities' of working in the public sector. These 'realities' might be conflict between profit and equity of treatment or use; between task execution and 'looking after' staff; or over, in relation to the 'enterprising manager', the appropriateness of treating some groups such as the ill, the unemployed, the offender or the student as a 'customer'.

Welcome to the 'enterprising manager'

If the 'accountable manager' is concerned primarily with cost control and intensifying the contribution of labour (which includes substituting relatively expensive labour for cheaper forms and more closely specifying and attempting to control professional practices), then the 'enterprising manager' augments this with recourse to a discourse of change, empowerment and liberation (Clarke and Newman, 1993). As Clarke and Newman (1997) note, the notion of *change* is deeply embedded here and powerfully colonizes space for debate about public services. Its narrative logic, which locates the local in a global order of inevitable and fast-moving change, positions those who might challenge a particular 'change' as being against change itself, and managers as the implementors of change. Those who resist the 'calling' to change are assumed to be personally, socially and organizationally engaged in protecting vested interests, traditional practice and bureaucracy (Clarke and Newman, 1997: 53).

Through this the 'enterprising manager' is constructed as concerned with liberating him or herself and her or his organization from the strictures of traditional practice, bureaucracy and entrenched interests. It is this particular issue which has proved so powerful and alluring for the Foucault-inspired governmentalists (Rose, 1989; Gordon, 1991; Burchell, 1993; du Gay *et al.*, 1996). The Thatcherite power bloc's attempt to suffuse an 'enterprise culture' elaborates a new field of governmentality where the micro techniques of governing oneself – in an enterprising fashion – intersect with and reproduce a whole political economic terrain. As Rose (1989: 115) notes in relation to management, the 'enterprising manager' promises 'economic progress, career progress and personal development intersected upon this new psycho-therapeutic territory'.

Meanwhile, the 'enterprising manager', charged as change agent might be read as a 'born again' 'accountable manager', fired with an almost evangelical desire to reconstruct the 'static frozen wastes', to use Issac-Henry *et al.*'s (1992) term, of public sector organizations with a zeal for the customer/user. This is Common *et al.*'s (1991: 121) 'champion of change', Issac-Henry *et al.*'s (1992: 42) 'effective change leader', who is concerned with the 'penetration and durability of reform', and Pollitt's (1993: 170) 'heroic cultural engineer'. Frequently this construction deals only with how *this* manager orchestrates change. Only occasionally do 'the people' or the objects of change appear. For instance, in Issac-Henry *et al.*'s text the authors suggest that the priority for the change leader is empowering staff. While there is a good deal of slippage between informing, involving and empowering, the relationship constructed is one of doing something unto 'the other'. Any response by 'the other' is seen as the fertilization of the manager's action. Instructively, these authors add a later rider to those who might take up the subject position of 'inseminator': 'One must be wary of assuming that negative attitudes toward change are necessarily irrational emotions' (Issac-Henry *et al.*, 1992: 48). Such a comment, while offering an 'olive branch' of rationality to 'the other', also implicitly assimilates rationality to the enterprising manager. Often it seems that rather than talk about people in organizations, this construction relies on particular metaphors – for instance, 'the body' as a metaphor for the organization. In Issac-Henry *et al.*'s text, Lewin's (1951) metaphor of the body in suspended animation is used. The manager, like a scientist or doctor, goes about the business of 'unfreezing . . . injecting . . . and finally refreezing to consolidate the new patterns' (Issac-Henry *et al.*, 1992: 48).

While the discourse of change and the enterprising manager might appear to simply reconstruct the way in which public sector organizations are talked about in official reports, in political speeches and the advice of the management consultancy firms, of key importance is the interdependence of this with the devolution of processes. This allows action and control to be attempted 'at a distance' (Miller and Rose, 1990: 1; Meadmore *et al.*, 1995). This involves the 'devolution' of budgetary responsibility and accountability to senior professionals particularly, but also includes various review, auditing and monitoring processes which provide the means by which professional practice is rethought, recalculated and thus reworked. This apparent devolution of decision-making power through the practices of audit, budgets and other monitoring devices has significantly 'transformed the governability of professional activity', as Rose (1996b: 351) notes. Through these devices professional practices are evaluated not in the knowledge of the profession itself, but in terms of output in relation to particular quantitative measures, customer 'satisfaction' or return from a market.

The 'beneficiary manager': a new self-interested élite on the 'make'?

However, the 'accountable' and 'enterprising' managers were not the only constructions engaged in providing rhetorical and practical material for the 'development' of public sector managers during this period. As an example of how potentially brittle and precarious such constructions are, I want to highlight a potent 'anti-managerial' construction elaborated during the period. Alongside the accountable and enterprising manager there was a critique which constructs the new public sector manager as a member of a favoured new bureaucratic class and self-interested élite. Media stories concerned with the proliferation, expense, exorbitant perquisites and alleged frauds of managers in the NHS particularly, but also in education, brought this construction to the fore.

Arguably the unravelling of the Thatcherite power bloc can be attributed in part to the problem of the 'beneficiary manager'. Scandals over the cost of management consultants, over managerial nepotism ('Quangoland') and fraud led eventually in part to the Nolan inquiries into standards in public life.

A startling example of how tensions over the 'beneficiary manager' reached across the Thatcherite power bloc and arguably led to its disintegration came in 1993. The Welsh secretary, John Redwood, put a stop to manager recruitment in Wales. In ways that parallel the then government's problems over European integration, Redwood questioned the government's enthusiasm for management, its cost and the growing legions of 'men in grey suits' (Brindle, 1994b). 'I want more operations, not slogans; and medicines, not glossy leaflets' (Brindle, 1994b: 3). His questioning followed the 'discovery' that the number of NHS managers in England rose from 6,091 in 1989/90 to 20,478 in 1992/3 while the number of nurses fell by 27,235 (Brindle,

1994a). Health minister Brian Mawhinney at the time was reported (Brindle, 1994b) to be concerned at the damage the issue was doing to the then government and to have called on NHS trust federation leaders for ideas to control management costs.

This construction of the manager as a self-serving beneficiary of government changes continued to gain momentum between 1995 and 1997 with reports of large increases in vice-chancellor and FE college principal salaries, of college principals employing spouses in senior posts, giving contracts to friends, and financial irregularities at the heart of the resignations of vice-chancellors and directors at Portsmouth University, Huddersfield University, Swansea Institute and Glasgow Caledonian University.

Constructing managerial stationings in FHE

Turning to colleges and universities I want to continue to use these constructs of the 'accountable', 'enterprising' and 'beneficiary' managers to explore the legislative, regulatory and financial changes which confronted both sectors, and worked to station senior professionals as managers.

To reiterate, a station is both a physical place where a particular social order is imposed and a social positioning in a particular set of social relations (Fiske, 1993). The term is used as a way of combining elements of social experience which are frequently conceptualized as separate: the interior dimensions of consciousness (identity, subjectivity), the socio-political dimensions of social relations and the physical dimensions of bodies in space and time (Fiske, 1993: 13). Following Foucault, Fiske argues that power operates not through the effort of a particular social class (Scarbrough and Burrell, 1996), but through sets of technologies and mechanisms. In the following I argue that the managerial station(ing) in FHE is produced nationally through the suffusion of particular funding, audit and planning processes (together with a raft of reports, forms of advice and a growing manager development literature). These processes or devices form what Rose (1996a) calls 'lines of latitude and longitude'. For example, audit, budgeting and planning devices form lines of visibility and thus lines of potential action. They form links between seeing and saying (Deleuze, 1992). Their intersection constructs the managerial station in FHE. Through them the senior post-holder comes to know her or himself and others in ways that are largely at odds with the knowledges and practices of the professional administrator, academic or teacher.

The 'accountable manager' and the 'enterprising manager' stationings in FHE do not directly map onto the two modes of managerialism in HE identified by Martin Trow (1994) and discussed by other commentators of various theoretical persuasions (Ainley, 1994; Parker and Jary, 1995; Harvey and Knight, 1996; Trowler, 1998). Trow (1994: 14) argues that 'soft managerialism' developed within the universities in response to budget cuts while 'hard managerialism' developed with the replacement of the

University Grants Committee (UGC) with the University Funding Council (UFC) and the HEFC, which 'aimed at introducing business-like attitudes towards work and performance into universities, changing the functions as it changes the motivations of their employees, not merely introducing more efficient rationalized structures of management as in the first phase'.

Trow argues that 'soft managerialism' is the best 'defence of university autonomy' (1994: 16). Yet the qualitative intensity of 'managerialism' suggested by this distinction, I would argue, leads the discussion away from actual practices and knowledges which are being drawn on, or pushed through, to accomplish particular objectives. As the following discussion highlights, positioning oneself as a 'soft' manager has a powerful appeal when 'hard managerialism' can be identified as a feature of the practice of others. Yet it nevertheless involves the construction of the 'other' as managed and oneself as 'managing' in a more palatable way, which attempts to enhance the efforts of others.

The 'accountable manager' in HE: cuts and funding

In HE the construction of the 'accountable manager' was massively boosted by the cuts to university grants announced in 1981 of, on average, 17 per cent (Sizer, 1988; Pratt and Silverman, 1989). Indeed it would be possible to read the construction of the 'accountable manager' generally across the sector as broadly induced by the politics of public sector funding restraints. While calls for 'better resource management' and more efficient use of resources in HE had been growing with the expansion in HE, and the increasingly active role taken by the UGC following the end of the five-yearly funding programme in the early 1970s (Fielden and Lockwood, 1973), the 1981 cuts provided the conditions for the early construction of the 'accountable manager'. Peter Scott, in a review of the 'Thatcher effect' on HE, argues that 'it was the cuts that forced institutions to operate as businesses rather than academic enterprises' and that the 'cuts . . . allowed the government, under the guise of value-for-money accountability, to extend its political control over the system' (1989: 206). To a varying extent, this was done by devolving financial accountability 'out' across institutions. Gareth Williams' 1992 study[1] of changing patterns of finances among 24 HE institutions confirms points made by Pratt and Silverman (1989) and Sizer (1988) that the 1981 cuts induced a wider devolution of resource management responsibility across universities.

These authors argue that this was done primarily as a way of showing university departments the proportion of institutional shortfalls that each was required to bear. While this in itself was unlikely to turn senior post-holders into 'accountable managers', the decisive change in this direction came in 1986 when the UGC split research funding from teaching funding, organized the first selectivity exercise through which research funds were progressively distributed on a performance basis, and at the same time introduced a formulaic method of funding teaching on the basis of student places rather than through a block grant. The specification of teaching funds based on recruited student numbers (on the basis of a particular unit of resource) is a key aspect in the construction of the 'accountable university manager' across HE during this period, and later in public sector FE.

While still under the control of local authorities, polytechnics were progressively being funded in this method through the allocation methods developed by the former NAB (Thorne and Cuthbert, 1996). As the 1980s progressed, both the NAB and the UGC/UFC made more transparent the formulas by which they distributed teaching funding. These processes, as a number of authors assert, aided by the development of accounting software, simultaneously 'broke' the pattern of previous institutional funding and allowed the income attracted by each polytechnic and university department from the funding bodies to be readily identified by senior post-holders (Thomas, 1996; Thorne and Cuthbert, 1996).

Williams (1992) argues that the previous incremental block grants system for universities had enhanced and developed collegial forms of management. The shift to increasingly targeted, contractual and tendered funding methods in the latter half of the 1980s had the effect of concentrating control of funds among senior university post-holders. Turner and Pratt (1990: 31) identify the bidding or tendering processes instituted by the former Polytechnic and Colleges Funding Council (PCFC) (established with the incorporation of polytechnics in April 1989 under the Education Reform Act), and continued in a scaled-down form by the higher and further education funding councils as powerfully increasing the centralization, secrecy and thus the managerial positioning of senior post-holder groups in the former polytechnics: 'The limitation on the number of people concerned in devising the bid has generated concern among senior managers as well as elsewhere about collegiality within institutions and the increased concentration of decision making in the hands of a small executive'.

At the same time this move to more contractual funding requires, in Williams' terms, a 'high degree of managerial effort and competence' (1992: 26) among senior academic and service department heads within institutions. Formulaic funding and devolved budgeting, while two different mechanisms not necessarily directly linked, more intensively individuate or station senior academics/administrators as 'managers' responsible for the efficient use of resources. At the same time they make such post-holders responsible for the organizational processes which secure the continued exchange of a particular level of output for a certain level of resource. The complexity and detailed character of the funding mechanism together with the state sector-wide efficiency drive has increasingly required FHE senior post-holders over the last ten years to be actively involved in generating, projecting, calculating and returning student/activity unit figures in such a way that maximizes the return from the funding council.

Funding: differences and details

The framework for funding post-compulsory education in colleges and universities in the UK is broadly similar across both sectors and has been converging in recent years. In general, funds are paid for a certified number of learning activity units in FE, and full-time equivalent students in HE. Differentials are paid on the basis of different subject areas and modes of study (full-time and part-time). Claims for income are made against a plan for the coming year agreed between the college/university and the funding council. A key difference between the two sectors is that FE is funded through activity units (rather than full-time equivalent students) and these carry an output element which is 'claimed/earned' following successful course completion. Colleges claim, on the basis of calculations made at three 'census' points during the year (one in HE), a certain number of units for enrolment, on-programme and achievement of courses. This more intensified funding method and the relative variety of programmes that colleges provide (a large part-time provision) together with the common problems of instituting a computer system which would cope with these elements, have constructed the terrain across which the manager in FE is required to manoeuvre.

In the case of HE teaching in England, the HEFCE formula is based on funding institutions on the basis of student numbers, taking into account subject areas (four price groupings), mode of study (part-time/full-time), and institution-related factors (e.g. London premium). Institutional grants are then adjusted for non-compliance with previous contracts (5 per cent leeway), inflation and any added funding for additional students. The HEFCE has adjusted its funding methods in recent years, adding elements which encourage institutions to widen access by paying premiums for mature students in their first year, for part-time students, and students on courses of longer than 45 weeks' duration.

In general, though, institutional funding is calculated on the basis of the previous year's funding with adjustments. This is then set against fee income, paid by local authorities in the main via the government. However, from 1998/9 this includes a compulsory, means-tested, element paid by full-time students themselves (to a maximum of £1000 per full-time student).

In both FE and HE the funding mechanisms allow a level of visibility across the sector, but more importantly across institutions. While funding councils point out that institutions are free to allocate funds according to their own priorities, the devolution of such mechanisms 'into' colleges and universities means that senior post-holders are able to judge their relative contribution to institutional performance and 'their' area's activity contribution in relation to that of others. It is through this nationalized funding mechanism, and the institutionally-specific devolutionary mechanisms which developed during the 1980s and into the 1990s in both FE and HE, that senior post-holders have been progressively stationed as 'managers' of fields of activity (Berry, 1994; Lawrence, 1995).

Of course, nationalized funding processes do not simply station senior academic and administrative post-holders as responsible for a 'cost centre'. They simultaneously attempt to position them as responsive to and responsible for a diminishing supply of funds upon which to resource that cost centre. This is the interface between the 'accountable' and 'enterprising' manager. The 'accountable manager' is positioned as responsible for the efficient use of resources. The 'enterprising manager' is constructed *between* the income and expenditure of a particular cost centre. This positioning requires the post-holder to take responsibility for securing, and preferably generating, a level of resource – for example, by increasing effort, reducing teacher contact hours, or finding alternative income sources.

The so-called efficiency gains which have been a persistent requirement of the secretaries of state in their 'advice' to the FHE funding agencies in recent years are made possible by these new funding mechanisms and the apparent autonomy of FHE institutions. Increasing student numbers have been achieved through a system of tendering for extra students (which could then be rolled into core funding) at a marginal 'fees-only' rate. The Labour government meanwhile has moved away from this method towards full funding. Yet during the early 1990s this method, together with 'efficiency gains' drove down the price paid while actual students numbers increased dramatically – particularly between 1989 and 1994 in the 1992 universities and between 1994 and 1996 in FE colleges.

As a result of these nationally orchestrated processes, student numbers in HE rose in the ten years to 1997 by 62 per cent to 1.659 million while the level of funding per student paid by the state has been cut by 35 per cent in real terms (CVCP, 1997a). The Dearing Report's account of this puts it in a slightly bigger light: 'while student numbers doubled in the 20 years to 1997, funding has increased in real terms by 45 per cent. While public spending on HE, as a percentage of gross domestic product, has stayed the same, 'the unit of funding per student has fallen by 40 per cent' (National Committee of Inquiry into Higher Education, 1997).

A productivity study of HE between 1980 and 1995, produced for the Committee of Vice-Chancellors and Principals (CVCP, 1997b) for the Dearing Inquiry (National Committee of Inquiry into Higher Education, 1997) shows that HE productivity increased by 4.6 per cent per year during the period, while on average productivity across the service sector was just 2.1 per cent per year (these figures were generated by dividing HE's total income by the number of people employed by institutions). The bulk of the productivity growth was between 1990 and 1995 (up 26 per cent over the five-year period compared with 8.7 per cent for the service sector as a whole), with the 1992 universities increasing productivity by 3.8 per cent per year against 2.3 per cent per year in the pre-1992 universities (CVCP, 1997b). These changes, particularly in the three years to 1997 where HE was required to produce efficiency gains of around 6 per cent per year without growth in undergraduate student numbers, helped to produce what the CVCP called 'the greatest financial crisis in recent memory' (CVCP, 1996) and the HEFC called a 'rapidly deteriorating position' (HEFCE, 1996). This situation had numerous effects, the most important being the shift to recover more income from students themselves. It underpins concern over the declining 'quality' of HE, particularly in relation to franchising programmes, and has intensified the controversy around the political nature of the mechanism of 'quality control' – teaching assessment and quality audit. Of course, there are wide variations in circumstances between institutions with the 'financial strength of the sector concentrated in a small number of comparatively wealthy institutions' (HEFCE, 1996: 6).

As a result of this financial squeeze, institutions have progressively looked for ways to reduce costs or increase funding. They indicated to the funding council through strategic plans and financial forecasts that they were reducing staff numbers, deferring capital programmes and long-term maintenance and limiting equipment expenditure to the funding council level. The council noted that many institutions had offset increases in pay rates with reductions in staff numbers (HEFCE, 1996).

Funding the 'system': constructing the 'manager'

In summary then, this broad approach to funding teaching which includes the close specification of funds on the basis of full-time equivalent students, or in the case of FE through activity units, has been repeated and refined across the post-compulsory sector.[2] The 1988 Education Reform Act, and the repeated remarks of ministers during this period, make it clear that rather than funding institutions, funding bodies were understood to be providing funds 'in exchange for the provision of specified academic services' (Williams, 1992: 13). The secretary of state instructed the new UFC in 1989 that 'I shall expect to see . . . a means of specifying clearly what universities are expected to provide for public funds' (quoted in Williams, 1992: 9).

This process of 'specification' through the formulaic means by which funds are distributed/'earned', together with the squeeze on funding, positions senior professionals as more intensively accountable for the financial return on particular levels of academic/teaching activity. Pratt and Locke (1994) argue in relation to teaching that the 'formulaic method of calculation means that it is difficult for institutional managers to make internal allocations of funds that differ significantly from the formula' (1994: 40). Thus, the more detailed the specification of the activity for the funding relationship, the more the process bypasses 'central' institutional personnel and directly stations the head of department/faculty/section.

The dominant reading of these processes is that the 'accountable manager' is an evolutionary aspect of the development of a necessary mass post-compulsory education system (Scott, 1995; Barnett, 1997). Yet this suffers, in part, from a systems theory bias (Becker and Kogan, 1992; Scott, 1995;

Harvey and Knight, 1996). Such accounts fail to capture the political character of such practices. If management were simply the effect of the system's need for expansion at a reduced cost, then it seems unlikely that the
energy and determination which have been engaged in spreading the knowledge and practices of management would have been necessary.

A more engaged explanation would be that the Thatcherite power bloc's
approach to FHE in the 1980s and 1990s amounted to a 'war'; an attempt
to 'tame the shrews' (Jenkins, 1995). This would suggest that a mass HE
'system' is more an effect of alliances between changing patterns of dominant and subordinate interests. Ascendant interests, in order to achieve some
degree of saliency, would need to be articulated through the seemingly
benign but strategic mechanisms of 'systems'. In this reading the managerialization of FHE amounts to more than simply the meeting of already existing systemic objectives. It involved a programme set of 'reforms' in the late
1980s and early 1990s whose strategic objective increased state control over
FHE and simultaneously attempted to subsume erstwhile opposition to this.

Be better managed! Advice and
the construction of the accountable manager

The 'accountable manager' perhaps finds its most cogent elaboration in a
series of reports aimed at the post-compulsory sector advising universities,
polytechnics and colleges of the need for more devolved and competent
management. In relation to universities such advice is found in the *Report of
the Steering Committee of Efficiency Studies in Universities* (the 'Jarrett Report')
(CVCP, 1985), and in relation to polytechnics in the NAB's *Management for
a Purpose* (1987). In relation to FE such advice is found in the Audit Commission's 1985 efficiency studies in FE and the Department of Education
and Science and Local Education Authorities' 1987 report *Managing Colleges
Efficiently*.

The Jarrett Report is perhaps the most well-known example of all these
documents. It explicitly recognizes the university as a corporate enterprise,
providing services to consumers, which requires effective management to
maximize the efficient and effective use of the public resource it 'con-
sumes'. The Jarrett committee recommended that vice-chancellors adopt
the role of chief executive and heads of academic departments be appointed
with 'clear duties and responsibilities for the performance of their departments and their use of resources' (CVCP, 1985: 36). The NAB report *Management for a Purpose* sent a similar message to polytechnics. As the material
from one of the two polytechnics that form part of the sample discussed in
this book illustrates, elements from this report provided the vocabularies
and practices which led to the weakening and, in some cases, removal of
faculty and institutional committee structures in favour of management
teams. In relation to the pre-1992 universities, Williams (1992: 19) notes
that when university personnel were asked the reasons for introducing

devolved budgeting, staff from 11 of the 14 universities visited in the study said that the Jarrett Report's recommendations and 'the need to give departments information of their predicted shortfall in institutional funds' were the main reasons.

In general terms, these reports explicitly signal the change of relationship between the state and post-compulsory education institutions, and prefigure the 'nationalization' of local authority FHE in the 1989 and 1992 Acts. In the case of pre-1992 universities, Salter and Tapper (1994: 132) argue that the Jarrett Report, together with the changing relations between the UGC and the universities, signalled the 'fall of the traditional liberal ideal of the university and the rise of the new managerialism'.

'I plan, and I am audited, therefore I am!' Constructing the accountable manager in audit and planning processes

Alongside new funding mechanisms, and calls through efficiency studies for 'better management', the construction of the 'accountable manager' has been boosted by the introduction of more intensively-focused auditing and planning processes. In relation to the former, the controversial Research Assessment Exercises (RAE – the first in 1986 following the UGC's splitting of research and teaching funding), the subject-based teaching quality assessment processes (introduced by the new HEFCs beginning in 1993) and the institution-based quality audit (established at the time by the university-sponsored Higher Education Quality Council) have each been crucially involved in the elaboration of the 'accountable manager' across the sector. Each of these processes elaborates and reproduces, through the need to produce and defend departmental or institutional submissions, the positions of departmental, service and institutional managers. Through them the senior post-holder is located as responsible for the processes which yield 'quality': 'excellence' in teaching, highly-graded research and effective quality audit. While nationally orchestrated, each of these practices has, with some changes, been mimetically inscribed into the review and auditing processes of institutions themselves, so that each area prepares itself for external inspection. Both the teaching quality assessment and quality audit were designed to review internal quality assurance processes rather than to conduct such reviews themselves. While the cost and duplication involved in these two processes has been criticized and, after some controversy, a new body (the Quality Assurance Agency) established (which will streamline teaching and quality audit), the actual practices themselves are unlikely to be substantially changed.

The lineage of all three of these assessment processes can be found in organizations such as the now defunct Councils for National Academic Awards (CNAA), the CVCP's Academic Audit Unit, and institutional processes of peer review (coupled with the government's enthusiasm for performance indicators, in the case of the RAE). Yet the decisive shift, which renders such practices constitutive of the managerial station across FHE, has been the nationalization of such review processes, their standardization across the university and college sectors, the tying of resources to them (in the case of the RAE) and most importantly their mimetic suffusion 'into' institutions themselves.

Alongside these nationalized but substantially devolved audit processes, institutional planning processes have also been engaged in constructing the managerial station. The crucial difference between audit and strategic planning as processes, and one reason why strategic planning can be read as engaged in constructing the 'enterprising', rather than the 'accountable' manager, is the different ways in which such processes address the subject (be it the senior post-holder, the institution, or the activity area). Strategic planning is future-facing. It involves, at an institutional level, detailed plans that position the subject in relations of difference with the future. In this way, rather than being positioned as accountable and responsible for efficient and effective use of resources, strategic planning, together with contract-based forms of funding, addresses the subject as having choice – that is, as being continuously engaged in a project of shaping and maximizing effort for success. Rather than producing an intensified stationing between a level of resource and particular objects, strategic planning powerfully stations the subject as an agent, albeit within a particular set of constraints. As will be developed in later chapters, this provides a seductive but perhaps somewhat illusory sense of control over the circumstances in which the subject is positioned.

While planning processes have a long history in HE (Thomas, 1996), strategic planning and the plans themselves have become a key item in the relations between FHE institutions and their funding councils. For example, the newly independent polytechnics were required by the PCFC to submit strategic plans as part of their desire for 'independence' in 1989. This practice was later embraced by the UFC and FEFC. All universities and colleges are required by the funding councils, as a prerequisite of funding, to submit detailed (in some cases annually updated) strategic plans. While offering the possibility of diversity and divergence across the sectors, Thorne and Cuthbert (the latter the assistant vice-chancellor at the University of the West of England in Bristol) argue that the 'requirement to produce plans can be seen as a managerialist control over institutions' (1996: 180). Like the devolution of funding mechanisms 'down' to the operating units, the strategic planning process is 'spread' out across institutions with senior post-holders setting the broad objectives and deans and heads of department/service 'filling out the corporate vision', as Thorne and Cuthbert describe it. Through the cycle of strategic planning processes, deans and heads of department/service are thus required to position themselves within corporate objectives, speaking for 'their' sphere of activity, but more importantly taking up an 'enterprising' relation to the future of both 'their' department (or faculty or service) and themselves. Through this requirement to fill in the 'blanks' of the strategic plan, they are required to detail how, when, and by whom corporate objectives, as expressed in relation to 'their own' sphere's activities, are to be achieved.

'I appraise therefore I am!' Appraisal and the manager

Alongside, and in most cases embedded within, strategic planning cycles are the requirements for senior post-holders to hold performance appraisal cycles. This in turn is underpinned by the introduction of new employment contracts across FHE, particularly in formerly public sector FHE following the 1988 and 1992 Education Acts. For many observers both contracts and staff appraisal represent the managerialist tide as they, unlike other more institutional and nationalized processes, have as their strategic intent the individualized orientation of staff to corporate objectives (Kogan, 1988; Townley, 1993a, 1997; Henson, 1995; Thomas, 1996).

Under the terms of the two acts the then polytechnics and FE colleges were removed from the aegis of local authorities and reconstituted as education corporations, with charitable status. As a consequence they acquired responsibility for their own finances, estates and the employment of staff. With the passing of the two Acts, staff who were previously employed by local authorities were required to become employees of these FHE corporations. This, in the context of new contractual funding regimes, and what R. Ward (1995: 157) describes as the market-orientated deregulation drive of the Thatcher paradigm at its peak, led polytechnic and then college employers to take action against the local authority-originating employment conditions of the sectors, and introduce new more 'flexible' employment contracts. As a consequence both sectors experienced significant industrial conflict over the introduction of these contracts during 1991 (in the case of the former polytechnics and HE colleges), and from 1993 onwards (in the case of FE colleges). The disputes included the use by the secretary of state for education of a controversial 2 per cent funding 'holdback' mechanism (R. Ward, 1995), to push through contract changes. This was also used in order to agree the introduction of a now defunct performance-related pay scheme for the 1992 universities.

Meanwhile, in both the post-1992 university and FE sectors, senior post-holders were among the first to sign new contracts. These 'management spine' (FE) or 'local management' (HE) contracts are broad documents that specifically re-designate senior post-holders as responsible and accountable either to more senior post-holders as their line managers, or to the institution's governing body in the case of the vice-chancellor or director. Such contracts also charged post-holders directly with managing the performance of particular domains of activity (e.g. the college, departments, sections or sectors). For example, the contract for heads of department and deans in one of the two post-1992 universities discussed in this book names the 'effective and efficient use of resources' as a key responsibility. Meanwhile the post-holder is responsible to the dean (or vice-chancellor in the case of the dean) for the 'leadership, management and development of department/faculty in line with the university's purposes, policies and plans'.

In FE colleges the 'management spine' contract for section managers and programme coordinators (found in one of the four FE colleges discussed in this book) identified similar elements. The job specification for programme coordinators for instance (fourth-tier managers), demands that post-holders 'deploy and manage staff and resources within programme teams' and 'contribute to (the) college's strategic planning process'. The section manager's contract meanwhile (third-tier manager) is more explicit. It demands that post-holders 'develop, implement and monitor a section's business plan', 'respond to the declared objectives in the college's strategic plan', and 'manage, monitor and control resources delegated to the post-holder on a regular and consistent basis in conformity with internal requirements to ensure that the resources are efficiently and effectively utilized in line with agreed targets'. The section manager is also 'responsible for generating new business for the section'.

Compared with the shift to new contracts for teaching staff, the shift of senior post-holders onto local management contracts was relatively smooth. It was aided in some, but not all, cases by financial 'sweeteners'. In the former polytechnics discussed in this book these were up to £5000 per annum. However, as the example in Chapter 6 shows, some found the terms and conditions of the new management contracts worrying. There was particular concern over the loss of a negotiating forum for senior post-holders who were required in many cases to negotiate salary increases individually with their line manager. This system of personal and 'secret' salaries has, as Farnham (1995) showed in his survey of heads and professors in post-1992 universities and colleges, led to quite wide differences in salary across the sector. Alongside this were concerns that these generally broad documents failed to recognize the professional standing and expertise of senior post-holders (there was often no mention of teaching and research in the contracts) outside of being positioned as managers of particular domains of activity. Embedded within the new management contracts was the requirement that those on such contracts would be both appraised by a 'line manager', and become an appraiser of the performance of staff.

Generally, individualized performance appraisal of university and college staff has, as House and Watson (1995: 14) note, 'been a feature of thinking of Conservative administrations since at least the early 1980s'. Appraisal was recommended for the university sector in the Jarrett Report (CVCP, 1985) and taken up in the late 1980s and early 1990s on an institution-by-institution basis, usually through consultation processes between local union branches and university management (Bryman *et al.*, 1991). The Jarrett Report noted in regard to universities that 'little formal attempt is made on a regular basis to appraise academic staff with a view to their personal development and to succession planning' (CVCP, 1985: 28).

Accounts of the impact of appraisal in pre-1992 universities suggest that it tends to be regarded as a meaningless bureaucratic exercise with very few tangible outcomes (Thomas, 1994). Appraisal was made a condition of the new 'flexible' staff contracts agreed in January 1991, while in FE compulsory performance appraisal schemes were established through the 1986 Education (no.2) Act. Here local authorities were required to establish processes that appraised the performance of teachers in schools and FE colleges (Scribbins and Walton, 1987). Such efforts had a strong staff development aspect to them. Since the incorporation of colleges on 1 April 1993 however, appraisal has been renovated and in many cases directly linked to strategic planning processes so that each individual is required to meet targets linked to college objectives.

Appraisal, as Townley (1993a, 1997) has argued, forms a key process in the construction of the managerial identity in HE. While there are wide variations in the ways in which appraisal is constructed across the FHE sector, performance appraisal, both of staff and particularly of heads of department/service, is explicitly engaged in constructing the subject position of the future-facing 'enterprising' manager. Individualized appraisal objectives across FHE in most cases explicitly position the post-holders as responsible for the productive and efficient use of department/service resources. In some cases this is to be assessed against particular targets and performance indicators (Townley, 1993a, 1997; Henson, 1995). In general staff appraisal documents and processes are involved in constituting surveillance relations between subjects. While often articulated in the language of 'staff development' they provide appraisers with 'guides for action and present information which prompts the need for decisions and solutions' (Townley, 1993a: 231) in relation to work colleagues. These micro edicts act as devices which at the same time construct the appraiser as the overseer or manager of both a particular subject and that subject's sphere of activity.

In summary, I have sketched out the key nationally orchestrated processes, practices and knowledges involved in constructing the managerial station across FHE. Alongside these processes must also be added the accumulated knowledge and advice found in the growing FHE management literature. This provides 'support' and 'help' for managers and is thus intimately engaged in the construction of the managerial station.

The higher education management literature: tracking a moving target

While a detailed review of this literature would distract the discussion here from its current trajectory towards the discussion of empirical material, there is a string of texts, many found in the Society for Research into Higher Education's catalogue, which chart the elaboration of the increasingly accountable academic and support service manager. Fielden and

Lockwood's (1973) *Planning and Management in Universities: A Study of British Universities* forms a good baseline text. While managerial in intent, its somewhat pastoral tone sets it apart from later works. For example, while arguing that universities pay 'more attention to the details of their management structures' (1973: 35), Fielden and Lockwood concede that 'lack of clarity in the allocation of responsibilities, for instance, has a latent function in that it can allow expertise or motivation to override authority; it might therefore be best to retain a lack of clarity in certain units (p. 35).

Twelve years later Geoffrey Lockwood with another co-author (Lockwood and Davies, 1985: 339) declared that:

> institutional leaders cannot now rely necessarily or exclusively on the good sense of the collegial processes to cope with the issues arising from a highly competitive higher education environment. Collegial processes . . . are not particularly environmentally aware; not particularly problem orientated, are conservative rather than adaptive . . . It is senior institutional leadership which has to define problems and structure the context of possible solutions.

Yet even this seems somewhat tentative and benign in comparison to the account of managerial practice recommended in a run of recent texts: Warner and Crosthwaite's *Human Resource Management in Higher and Further Education* (1995); Warner and Palfreyman's *Higher Education Management: The Key Elements* (1996); Bocock and Watson's *Managing the University Curriculum* (1994); and Ford *et al.*'s *Managing Change in Higher Education: A Learning Environment Architecture* (1996).

This last text represents a clear elaboration of the new managerial positioning for universities. It recommends not simply a renewed emphasis on management, but a thorough re-engineering of the university's core 'business processes'. Senior post-holders become enterprise managers charged with maintaining learning architectures. According to Peter Ford and his co-authors, this includes the development and evaluation of learning 'chunks'. A learning 'chunk' is a bounded learning activity with a specified set of learning objectives and assessment procedures. In their approach, chunks are put together by a 'learning chunk development team' and would be offered to students through different 'learning vehicles' (1996: 57). In relation to the need to re-engineer the university, the tone is stark and uncompromising:

> an HEI [higher education institution] must understand which core processes it needs to put in place. These processes must be designed to support the objectives of the business. Achieving the objectives must not be subservient to the processes. In other words, processes that do not contribute to the achievement of the stated objectives of an institution will require examination to determine whether they can be modified or need to be replaced.
>
> (Ford *et al.*, 1996: 21)

This functionalist and systemic approach to the reconstruction of the university draws heavily on the prescriptions of business process engineering (Hammer and Champy, 1993). Taken together with other texts in the field (e.g. Bocock and Watson 1994; Thorne and Cuthbert 1996, particularly chapters 3, 4 and 7) and the renewed emphasis on teaching in the Dearing Report (National Committee of Inquiry into Higher Education, 1997), these texts provide an outline for what Roger King (1994: 71), vice-chancellor of the University of Lincolnshire and Humberside described as an increasingly corporate 'curiosity' in the learning process:

> It is an interesting and perhaps remarkable fact that in higher education the core of the academic enterprise (the course or programme or product) lies largely outside corporate control . . . The search for growth, efficiency, and quality are essential organizational requirements that will take senior management more directly to the heart of the academic domain.

Constructing the FE managerial station

The FE sector has been broadly subjected to similar mechanisms and practices which were applied to public sector HE in the late 1980s and early 1990s (Phillips, 1994). Similar funding, strategic planning and inspection processes were applied to the new sector, which was created by the 1992 Further and Higher Education Act, as those applied to the newly 'independent' polytechnics following their removal from local authority control under the Education Reform Act 1988. As a condition of their 'independence' the 452 tertiary, FE, specialist and sixth form colleges which make up the sector, are required to provide detailed three- and five-yearly strategic plans supported by annual operating statements. These include plans for each year's projected student recruitment together with bids for growth in activity units for the following year (FEFCE, 1999). It is through this mechanism that historically different levels of income for each college are being equalized, 'efficiency gains' for the sector are being accomplished alongwith spectacular growth in student numbers. In the three years between 1993/4 and 1996/7 colleges were expected by the FEFCE[3] to grow by 25 per cent. However as the price paid for such growth was at less than existing levels of funding, the so-called 'efficiency gains' were achieved. The National Audit Office (1997: 24) recently reported that 'in the three years since 1993–4 [the funding methodology] asked colleges to expand numbers by some 17 per cent with an increase in funding of five per cent. The implied efficiency gain is over four per cent a year'. Added to this is a differential where colleges with historically higher than average levels of funding faced a faster rate of income reduction than colleges with historically lower levels of funding, although this has been slowed by recent government announcements (FEFCE, 1999).

To achieve these 'efficiencies', colleges have been forced to remove, intensify, substitute or re-skill the labour of teachers and administrative staff across the sector. Upwards of 80 per cent of the sector's costs are in staff salaries and wages. The National Audit Office's survey of colleges found that in response to this methodology, 'nearly all [those surveyed] had reduced their staff costs, for example through introducing more flexible staff contracts, reducing direct teacher contact time and increasing class sizes' (1997: 27). The new funding practices together with wide disparities in the historical circumstances of colleges has contributed to the rising number of colleges in serious financial difficulty. The FEFCE admitted in 1997 that 20 per cent, or 80 colleges, were in serious financial trouble (Russell, 1997b), and only continued to operate with the goodwill of banks.

These conditions, as well as the new practices, provide the 'bed' in which the managerial station has become established as the common-sense solution to the problems. The problems tend to be attributed to a lack of management or lack of effective managers. For example, the National Audit Office (1997: 66) argued that 'management and governance appear to be key factors in financial health'. This follows similar comments by FEFC inspectors. Former chief inspector Terry Melia called for 'imaginative management' to stem the 'downward funding spiral' for many colleges. College principals also seem to concur that 'mismanagement', not underfunding, is largely to blame for the rising number of colleges struggling with deficits. A newspaper telephone poll of about 10 per cent of college principals (Utley, 1995) suggested that three-quarters of principals, when asked, thought that funding problems were caused by 'managers' inability to keep control of labour and other costs'.

Alongside the strategic planning and funding methodologies a new inspection regime was also established, which again mirrors in some ways that applied to HE institutions through teaching quality assessment and quality audit. The FEFC's inspection process aimed to inspect each college every four years. The inspection regime assessed cross-college provision (including governance and management) as well as each curriculum area.

Yet the construction of the managerial station in colleges was intimately linked to their incorporation effective from 1 April 1993. Like their public sector HE 'cousins' before them, colleges were required to establish 'inhouse' services previously provided by local authorities (e.g. finance, personnel, estates and information systems). In the build-up to incorporation, colleges received advice from the management consultancy arm of Touche Ross and, as a condition of 'independence', were subjected to a series of 'health' checks by management consultants Coopers and Lybrand, hired by the then Department for Education. In general terms these processes were aimed at ensuring that financial controls were in place for receiving FEFC funding. However, the introduction of new processes together with these checks and advice had the effect of putting large numbers of senior college post-holders together for long periods and subjecting them to a new way of considering FE and their 'role' within it.

Burton (1994) suggests that this whole process of incorporation, which involved numerous surveys and assessment processes carried out on and by senior post-holders, was likely to have 'produced' managers with the 'perspectives of the commercial world as the ones most appropriate to the new further education environment' (p. 358). Burton notes that 'for many months [prior to their incorporation as self-managing institutions] a large proportion of managers were engaged almost exclusively in processes which would have exposed them to such influences, or in directly analysing their roles and evaluating how they compared to their counterparts in the private sector' (p. 358).

Through this, managerial knowledges and practices have isomorphically suffused the sector as senior post-holders have engaged in a process of comparing their work in the new FE corporations with private sector practices. Burton goes on to suggest that these processes almost certainly would have inclined some senior post-holders to a managerialism which, using Cuthbert's (1992) definition, can be described as 'elevat[ing] the activity of managing above that which is managed, instead of recognising that the two are inseparable' (Cuthbert, 1992, quoted in Burton, 1994: 359).

Following what might be termed this 'conversion' process, senior post-holders have since been, to varying degrees, engaged in 'cascading' management practices across colleges (Whyte, 1994). The handbook from consultants Touche Ross, for instance, advises senior post-holders on how to draw up strategic and operational plans, to instigate value for money studies with appropriate performance indicators, 'to define how the college will measure whether it is delivering value' (Touche Ross Management Consultants, 1992: 30) and to develop marketing and quality assurance programmes. Colleges were also advised to develop 'a formal management system for assuring quality' (1992: 32). Each of these processes progressively constructs the managerial station in FE colleges, and attempts to increasingly tie senior professionals into these processes.

However, arguably the sheer diversity of the sector and variety of college experience under local authority control means that the degree of suffusion of management knowledges and practices is highly mixed. One of the principals interviewed for this study, who is a member of a number of FEFCE advisory committees, suggested that the suffusion resembled a 'normal distribution curve' where some colleges are 'organizationally pushing the boundaries and others are doing sufficient to keep up with their environment and the demands made on them'. While there are significant differences in the 'operating environments' faced by colleges (e.g. degree of direct competition with other colleges), there are also significant differences in historical experiences. Cowham (1995) described how prior to incorporation many colleges had become accustomed to a more 'entrepreneurial' or 'opportunistic' approach to managing substantially devolved resources under the local authority. Others clearly had differing relations with local authorities which inclined them to a more public sector educational ethos. For some, incorporation was clearly a 'shock', while for other colleges and personnel much of the groundwork had been done. Thus the extent to which senior post-holders were constituted as 'managers' prior to and following incorporation was mixed.

This chapter provides an account of the nationally orchestrated funding, planning and auditing practices constructing the managerial station in FHE. The purpose has been to read these practices as acting, not simply out of the inexorable logic of a 'system' but as part of the imperializing strategy of the Thatcherite power bloc. Chapter 4 moves to examine in a more detailed way the construction of this managerial stationing in colleges and universities themselves. It draws on empirical material from eight FHE institutions.

Notes

1. The study discusses changes between the 1981 cuts and the publication of *Higher Education: A New Framework* (DES, 1991). This government White Paper pre-figured the changes instituted in the 1992 Further and Higher Education Act. This Act abolished, formally at least, the divide between polytechnics and chartered universities, established a single funding council for the HE sector and set in train the removal of FE colleges from local authorities' control and the creation of the FE sector funded by its own funding agency on 1 April 1993. This repeated changes instituted for polytechnics by the 1988 Education Reform Act.
2. Changes to the national funding formulas for formerly public sector FHE were notably advanced by the same personnel. Sir William Stubbs, now director of the London Institute was chief executive of the PCFC under the chairship of Sir Ron Dearing, before moving on to the same post at the FEFC in 1992, when the PCFC and the UFC merged.
3. The FEFCE plans to distribute £3.205 million in 1999/2000 to 452 general and specialist colleges. This will fund the attendance of around 3 million students. Recent figures for the academic year 1996–7 note that UK colleges employed 218,500 people, or 134,500 full-time equivalent members of staff, of whom 97,300 are full-time, 121,200 part-time and of whom 56 percent are female and 44 percent male (FEFC, 1998: Table 1).

4

'Doing the Business': Constructing the 'Manager' in Further Education

This chapter and Chapter 5 offer a more detailed account of the knowledges and practices involved in the construction of the managerial stationing in FHE institutions. As a means of addressing this stationing, however, I first offer the reader an example of how such a stationing is achieved, using the parallel example of the construction of an element of academic identity. This chapter then discusses the construction of the managerial stationing by exploring the reconstruction of the 'college' and then discussing how the new practices of managing work assemble the grid aimed at constituting managerial subjectivity.

Approaching managerial identity through a parallel example

The discussion up to this point in the text may seem to some readers to overplay the determining characteristics of the 'power bloc' and to underplay the precarious and unstable aspects of the dispersal of the mechanisms of power, or the ability of actors to mediate such processes. The forthright criticism that Watson and House (1995: 9) make of 'critical' accounts of the reconstruction of HE might be levelled at the discussion up to this point:

> There have been several crude attempts to characterise the strategic tendencies and management styles of the post-Jarrett universities, the 'higher education corporations' under the Polytechnics and Colleges Funding Council (PCFC), and most recently the Further Education Corporations of the Further Education Funding Councils (FEFC) . . . The critics focus on the motive and qualifications of what they regard as a new breed of manager, as if the Education Reform Act and the Further and Higher Education Act of 1992 swept away the senior and middle management cadre and replaced it overnight with government placemen and women.

The remaining chapters of this book address this issue of 'replacement'. The crucial difference between this work and the work House and Watson regard as 'crude' is the attempt to read this 'replacement' not as a replacement of personnel but as the tense and unstable dispersal of the managerial stations in FHE institutions which is nowhere nearly as 'neat' as the 'replacement' of personnel, but nevertheless does bring to bear a different set of demands alongside more traditional dispositions and directionalities. It is however important that this issue of 'replacement' or learning to be/become a 'manager' is addressed. As well as doing this in detail by drawing on material from interviews, I begin this chapter with an example of a parallel 'stationing' process. It revolves around the construction of 'my' academic identity. This also serves as a means of positioning 'myself'.

As suggested above, a relational account of identity collapses strong claims to entities such as the 'observer' and the 'observed', arguing instead that such identities are constituted through discursive practices. A book such as this forms and reinforces the discursive practices which in part produce academic identities – of both reader and author. One cannot stand neatly outside these processes. For example, at the same time as offering an account of the development of managerial subjectivity in FHE, one is being constituted through the positionings available in discursive practices locatable in academic settings. It is crucial, given the epistemological priorities outlined above, that this be highlighted and acknowledged. A form of doubling is therefore under way where a relation to oneself develops in the midst of attempts to describe those practices which constitute managerial subjectivity. This doubling includes, for instance, the construction of 'my' academic identity within the power-laden discursive practices of authorship and attendance at academic conferences. Through these practices academic reproduction, socialization or learning is achieved. I want to argue that a similar process is under way for those positioned as senior post-holders in FHE in their constitution as 'managers'. The discussion below shows how the constitution of 'me', as an 'apprentice' academic, is an outcome of 'my' stationing within the discursive practices of, for example, ' the conference', just as the manager is an effect of the stationing of the senior post-holder within the discursive practices of managing corporate colleges and universities. This stationing is, however, an altogether more dispersed, subtle, fragmented and multiple process than the discussion of the Thatcherite power bloc and its imperializing strategies might at first suggest.

The academic station comprises forms of communication and actual bodily practices with previously inscribed power relations – for example the surveillance and examination aspects of academic paper-giving. These have the effect of reproducing dominant alliances and interests which are not explicitly present. They are an effect of the precarious mimetic processes of developing a particular relation to oneself among large numbers of people. For example 'I' was not *told* my place in this 'organization' (the academic conference), I *took* my place, both by imaginatively positioning myself within particular narratives and by taking up a position within particular practices of academic paper-giving. This taking up of 'my' place, that is, playing the variably pleasurable power–knowledge practices across 'me', sets up lines of coherency which reproduce particular dominant interests and groups.

In the same way, 'managers' are not 'told' or forced to take 'their' place. They take their places by 'playing' the knowledges, discursive and embodied practices upon themselves. These form an unstable 'grid' which signifies as 'the manager' or 'managing', but whose effectivity in relation to embedded locales is constantly problematic. Thus claims, for example by Longhurst (1996), that managers are motivated by their own survival to exploit and oppress staff are analytically incorrect (and confirm Howe and Watson's criticism) in the approach taken here. Longhurst's approach might be said to overplay the attribution of coherency to 'managers', by misreading the intent of managerial practices as the effect. Imperializing knowledges, as Fiske (1993: 71) argues, seek to totalize and refine the station so as to 'minimise the gaps through which locales can be established' or reproduced. Longhurst's work, like other labour-process orientated discussions of public sector education (Sinclair *et al.*, 1996) could be said to have become ensnared in and give undue coherency to the imperializing power–knowledge strategies that are at work in constructing the 'manager'. Longhurst (1996: 65) argues that 'college senior managements are under pressure to oppress and exploit staff and those that fail to do so are likely to be unable to balance the books and thus face dismissal'.

The analytical division Longhurst makes between 'management' and 'pressure' is unwarranted and misleading. It attributes to 'management' a functionalist and structuralist coherency, which as well as supporting the imperializing knowledge practices, largely denies the incoherency and fragmentation of 'management' and the 'manager'. This is precisely the advantage of a postdualist approach exemplified in critical work on education by the likes of Ball and his co-authors (Ball, 1994; Gewirtz *et al.*, 1995) and supported here.

'Managers' are not directly motivated by their own survival. Powerful individuating discursive practices are at work which separate the 'manager' off from others and attribute to that body a responsibility for certain domains of activity. This is achieved particularly through various mechanisms of visibility (e.g. quantitative returns, reports and the like) which seek to measure activity against particular norms. Also, these practices tend to induce both a seductive or exhilarating effect interdependent with a fear of separation and intensive judgement. These responses intensify the 'playing' of particular ascribed identities upon the body (in the sense of both body 'surface' and 'depth') of the FHE senior post-holder. This can be said to construct the managerial 'station' in FHE. However, its hold is problematic. The 'manager' is not just a 'docile' reproducer of top-down Taylorite practices but a site of contradictory positionings within various discursive practices – not just those individuating practices of top-down imperializing managerial discourse. The compliance, commitment and effort in extending top-down Taylorite practices, for instance, is not forced from us through domination, or collected from us through some simple exchange relation (work effort or skill for money) (Grey, 1994). It is *variably* 'extracted' to a large extent through practices which produce 'us' and progressively tie 'us' to particular identities – that is, particular ways of being a 'self' or 'selves' (Knights and Willmott, 1989). These 'selves' or ways of being encompass the wide range of contradictory dispositions, desires, perceptions, emotions, physical coverings, positionings, practices and knowledges which make up the flows of embodied life in FHE corporations. As Chapter 6 shows, some of these ways of being are intimate, deeply embedded 'horizontal' identities which variably, and tactically, challenge the construction of the managerial station in FHE.

In order to discuss this process and also to highlight the problematic of 'my' own voice (see Appendix for further discussion of this), I shall change the text format here. By placing the discussion in extract form I am indicating that analysis found in the text is, itself, 'up' for analysis as a discursive practice which enfolds identities and power relations.

Conference going and the construction of academic identity

> Scene: A university classroom. About 25 men and women are seated at tables which form a square in the room. On one side of the square in front of a whiteboard and beside an overhead projector, a speaker sits. He stands, introduces the person to his right and sits again. The person on the right then stands and begins to speak.
>
> 'Thanks, Martin for that. First I appreciate your coming to listen to my paper. I want to begin with a brief account of its development. To be honest the thought of actually being here before you and talking with some conviction filled me with major *feelings of dread and anxiety*. In fact these feelings led me to put off writing this paper for some weeks. Eventually I got to a point where the anxiety of not getting the paper done crashed through the anxiety of actually doing it and I found myself in front of a PC desperate to start. The only way I thought I could possibly start, though, was to literally write my fears out of myself. I thought that by addressing my anxieties I could silence them.
>
> 'I was able to track down two possible explanations for my anxiety at writing. First, *I feared being mocked* by my dear audience. While you might regard yourselves as my peers, prior to the conference I felt more like an apprentice about to confront the tradesmen during my first day on the job. I imagined the conference to be the site where I would be symbolically taken out behind the academic workshop and set upon by the intellectual bullies.
>
> 'My fears were to a degree confirmed when a colleague who was involved in this conference last year said that some people had been reduced to tears when presenting their papers. He described this

conference as a "rigorous conference rather than one at which you could just give your life history". His comments confirmed that I was entering a place where spectacles of punishment were to be enacted and where particular identities and knowledges were perhaps policed by the intellectual *tradesmen*.

'A second reason suggested itself. I was convinced that the abstract I wrote for the conference had in fact duped the conference *managers*. I thought that they thought that after reading the abstract *I was someone who I was convinced I was not*. I guess I felt an outsider. This feeling of being outside I justified on the grounds that I don't have a research degree, I'm not a lecturer and I haven't published much before this. Initially I had thought that the abstract would be rejected but it would nevertheless satisfy my department manager, who is concerned to ensure that I am at least seen to be delivering the research 'goods'. Anyway the shock came when the abstract was accepted.

'You're all probably thinking: "Why is he telling us this?" Well, the key reason is that it can be used to illustrate how power relations, subjectivity and discourse are interdependent and how reflecting on the stories and practices at work in particular locations can tell us a lot about how particular effects like the academic or the manager are produced. Using some tools from the kind of discourse analysis methods outlined by Fairclough (1989, 1992) I want to prise apart the above.

'First, I want to suggest that this conference can be read as a tax-payer-funded public sector organization reproduced by "managers" through their privileging of certain discourse practices – e.g. paper-giving. These practices can be seen as made up of certain bodies of knowledge, subject positions and embedded relations. These discursive practices do not just operate here and now in this room. They are widely dispersed. They organize time and space use, identities and relations down to the most intimate of levels in people's lives.

'These explanations of my feelings amount to a set of readings of this public sector organization; or, to put it another way, they are readings of texts available to me which construct this public sector organization. In these texts the "managers" are positioned in certain ways in relation to "myself". In my first reading the organization contained a dominant bloc of academic "managers" who use the spectacle of public confessional, i.e. paper-giving, as the process to accomplish relations of power and to patrol the definitions of what knowledge is. I read/constructed the spectacle in highly masculine ways. I framed paper-giving as the academic equivalent of the punch-up behind the work-shop. I positioned myself on the receiving end of this "justice" and the academic managers as the toughs. My colleague confirmed the dominance for me of this reading by suggesting that the necessary skills for a "confessor" so as to survive the spectacle were rigour, also known as strength, and invulnerability to feelings. Both these I suggest are the very "pillars of maleness" (Middleton, 1993: 120). In this reading then, paper-giving amounted to a ritual to test one's (male) identity, as well as to constitute one's academic identity.

'In my second reading I positioned myself as being outside the conference altogether. I did this through a liberal credentialist discourse. In this I assumed that conference subjects could legitimately hold certain definitions of self through the possession of certain "goods". For instance, a research degree or publishing track record. The conference's academic "managers" in the discourse are positioned as the arbiters of these definitions of self through control of the discourse practices which define what publishing is at conferences and, on other sites, how one gains possession of a research degree. The effect for me of reading the organization in this way and placing myself outside its domain of the legitimate was this intense feeling of lack, of being without the necessary credentials. Broadly, both these readings problematized an identity. The combination of my positioning within this credentialist discourse and the first which problematized my maleness or masculine identity heightened this sense of anxiety. From within these positionings it seemed unlikely that I would rid myself of these feelings of lack.'

Making academics and making managers through the construction of stations

The above illustrates how a poststructural or postdualist account of the constitution of identity can be approached. There is no 'organization' and 'individual', as such. There is a 'power bloc', but this is largely the effect of the suffusion of particular practices and knowledges (rather than the direct origins of domination) which are located and reproduced in certain spaces (e.g. the conference session). Mostly, however, these practices and knowledges are dispersed and embedded in the 'paper structures' of organizing. These are reasonably durable and provide ways of making certain judgements and decisions. They provide guides for action and organize ways of responding to particular 'problems'. The 'individual' identity is thus an effect of insertion into the subject positions available in particular knowledges. Yet one's insertion into such positions is variable. This could be said to depend on the resonance of such subject positions with patterns of desire collected biographically through engagement in other political processes (in this case schools, worksites and families). The example above illustrates how this is often deeply gendered. The 'significant others' in the example are all men: conference organizers, colleagues, 'tradesmen', a head of department. The desire for acceptance and positive evaluations by these men (fathers!) is crucial and fuels efforts to find subordinate positionings in credentialist and masculine discourses. One effect of these processes is the construction of dominant male groupings in 'organizations'. In this sense, power is diffuse and ingrained. It has material effects, but is mirage-like. It is neither held nor exercised by these groupings directly. It is embedded in the seemingly synaptic responses of people who have been inscribed with a particular relation to the self through particular practices which, in effect, project power and authority onto these groups. Power relations are thus at work constituting and articulating particular powerful positionings, even if those who might be ascribed such positionings – the post-holders in other words – would reject such a positioning.

The 'manager' in FHE is, I want to argue, constructed in ways similar to, though more complex than, the academic identity and the conference 'managers' discussed above. The FHE 'manager', like the academic identity, is an effect of particular discursive practices that operate in particular spaces (e.g. the management team meeting, the appraisal interview, the inspection audit). Like the conference paper-giving process described above, numerous overlapping practices work to constitute the FHE 'manager'. For example:

- strategic and operational planning documents which require 'managers' to suggest and commit themselves to particular new programmes, targets and review processes;
- the income and expenditure spreadsheets which construct the manager as between units or full-time (student) equivalents 'earned' and the costs of such activities;
- assessment and inspection processes.

As I mentioned, the managerial 'I' is not an outcome of oppression and domination, but of subjection: the seemingly subtle processes of becoming both subject to and a subject of a particular regime of knowledges and practices. This occurs as we are drawn into the seemingly benign knowledges and practices which dominate particular sites. These in turn prescribe an appropriate relation that one has with oneself in these settings (which simultaneously constructs relations with others). The intensified processes of audit, planning and budgets, which make up the 'paper structure' of 'managing' colleges and universities, insert and mutually produce the subject position of 'manager'. Through these knowledges and practices, particularly the multiple guides to action, and the demands and forms of reflexivity that they contain, a position is constructed which is engaged in evaluating and taking responsibility for the performance of a particular area of activity. This positioning is supported to varying degrees through a set of embodied positionings – for instance in the management team meeting or appraisal interview. The process of becoming a 'manager' is a subtle one of inducement and suffusion of, primarily and initially, relations to oneself, linked and reproduced in 'paper' and people formations. These relations to oneself also have the effect of constituting relations with others.

Of course the local effectivity of such knowledges and practices in constructing the managerial stationing is by no means stable and secure. It is mediated by the interconnections and conflicts between the localized and the imperializing. How these multiple practices cohere, coalesce or conflict is locally contingent in relation to each college/university and to all those localized sites and ultimately working bodies that make up these 'organizations'. The managerial station may conflict with, run over or around other established stationings (e.g. professional or administrative), which are read in the approach taken up here as 'locales'.

As I mentioned at the beginning of this book, the imperializing knowledges and practices of management meet the flows and contours of the crumbled terrain of sedimented identities and professional and administrative practices. At the same time, these rather technical imperializing practices work to extend their reach by simultaneously setting the subject position within a particular field or terrain. The practices of audit, budgets, contracts and performance appraisal provide, as Rose (1996a) outlines, grids of visualization, vocabularies, norms and systems of judgement through which the subject position 'manager' and the terrain that is required to be managed are produced. It is to this, in relation to FE, that I now turn. But first, Stephen Jones (1997a), further education columnist with the *Times Education Supplement*, offered the following description of the tension between managerial station and teaching locale:

> So given that it's the managers who are the future, what will the future 'my best' columns be like? I tentatively offer the following . . . My best manager thirty years on, Tracey Trumpeter, pays tribute to Richard Brain, the FE manager and administrator she remembers most vividly from her teenage years.
>
> 'He changed my life. He really did. You see, up until that point the only people I came into contact with at the college had been teachers. Richard – Dick we called him – was different.
>
> 'For a start, he convinced me I was worth something. He used to refer to me not as a student but as a unit of activity (the teachers had only ever implied I was a unit of inactivity). And with Dick I was not just one unit but lots of them – a walking bundle of units was how he saw us . . . Dick explained he was only dealing with us units temporarily, until they had persuaded the teachers to accept their latest pay cut and come back to work.

Stationing the further education college: identities and relations in principals' interviews

The accounts offered by senior post-holders in colleges and universities of becoming a manager involve similar elements to the account above of the development of the academic identity. There is fear and anxiety over how to be in relation with others and with oneself. There are the new discursive practices and knowledges of 'managing'. There is an intensifying emphasis on credentials (particularly educational credentials, MBAs and the like, or 'real' management experience) in order to 'shore-up' the new identity. And there is the need to reproduce a managerial identity in order to 'fit' in with and continue to gain the support and patronage of the next hierarchical tier of 'managers' in universities and colleges. These elements induce the demand for ways of talking and ways of working which differ from the established and traditional. Of course there is the fear and anxiety for one's job, for the future of one's college or university, but this is more directly and powerfully read as anxiety over the identities one embodies, and which receive approval and support. The 'college' and the 'university' might seem powerful 'entities' outside the 'individual', yet from the perspective adopted here they work to support and elaborate both existing and new identities. Of course they are just one part of the new knowledges and discursive practices which come to dominate 'meetings' and relations between people in the new FHE. It is here that the managerial station with its panoply of techniques of reporting and review attempts to establish itself. I shall turn in the second half of this chapter to the processes at work in 'meetings', but first I address the 'college' through the texts from interviews with college principals.

At interview all four principals identified colleges not as *businesses* but as using business practices. As City College's[1] principal said: 'We are effectively running as businesses now. We've got accounts that have to be signed off by external auditors. We are exposed to the process of audit and inspection and accountability in a way that is fundamentally different from anything that happened before'.

The principal of Urban College meanwhile described senior post-holders as 'Effectively running small businesses now with considerable amounts of delegated authority'. Through this move, business and management discourse was drawn in and took a number of forms in these texts. Tower College's principal stressed the provision of services for customers and payment by performance:

> A college's *core business* is providing excellent education and training *services* . . . the difference today [compared with pre-incorporation] is that the funding that we receive very much reflects our *performance* and in the past it didn't . . . to provide excellent services we need to have very good information about what our customers want, and by customers I mean the users of the college in the widest sense.

In general terms all four principals drew on the dominant functionalist discourse to discuss the identities and relations of senior post-holders. This prescribes the necessity of colleges to be managed by managers who have a variety of 'skills' depending on their 'level' in the new organizations. Hillside College's principal said the 'key role [in the college was] the middle manager'. City College's principal meanwhile drew on team discourse (Sinclair, 1992) and positioned the manager within the team. She suggested that incorporation required a 'paradigm shift' where senior post-holders were required:

- to become 'effective resource managers, human, financial and physical';
- to be increasingly accountable ('they have to produce evidence to prove they were doing what they said they were doing');
- to be exposed to a funding methodology which could 'threaten the life of a college'.

In response to this, particularly the fear and anxiety produced by the funding methodology and independence, she counselled the 'importance of the process of effective team management'. This, she said 'helped managers to make the paradigm shift': 'We have gone through some very hard challenges, I mean the putting together of college teams and the teams themselves working together on the ground has been extremely powerful. I think that is [shows] mutual support from colleagues at every level of the college and trying to avoid people feeling that it is all their fault'. She even prescribed the 'team' as a response to her own anxieties: 'I'm not afraid to acknowledge that I'm frightened at times by the responsibilities that I face and I think that putting that on the table with staff and managers helps. I haven't got all the answers. This is a team effort. We can only do this if we are rowing the boat together and that is how you can allay some of that anxiety that follows from that fear'.

Meanwhile Urban College's principal spoke of management in much more combative and controlling terms, reflecting a much more competitive masculinity at work in his construction of the college and the manager (Whitehead, 1996b): 'In a sense it has taught me that management is about propaganda to some extent, a selling exercise. You have not only to sell ideas and change to your staff but you have also to make sure that if there are people internally and externally who are working against you then you have also got to sell it more widely to get a better understanding'. He recounted how prior to incorporation colleges were 'loosely administered' as neither local authorities nor principals controlled colleges: 'they weren't allowed to', he said. Gaining control, given that around 70 per cent of expenditure is on staffing, involved 'gain[ing] control of the deployment of staff, their pay and their outputs and how you manage them and deploy them. The name of the game is managing colleges rather than administering them'. The principal went on to argue for two ways of managing colleges, by authoritarian 'dictat and fear' and by 'delegation, understanding and skill development': 'we are very authoritarian about the plan, the direction, the strategies. We are very authoritarian about those. Also we are quite clear about behaviours. Nobody is entitled to create their own management style, I don't want mill owners running parts of the college; there is a house style'.

The 'house style' was said to be 'leading people, developing people, creating enterprising environments, not delegating tasks and not managing by fear'. Yet this was at odds with later comments made in the interview. The principal suggested that:

> control comes up against a number of things. First of all it comes up against the debate about professionalism, particularly about academic

staff and academic freedom . . . it has not been argued to my satisfaction that an approach to delivering education and training to students, and good value for money and constant change is compatible with what I understand to be professionalism and academic freedom'.

He then went on to define the 'new' professionalized station, drawing in the terms 'professional' and 'academic freedom' in the context of the new constraints in FE:

I think the facts are that there are parts of this organization that are very cost effective, very entrepreneurial, very enterprising and where staff would say that they have got professional approaches and a degree of academic freedom. Given that they expect payment on a certain day of every month, I expect something in return. If people think it is optional to do some work then I think it is optional to pay them, an option that they don't like [laughs].[2]

In this last comment the principal's text works to construct his own identity as a manager and employer, and to reconstruct the professional as an academic labourer in a new competitive environment. This reconstruction has been hotly contested through the lecturers' dispute over new contracts in this college. Whereas City College's principal relies on team discourse to reposition and construct discursively the new conditions for academic workers in FE, this principal preferred to remind academics of their financial vulnerability. This suggests that the principal's regime, despite his suggestions of a contrary 'house style', operates on the basis of fear about redundancy and dismissal. This was supported by examples and comments from other senior post-holders interviewed at the college who described the senior management as aggressive and heavy-handed.

To summarize, the above illustrates the dominant commercialism and managerialism in the texts of FE principals. It suggests, however, that there are significant differences in the mix of managerial discourse drawn upon in FE and that this both confronts and reflects different historical contexts. It also suggests that the suffusion of managerial knowledge and practices is not simply smooth and unproblematic. Indeed, Urban College's principal said that in many cases senior post-holders themselves, to say nothing of academic staff, had been brought 'kicking and screaming' into the 'new culture'. Nevertheless the principal was proud that the college had not removed those with what he termed 'incompatible values':

interestingly we haven't swept out, there has not been a night of the long knives here. People have sometimes recognized that they are incompatible and they have left us. We have not actually swept people out in that fashion and I'm pleased to say we have not sort of hand picked the red-blooded, meat-eating people from outside and created a college on the basis on this new culture.

This may be true. Yet there has been a significant 'replacement' of senior staff in colleges and universities. Right across the post-compulsory sector there has been a significant 'reshuffle' of personnel at senior levels with the restructuring and reorganization of academic units, replacement of senior staff, and the reallocation or rotation of responsibilities. More than a third of FE college principals left their jobs or took early retirement in the three years surrounding incorporation (Ashton, 1995). All four colleges in the sample have appointed new principals since 1992 (all external appointments).[3] However it is not necessary, as Urban College's principal asserts, to 'replace' people in order to reconstruct identities and relations. What is required is that one set of dispositions, practices and knowledges substitutes for others. As Smith *et al.* (1995: 37) argue: 'The substitution of a management for a professional or curriculum-led further education sector is potentially one of the most far-reaching consequences of recent reforms'.

The argument here is that new practices and knowledges construct a particular station for FHE senior post-holders which differs significantly from past positionings. From being administrators of predictable income flows, senior post-holders in colleges and universities have been stationed as responsible for processes which are deemed to influence these flows. They are positioned particularly by devolved budgetary processes and between income and expenditure. Such knowledge practices do not simply position, but individuate and divide senior post-holders off from one another. Through such exposure, anxiety seems to fuel desire for competency in the new knowledges which in turn helps to solidify new hierarchical relations and problematizes existing identities. This is outlined explicitly in the comments from Urban College's principal which open the next section. The next section continues the discussion in relation to the construction of the managerial station in FE, drawing on interview and documentary material from the colleges.

Stationing the manager: an embodied nexus of grids, guides for action and forms of questioning with examples from further education

> To survive this college had to move very quickly. We started with a lot of training on the managers, on enterprise and enterprise skills, leadership skills. The first thing we came across was language which reflected a certain attitude: like the denial of the use of the word manager in relation to some academic leaders; a preference for administration, side-stepping of responsibility – with some alacrity I would have to say. So part of the process was unequivocally pinning on people an accountability with an appropriate authority and the responsibility and over time delegating that down . . . Heads of school now operate a performance management scheme . . . they are responsible for delivering on an annual contract a volume of work at the right quality on each area's business plan. They are effectively running small businesses

now with a considerable amount of delegated authority. Some of that is uncomfortable for them, some of that is still in transition . . . running through the organization is a new culture; some people find it hard and some people take to it easily – it depends on their attitudes, their personality and their employment experience and background . . . the college's survival in this new environment was very much about value for money, customer care, responsiveness, it was about reorienting staff values, manager's values.

The uniqueness of this quotation is its brevity. It compresses into 200 or so words many elements which address both the new practices at work in post-compulsory education institutions and particularly those engaged in constructing the managerial station. A station, as Fiske (1993) suggests, is constructed by detailed imperializing knowledges and practices that work to control simultaneously the interior dimensions of subjectivity, socio-political relations and the physical dimensions of bodies in time and space. The quotation can be read as offering a detailed account of the construction of these dimensions of the managerial station in FE colleges.

The first thing to draw from the quotation is its grounding in the common-sense, but politically complicit, ontology of the 'individual'. The principal's text assumes college 'managers' to be a population of 'individuals' with *attitudes* shaped by 'employment experience and background' which will in turn shape adaptability to the 'new culture'. The assumption of a group of 'individuals', however, is used to buttress the construction of the *individuated* manager – a manager who is divided off from his or her colleagues and can be subject to particular techniques of measurement and judgement. In order to achieve this, however, forms of knowledge and practices are required which construct senior post-holders as individuals in the first instance. As Foucault (1983: 212) argued (unfortunately using the male pronoun) the power process of subjection 'categorises the individual, marks him by his own individuality, attaches him to his own identity, imposes a law of truth on him which he must recognise and which others recognise in him'.

The second point to draw from the text is the assumption that it is the new 'culture' (the 'station' in the approach used here) which is stable and the individual whose adaptability to it who is variable. Thus each 'individual' becomes a case that can be assessed against the station's (culture's) norms. Through this decisions can be made about each individual's suitability or need for special attention.

Yet the managerial station which involves these new ways of relating to a 'self' as a 'manager' (located in the principal's text in the notions of enterprise, leadership, customer care, value for money and responsiveness), is highly unlikely to be taken up simply through the principal's act of will or through training exercises that challenge the 'denial of the use of the word manager'. What is required is that these same relations be distributed so that there are multiple points, moments and events through which the designated 'individual' is required to address her or himself as a 'manager'.

One strategy of imperializing top-down power, as Fiske (1993: 71) notes, 'is to construct its stations in as fine a detail as possible to minimise the gaps so that locales can be excluded'. This requires a whole panoply of seemingly mundane technical devices or 'forms of communication', to use Foucault's term. These act continuously and at a distance aiming to produce new ways of being a subject, new identities.

Miller and Rose (1990: 7) highlight this directly in their discussion of the practices of modern statecraft. In order to govern, states must translate the events or phenomena to be governed into:

> information – written reports, drawings, pictures, numbers, charts, graphs, statistics. This information must be of a particular form – stable, mobile, combinable and comparable. This form enables the pertinent features of the domain – types of goods, investments, ages of persons, health, criminality etc. – to literally be re-presented in the place where decisions are to be made about them (the manager's office, the war room, the case conference and so forth).

Thus the managerial station in FHE can be read as a point of both collection and translation; where events are translated into forms of information which can then be acted upon given certain criteria or norms. Perhaps most importantly it is the site where all these processes are going on at once and seemingly automatically. The managerial station is where information is collected, translated, judged against certain norms and actions and applied on a continuous basis. This is done not through processes of domination but where 'individuals' are continuously judging themselves and others and adjusting their actions on a continuous basis. Indeed, the whole suffusion of the 'manager' across the sector is intimately linked to the increased need for information, and, through this, control. The seemingly mundane practices of 'managing', what one section manager interviewed called her 'housekeeping jobs', have multiplied and now require a large commitment of time. Alongside tasks such as recruitment of staff (particularly part-time staff), timetabling and room allocation, a whole raft of more detailed monitoring processes have been assembled and introduced which address, for instance, student numbers, courses, attendance, staff hours, sickness and holidays. As the discussion of the 'meeting' in this chapter shows, colleges are now required to more intensively monitor themselves and particularly to attempt to ensure some degree of 'equalization' between the total staff hours available and the staff hours used, while at the same time attempting to maximize the return on each of those used hours. This requires intensive information collection, particularly in relation to staff hours, holiday usage, staff development time and sickness.

The managerial station as a point of translation is succinctly illustrated in the following text from Hillside College's principal. The quotation also shows again how common-sense notions of the 'individual' are used to ground the individuating practices which work to produce the managerial station.

The key role is middle manager development, middle managers who can handle resources, you know, in terms of understanding in their heads that they have got a block of activity, how much that block of activity costs and what is the revenue generated by that block of activity, and they can resolve issues to do with resource allocation and issues to do with managing people. They are the key things. In some colleges like this one it has taken longer because middle managers were never appointed as middle managers. They were Burnham senior lecturers, and the only distinction between them and ordinary lecturers was that they got paid more and they taught less.

While this comment might be read simply as a graphic way of expressing the characteristics of the middle manager, such a discourse is crucially involved in the construction of the managerial station. The key element in the text is the positioning of the 'block' inside the body of the middle manager. This establishes ties of responsibility and accountability between the characteristics of that 'block' and the particular managerial body. An alternative reading would suggest that this 'block', which includes the multiple locales of students and staff, is not a 'block' at all, but a set of variably fragile social relations. The politically significant element of the principal's description is then the collapsing of these relations into a 'block of activity' (which costs a certain amount, generates a certain amount of income and generates certain staffing and curriculum issues), which is then enfolded into the body identified as a 'middle manager'.

The text also notes how this 'understanding' (the political significance of which is denied) differs from that of the 'old' Burnham senior lecturers, who were senior academics in FE colleges. This is a crucial distinction, yet the principal's text suggests that the difference between middle managers and senior lecturers amounts simply to the specification of the job at appointment. It denies the problems of such a reconstruction, given that all the six section managers now on management contracts in the college were previously senior lecturers. It also underplays the complex nature of the repositioning.

However, both Urban and Hillside principals' texts highlight how the managerial station is produced. In the text from Urban College's principal, the *mechanisms* of 'performance management', 'annual contract[s for] a volume of work at the right quality on each area's business plan' and delegated authority for 'running small businesses' are used to 'unequivocally' pin on senior post-holders a new way of being a subject at work. Embedded in these mechanisms are numerous more detailed paper- and computer-based systems such as strategic planning, budgets, timesheets and taught hour plans (which take the form of computer spreadsheets and databases). Significantly, it is the elaborateness and the overlapping character of such mechanisms which enhances the construction of the managerial station.

Two further examples highlight this. The first deals with new strategic planning processes and the second with performance management programmes. In the first quotation the principal of City College (which in 1995/6 reported a £1 million surplus on its work up from £460,000 the year before) explains how the college's planning process operates:

> The cycle of strategic planning which we have just initiated begins with the governing body of the college setting the direction of the organization. That will be communicated back at the residential conference next week with about 50–60 middle managers. We will then determine our corporate management priorities against the direction the governors want us to move. That will be taken back down into teams. Teams will then develop their own strategic planning priorities to help contribute to those corporate goals and individuals will identify their particular contribution to that. That goes right down to individual operating statements which are the basis of the review. The annual development review with the individual seeks to identify the individual's staff development needs. Now that is the process. Putting that process in place over a three- to four-year period, which has been about aligning people with the mission and the corporate goals and developing team management skills, *has helped* the process of taking managers to make the paradigm shift.

The 'paradigm shift' is the principal's shorthand term for the move, initiated by the incorporation of colleges, to a more commercially orientated mode of operating. The example illustrates how the new discursive practices of planning, personal review and team working, with their embedded subject positionings, particularly that of the 'manager', are linked together in the attempt to produce particular stations at work. Through these multiple practices the goals and objectives of the individuated worker are aligned, via the discursive practices of individual review and the 'team', with the strategic objectives of the college, which of course are tied directly into the sector's objectives of reducing costs and increasing educational participation.

At Urban College the annual review is known as the performance management system (PMS). The emphasis here is not directly upon 'teams', but on individuated performance and reward. The college's personnel officer outlined the system:

> At the beginning *you* set down *your* principal accountabilities, what are *you* here for and what are *your* main accountabilities to the college, and *you* usually have four or five of those . . . From these *you* are expected to set PMS objectives for that annual cycle. Those are done in consultation with the manager, they are things that are going to move the area of *your* work on, they have got to be above *your* job description . . . These are then compared with others in *your* phase to make sure that they are not too far-reaching or too below everybody else . . . With objectives we also have to put together some form of performance indicator; so how are we going to meet it and how will *you* assess that *you* have met it. Usually that has to be completed by a certain date. *You*

go through the year, trying to achieve *your* PMS objectives, obviously not at the expense of *your* day-to-day role, and at the end of the six-month period, *you* are assessed on how *you* are meeting it. Whether *you* are meeting it or whether it is an unfair objective [or] whether it needs to be changed or whatever. And then at the end of the year *you* are then graded as to how far *you* have got, graded by *your* manager initially. Then it is countersigned and then there is a moderation panel, picked from the college for each phase, and they actually moderate the assessment. It is a fair system.[4]

Read from a Fiskean position, this text highlights the multiple and overlapping discursive practices which seek to construct in fine detail managerial stations in colleges. As is apparent, these practices combine particular knowledges, identities, relations and physical aspects. The PMS scheme addressed here, for instance, provides a mechanism by which workers can self-discipline themselves in relation to college objectives. It both provides a means for individuating workers and offers devices through which they can closely discipline and monitor, on a continuous basis, their own performance. This is then assessed by, and in the process constructs, their 'managers'. Note, for instance, the terms 'you' and 'your' are used repeatedly in the text (this suggests that there is perhaps a degree of struggle over the attachment of this particular 'you' to particular bodies). This 'you' is obviously top-down. It is a 'you' stationed by imperializing discursive practices in the interests of a Thatcherite power bloc. As Fiske (1993: 74) notes, such a 'you' is not extending that person's control over him or herself, but extending the power bloc's control over that person: 'The control is "hers" only in the sense of her individuation, not in any sense of her identity that she might recognise as her own'.

Detailed and intensive strategic planning processes operate in much the same way as the PMS. Through them senior post-holders are stationed as managers. The managerial 'I' is embedded and required to articulate itself in relation to objectives, targets and deadlines. These 'I's' are recorded in the operating plans which are held by the senior post-holders them-'selves' through which control is extended over them-'selves'. In HE this is often linked to particular quantitative measures through the research assessment exercise or grading in the teaching quality assessment process. These measures are in turn linked back into appraisal and reward processes.

Distributing the managerial station: examples from FE

The previous section highlighted the construction of the managerial station through the interdependent regimes of practices, to use Foucault's (1991) term. These are translated in and provide ways of being a particular 'you'/ 'I' in particular sites. The following provides detailed examples of the distribution of these practices, drawn from interviews and observation in the four FE colleges.

Hillside College's principal provided a compelling example of how imperializing knowledges are taken up and become naturalized as that 'person'. In this text it is possible to hear how the 'I' of the power bloc's imperializing knowledges is enfolded into the speaker to the point where the 'needs' of the power bloc become 'his' needs. The principal is here discussing the requirements of the senior manager and middle manager (section manager/programme manager) positions in the college. As he highlights, '*I* need people who can work strategically at senior manager level and leave the detail, leave a lot of the resolution of staffing issues and staffing conflicts with their middle managers, and *I* pay [middle managers] more and get them teaching less, much less'. This principal had earlier suggested that encouraging middle managers to take on issues surrounding staff conflict involved 'empowering' them. This did not, however, mean empowering the middle manager to challenge the imperializing knowledge and practice. It involved, as the following quotation in answer to my question 'What do you mean by empowering?' shows, positioning the middle managers with particular reporting and monitoring practices and in-built norms:

> Well it is giving them the authority to carry out fairly closely defined activities in terms of meeting targets for managing resources and in terms of resolving personnel issues because the natural reaction of a typical senior lecturer if a member of staff wasn't performing was to 'move it upstairs'. What I want them to do is to try and resolve those issues . . . when it comes to deploying resources each section of the college has a target in terms of units to be earned, that is its income side, and a target in terms of taught hours, that is its expenditure . . . it is up to the *managers* to maintain the balance. The ratio is 2.4 units per hour and if *they* stick to that then we balance the books . . . if it starts drifting down to 1.8–1.6 units per taught hour, then *they* have got real problems.

We can note here how 'they' is used to shift responsibility for balancing income against expenditure to the 'manager'. The text assumes this positioning to be a seemingly technical, unproblematic and autonomous process. As the examples from the 'meeting' later in this chapter and events in this college outlined in Chapter 5 show, this is far from the case.

One of the most prominent 'technical' processes at work in this college, however, is the computer-based unit efficiency process identified in the quotation just above (similar but less developed forms of this were found in two of the other colleges). This process attempts to intensively monitor the funding council income earned for each hour of teaching time across the college. In this college the spreadsheets are called 'taught hour plans'. They are maintained for reporting purposes by those in section manager posts (the equivalent of dean in the 1992 universities) but also distributed to programme coordinators in the various curriculum areas in most cases. The spreadsheets allow programme coordinators and the section manager to model 'virtually' the section's teaching hours, modes of teaching and class sizes so as to produce a certain average ratio of unit income per classroom contact hour across the section. Through this, section managers can explore the effect on income of particular changes to teaching programmes, for instance combining classes, reducing class contact time, increasing the use of cheaper workshop instructors or open learning time. The section manager can then act on those options that produce the best result – the best target ratio. In effect these processes are engaged in condensing, quantifying and then removing decisions about education processes from the sites where they take place. They provide the means by which learning and teaching can be speeded up, intensified or disposed of if they fail to meet particular levels of return. At the same time these processes constitute the managerial station, as the senior post-holder is positioned through them between the 'power bloc' and the 'people'.

In the case of Hillside College, its target ratio for 1994/5 was 2.4 units per hour. By 1996/7 this had been increased to 3.25 units and rose to 3.5 for 1997/8. The move from 2.4 to 3.5 in the space of four academic years is directly linked to the driving down of college funding levels through both convergence and efficiency gains. The college's curriculum director, however, proudly suggested that she had 'managed to get the senior management team to set 3.5 as the limit', although she also admitted that this was probably 'too far anyhow'. Programme coordinators and section managers across the college were highly critical of this efficiency drive. For them it was seen to be highly detrimental to college learning programmes, and likely to lead to more redundancies – particularly in A-level subjects and particularly A-level science!

Here we can see how the seemingly benign taught hour plan calculations are actively involved in both constructing the 'manager' and translating broad political economic alliances into the micro stationings of college and university classrooms. All section managers in this college are required through the computer-based taught hour plan to 'bring' their courses up to this level of return. In the first instance this required increasing class numbers, reducing contact time and increasing the number of classes lecturers teach. To give an example, the workload of A-level teachers in science in this college increased by 50 per cent during the period. While actual teacher contact time had only increased by about two hours a week, teachers were now teaching five A-level classes compared with, on average, 3.5 classes in the early 1990s. Class contact for A-level science students had dropped from six hours per group in the early 1990s to 4.5 in 1996/7. The effect of this is similar to speeding up a production line, forcing the workers to work faster. The programme coordinator for science noted: 'Our argument in science is that you can speed up the theory work if you like but you can't speed up doing practicals; that is fixed. And there is no way that you can speed that up. So we have to actually speed up more on the theory than other people'.

The taught hour plan thus provides a means for the speeding up of learning and teaching labour right across the college in order to meet the convergence and efficiency demands of the sector as a whole. The second phase of 'efficiency measures' required college section managers to substitute labour. Despite the principal's claims at interview that this would not be done, section managers, in an effort to meet taught hour plan targets, were moving technicians into workshop and laboratory 'manager's' posts, and replacing lecturer hours with instructor and assessor level staff as well as increasing the level of course project work.

In the case of science, the section manager was positioned in such a way by these processes that they signalled a major problem. The college's sixth-form programme was now competing with a new sixth form opened at the school not far from the college. This had 'eaten' into enrolments. Efficiency and convergence processes, plus competition from this new local sixth form, meant that when the section manager for this curriculum area looked at the projected taught hour plan ratios for the coming years, the ratios were significantly below the expected college norm and thus suggested that a significant number of A level and GCSE teachers' jobs would be at risk. The section had been through the redundancy process in the preceding year, when a number of jobs were lost, so it seemed likely that it would be used again – particularly in science.[5] The section head elaborated this as follows:

The single issue that engages my attention most, especially where sciences are concerned and maths to a certain extent, is trying to think how I'm going to take these people and this curriculum and ensure that they survive, because they are not going to survive. I don't know the extent to which some of the people whom I don't know very well realize this. I know that the programme coordinators, who are the line managers operationally for them, know because I meet with them regularly, we all meet together once a week and I meet each of those once a week, so I know what they think, but I do wonder sometimes if the people who go in there every day and teach the stuff actually realize that they are sitting on a boat that is sinking very very slowly. At the moment it is slowly: we don't want any sort of *Titanic* sunk in ten minutes sort of thing . . . in a year's time, possibly two years' time, we will not be employing as many people to do that as we now have. I would like to think that there would be some that were beginning to do some different things, they were beginning to think 'well what else can I do besides teach A-level biology, what else can I do besides teach chemistry? I must have some skills'. I'm convinced that my biggest problem with them is to get them to think creatively and very innovatively about what they do. The odd conversation I have with people at the chalk face is 'well what can we do to get more A-level students'? 'Well yes that is a fair point; if that will make you feel more secure then we will talk about it and possibly there are some things we can do to make sure we can go on'. [CP: but that's not the direction] Well it's small stuff. I think beyond that, if there is no A level tomorrow what will we do with you, what *can* we do with you, what would you like to be involved in doing?

> Clearly it is not something that you can just do overnight; you can't just spray this kind of stuff on. Some people have been here a long time and always done the same things . . . I don't know what it is going to take to make some people realize that this can't go on. How do you do that? How do you manage that without traumatizing them to death? How do you manage it without them running down the corridor with their hands in the air saying 'what are you going to do?'

This is not, as Longhurst (1996) suggests, a 'manager' motivated by her own survival to exploit and oppress. It is more a 'manager' constructed within and stationed by a particular set of knowledge practices which produce certain strategic implications – which prove troubling and highly problematic not just because they threaten college survival. They are troubling in part because the 'manager' is not a coherent distinct human being, but a multiple of subject positions within various discursive practices, which in this case sit uncomfortably together. The 'me' the section manager refers to in statements like 'my biggest problem with them' is *not* the 'me' that is the access studies teacher, the mother of two children, or the magistrate, in this case. It is the 'me' constructed through the knowledges and practices of the managerial station. Other subject positions are available, particularly localized knowledges which address professional and academic expertise. A key reason why the section manager lamented the 'slow sinking' of science A levels is that professionally the teaching staff were 'excellent'. As she said:

> they are good at what they do. Students who come here have a good deal. They get good results which is what they come for so I know that they are good. I suppose I should say they are good classroom managers. They get good results for their students and that is what they consider to be most important. It is what most students consider to be most important. But really, I don't know, I don't know what it is going to take to make some people realize that this can't go on.

Clearly the interview provides a space where such 'troubles' can be exercised. In the quote we hear how to some extent the section manager identifies with the professional identity, and its experience, but the speaker is also positioned by the unit yield methodology. 'Behind' her are the college's curriculum director and accountant who monitor 'her' efforts to bring courses into line with particular yield ratios. In this we can also hear something of the problematic processes involved in the extension of the managerial station out across the college. We can read in these quotations the politics of knowledge and knowledge practices at work which construct the positions of 'manager' and the 'academic professional'. The section manager speaks of how the 'programme coordinators' (those given responsibility for teaching staff in each of the four curriculum areas in the section) are said to 'realize' the current circumstances. But those whose knowledge practices position them as teachers continue to read themselves through these identities. Of course, as the above suggests, to the section manager positioned by the discursive practice of managing (i.e. the unit yield processes) this seems like resistance. However, what has occurred is that what previously might have been considered the 'teaching' station, has, in the framework suggested here, become a locale, as it has become the target of imperializing knowledges and practices. The section manager's own text reflects this shift as she positions the teaching staff differently in the quotations. She moves from a more 'horizontal', distanced and professional positioning with 'I don't know what it is going to take to make some people realize that this can't go on' to, 'I don't know how *I'm* going to take these people and this curriculum and ensure that they survive'.

Read in another way, the section manager's particular concern here is to enjoin the science teachers to 'read' themselves through the knowledges and practices of the managerial station. Yet their professional identities, those that engage with the student and not the funding council and the 'manager', continue to take precedence as it is these identities which are confirmed and reproduced on a day-to-day basis at work. The programme coordinators, meanwhile, those who were stationed at weekly meetings with the section manager, either individually or as a group were engaged in reconstructing their professional identities.

Programme coordinators/managers at Hillside College and across three of the four colleges (although different terms are used for these posts) represent the 'new managers' and the extension of the managerial station into the professional locales of the colleges. At Hillside this comprised a group of 30 former senior lecturers. Each had been repositioned as the 'line manager' for up to ten teaching staff in each of the college's curriculum areas. The pattern of this repositioning, as might be expected, was largely identical to that of the section manager. As programme coordinators their teaching load had been reduced slightly (by three hours per week). They had been given a small, flat rate, pay increase of £750 per annum and had all been positioned at the top of the lecturer's payscale, thus removing any differences between programme coordinators. Part of the work required of such post-holders is the provision of detailed monitoring information on each curriculum area (e.g. staff hours, student numbers). They are also required not only to input this into strategic plans, budgeting, unit yield and audit processes, but to reformulate plans and programmes on the basis of information returned from these processes. At interview the college's curriculum director added a positive gloss to this by suggesting that such processes allow control for 'two aspects of the job – curriculum and resources – to be *given* to the staff'. However, these processes were having a profound and highly variable effect on their professional identities.

One section's programme coordinator noted that since incorporation:

> it has gone like a business. What use to be student centred, is now, you look at a student and you see them as a unit of funding. You have to

look now at the viability of the course in terms of funding. Before you looked at it in educational terms. You shouldn't do but that is now what we do. We close classes on the basis of whether your funding units are up or down. Also I find it difficult to actually line manage people I've actually worked with on the same basis.

While this programme coordinator found the stationing problematic, her colleague (an A level and GSCE maths teacher), whom she described as 'one of life's perpetual optimists' by way of contrast, appeared to have embraced the positioning. In response to my question 'What does the programme coordinator's job consist of?' he said:

Planning for the future, trying to keep the unit yield up. Trying to think about new schemes, and keeping people motivated in the job, keeping the morale up. In this job you are more in touch with what is going on, with the problems, perhaps with planning for the future . . . you can see the possible openings. In terms of the future we're hoping to move into distance learning education. In part it is to do with keeping our jobs . . . we could see that with A-level classes opening up we needed to do something. So we are going to go for the distance learning market and hope to pilot the GCSE maths programme next year with 50 students. This would be learning packs and videos. We hope to run it so that it acts as a backdrop to any fluctuations in our classroom numbers. We could raise and lower this depending on classroom numbers. We could go nationally or even further afield. Last week I had to say how many students we would be recruiting onto it – because of the funding mechanism, if you overestimate they claw back but if you underestimate you only get the exit funding part of the unit. We estimated that we could give three hours for each student for each member of staff. If we were successful we could grow it enough to secure our jobs. So it is to help secure our own jobs for the future with the falling numbers of A-level students, although the numbers [in the new school sixth form] have not been escalating as expected, and with the publication of the first results this year, there may be a backlash against the new A levels in schools.

Here is a different subject at work, one with global ambitions! The speaker is engaged in attempting to reposition his professional identity in the discourse of distance learning so as to 'secure our own jobs'.

The last example shows how devolved funding processes station the senior academic and administrative post-holder as an accountable manager. They form a point of translation and enactment in a seemingly unbroken line of visibility and potential action from national funding body into the classroom/ lecture theatre/seminar room/laboratory. They provide the means by which a unit of resource is consumed through each hour of teaching/learning time and is made visible and thus equalized through various tactics, with the declining unit of resource available to fund that activity.

Meetings: putting 'flesh' on the bones of the paper structure

As a piece, then, the 'manager' can be said to be a station comprising a nexus of practices, vocabularies, norms and systems of judgement which form particular directionalities across the institutional terrain of FHE institutions. It is also clear that fear and anxiety for a relatively stable self – as a manager – informs, even fuels, the dispersal of these identities. Each of these practices (e.g. budgetary, strategic planning and performance appraisal) includes detailed guides for action, questions to be asked, decisions to make, solutions that can be suggested, forms of recording, listing and categorizations. These in turn are all embedded in yearly, six monthly, monthly, weekly and in some cases daily repetitions of forms of reporting and submission of results in various forms (e.g. in person at meetings, in paper form, in spreadsheet returns). These form what Tower College's personnel officer called the college's 'paper structure'.

> Yeah, that is the paper structure, that's what your role is, these are the people that you've got under you, here's your contract, here's the contracts of the people you manage, this is the discipline guidelines and some notes of guidance but *if we left it at that we are bound to fail. I think the other important facets are team meetings.* That is one of the things that [the principal] is very keen on, working as teams and then we support each other and *we work face to face rather than sending out pieces of paper.* So on the strategic side there are the team meetings. You could have a sector meeting, then there might be a curriculum meeting, which might be anything to do with, say, IT. That will cross over a number of sectors.

Here the personnel officer identifies the importance of the stationing of people physically, and thus in particular social relationships, in the construction of the 'manager'. The quotation highlights the importance of body topography to the development of the 'manager'. If this were left to the 'paper structure' – the knowledges, in other words – 'we are bound to fail', he suggested. Meetings, he argued, are the single most important aspect for stationing both the 'manager' and the non-manager within what is read here as imperializing knowledge practices. It is through these that the 'paper structure' is literally made 'flesh', as the personnel officer had earlier noted in the interview. He said that the principal had a current favourite saying: 'structures don't deliver courses, people do'. He then related how the principal himself was involved in personally elaborating this: 'I mean we had a meeting, personnel team with [the principal], another good example of putting flesh on the bones of getting people to work at managing change'. He then went on to talk more directly about 'putting flesh on the bones' of 'managing change':

> How we interacted is finely tuned. It comes down to the key word – communication. You've got your structures, you've got your rules and

regulations with the paperwork and then it is about *making that come to life* and that is through knowing what your role is and then going out and doing it and communicating that. I think the meeting structures play a very central part.

In sum, these quotations highlight the power–knowledge processes which construct the managerial station, and the managed college. As Foucault (1991) outlined, the first application of power–knowledge is enclosure – the physical enclosure of bodies in time and space. From these social relations and identities, those provided in this case by the 'paper structure' follow. The 'meeting' is a key site where power–knowledge practices are applied, and it is in these sites that particular identities found in the 'paper structure' are ascribed, reviewed and thus reproduced, all of course in the context of a general fear of college survival, and of one's own variably unstable identity.

'Making it come to life': managers and meetings, an example

Managing, as the above suggests, can be read as an attempt to construct stations through which particular knowledges and practices can flow. These provide particular ways of being oneself and relating to others. The crucial translation of managerial knowledge and practices, that which involves 'putting flesh on the bones' of such knowledges, occurs at 'meetings'. The personnel manager, along with others across the sample, highlighted the crucial importance of multiple small-scale meetings as sites where the body topography of the station is constructed. In order to illustrate this, I offer here an account of one of these meetings. The example provides a detailed account of the embodiment of the managerial station in meetings. The particular event was one of the weekly meetings a section manager at Hillside College holds with the four programme coordinators in this section. According to the programme coordinators, who were interviewed after this event, the particular meeting I attended (and report here) was very typical of section meetings. The following account is written from the point of view of an outsider 'listening in' on the multiple practices and knowledges that make up these meetings.

The meeting

The 'set': an FE college classroom mid-afternoon, late November 1996. Six people sit around a collection of tables joined together to form a square. One side of the square is occupied by M, the section manager, who has in front of her piles of folders arranged neatly in an order. Some of the folders carry the names of the four programme coordinators (PCs) who occupy the other sides of the table. An administrator also sits at the table taking notes.

The meeting: the meeting was jovial and punctuated by jokes, irony and sarcasm, supplied mostly by M. This overlaid, however, the main 'business' which was the distribution of a great many forms and requests from M to the PCs. These requests and forms had in turn come to M from the meeting she attended with the college's curriculum director and other section managers the day before. M punctuated her delivery of the forms with comments and asides which appeared to lighten the tone of this distribution process. For example, M made regular recourse to her intimate knowledge of what would make 'Big Sylvia', as the programme director is known, and 'George Bain', the finance director, 'happy'. The agenda was a mixture of reminders that such and such a process needed to be done/completed by such and such a deadline, overlaid with a raft of new paper-based demands each with their own new deadlines. The monotony of this process and the loading up which occurred led one PC to mime banging his head on the desk as yet another request for forms to be filled, and initiatives to be generated and inserted in the correct document, was handed out. Another PC screwed up his face and the lines upon it appeared to get deeper.

M meanwhile ignored this. She ran the whole affair with a crisp, focused efficiency, moving quickly from one element on the agenda to another. It was clear that this was also aimed at avoiding debate and critique from the PCs, who appeared to barely tolerate the requests and demands for figures, comments, plans etc. She clearly orchestrated the whole event. She kept the 'paper moving', interspersing it with almost constant, sometimes humorous, sometimes sarcastic comments about this and that manager or this or that deadline. She thus filled in verbal space which might have allowed comment to flow the 'other' way. When some question or comment did come 'back' she often put the responsibility back on the PC: 'Oh I don't know that, ring so and so, you ask him'.

Again to smooth the procession of paper, M occasionally played teacher and mum. After she had handed over a pile of documentation she said to the PCs, 'Now don't say that I don't ever buy you anything'. When another asked for something she quipped back: 'I'm not your mum!' 'Yes you are', came the laughing pantomine-esque reply. 'I don't want to be your mum, they don't pay me enough'. 'I' was used occasionally to deflect comment and potential criticism: 'You see what I have to put up with Craig', which followed a joke that had come 'back'. After the 'important' bits of paper were passed around, M also passed out brown folders for each of the PCs filled with more paper. (These included less pressing material, invoices and the like, as well as newspaper clippings and information sheets from other institutions aimed at giving the PCs ideas for projects and actions. The PCs said at interview that they largely ignored these folders.)

The main 'requests' meanwhile included: requests for updated taught hour plans and unit yields from the finance director. These had to be returned in two weeks' time. As these figures had been returned on an earlier form by the PCs two weeks before, M recommended simply lifting these figures for the updates.

The programme coordinators complained vocally at a training event, described in Chapter 7, about this duplication which they claimed was a regular occurrence. At interview a number said that they found this seemingly thoughtless duplication 'oppressive'.

The taught hour plan and the unit yield updates meanwhile would be fed into the college's spreadsheet programmes and then returned to M [and other section managers] on computer disks so that she could see how the section's figures were shaping up against the target. As a way of encouraging a response to this request M reminded the PCs that this update would be used to 'convince George [the accountant] to release the college-wide performance-related pay increase of 1.5 per cent. 'I wouldn't normally push this, but when people's pay increases hang on it, it needs to be done', she said.

The strategic planning documentation was the next agenda item. Each of the PCs received a five- or six-page collection of papers upon which they were to insert, under the appropriate strategic plan object-ive, 'their' subject area's contributions. The first page was for new courses, the second for full cost work. M began her 'pitch' on this by softly shifting responsibility back to the programme director: 'You know what Sylvia is like with boxes. There are loads of boxes on this sheet. Now I don't expect you to want to or be able to fill them all in; if you can fill in one or two maybe that will be fine'. She was harder on full cost work: 'We really have to go hard on this; if we don't then it is highly unlikely that the £3000 on the budget that George has held back will be released to us, unless we can come up with something on this. And some of us want £2000 of the £3000 anyway', M said, looking at one of the PCs.

One can note here how the same hold-back process exercised by the secretary of state across the sector in relation to contracts had 'migrated' into colleges to enforce compliance to particular objectives. There is a connection here to the college's inspection report of 1995, as it mentioned 'poor performance' by the college in generating 'full-cost' work.

One of the PCs later said, clearly bewildered by M's instructions regard-ing form-filling: 'So you want us to write something in every one of these'. 'As many as you can', M replied, and then covered: 'I could do it all myself and make it up, but then it would be you who would have to do it, so what I suggest is that you put them in in the first place'. Although M shifted responsibility for this demand for initiatives and reporting to Sylvia, she herself had in fact been involved in drawing up the broad objectives for the section which were now being 'fanned out' to the PCs who were required to 'fill in the gaps'. The broad objectives had gone to Sylvia and then, once she had checked them, they were sent back to M for her to 'cascade' to the PCs for specifics, deadlines and people to whom responsibility for them would be attached. However, M didn't put herself in the frame on this at the meeting, preferring instead to take up a more collegial, facilitating position. She positioned herself as the messenger from Big Sylvia and implicitly denied her own direct engagement. In terms of a deadline, again, she used Big Sylvia: 'I have to have this to Sylvia by 20 December so I thought we could negotiate on when to have them to me'. 'What about Friday the 13th?' said one of the PCs. 'OK, which means the 15th, OK?'

Through this one can hear how the programme coordinators are being progressively enrolled into the drive to increase course provision with higher income potential. The shift was directed towards full-cost recovery or higher earning courses and away from what a number of programme coordinators described as the more academically demanding but less well-financed courses, namely A levels. The meeting then went on to discuss the following:

Two hundred days: the lecturer's contract set a maximum of 200 days' work a year of which 190 were teaching days. The extra 10 were for other events, particularly staff development and curriculum development events. M wanted each of the PCs to return to her a list of how these 10 days were to be organized in each curriculum area. This flowed into the next two agenda items.

Staff development action plans: this form asked for details on the staff development activities to be undertaken by each full-time member of the teaching staff. The form stated that this must be done 'in liaison with their line manager' (PC). 'Their line manager, that's you', said M emphatically to the PCs. One of the PCs then asked whether this did not duplicate another form, previously 'transferred', which included staff development activities. 'I rang her this morning and tried to get clarification from Sylvia on that, but I haven't been able to find out', said M. 'If it is on the other form, then file it under "D" for duplication, OK?'. She then quickly moved on to the next item, anxious to avoid more criticism of duplication and overloading.

Curriculum development bids: 'You will see this is on double-sided paper so you won't be able to photocopy it as the photocopier doesn't like doubled-sided copies without a lot of coaxing', said M. [Note that through this she was suggesting that the PCs distribute such forms to lecturers themselves, thus encouraging lecturers in each programme area to reposition themselves. The forms were bids for money to 'pump-prime' curriculum workshops. An example was given: money to investigate resource-based learning materials for psychology and sociology. Deadline: 12 December.] 'The deadline for this is short, but that's because Sylvia "knows" that you all have projects in mind that you have been waiting for the chance to write down', said M. This cajoling humour fell very flat at this moment.

Logging cover time: the lecturers' contract stipulates 801 teaching hours per annum. It is possible to transfer hours from one lecturer to another on the basis of sickness. The PCs were reminded to make sure that this cover was noted and adjusted, and that it was for teaching, not the supervision of classes.

Study reading weeks: M suggested that each PC give some thought to the idea of running study reading weeks on each course which would be used for staff development/curriculum development activities. In one way this could be seen as a way of structuring in the ten non-teaching days in the lecturers' contract, of reconciling reduced teaching hours with curriculum, and also giving space for the teams to work on strategic plans, objectives and targets.

Part-time hours: there was a request for information on contracted part-time hours for each section, so that cross-college teaching hours could be scrutinized. Obviously this was being checked against the section's taught hour plans and unit yields.

All the items show how programme coordinators are positioned so as to more intensively monitor teaching staff time and activities.

PC staff development updates: the college had block-booked a hotel conference suite for section manager and PC groups for the following January. M had decided that this 'away day' would be used to work on 'filling in the gaps' for new courses and programme areas of the 1997/2000 strategic plan. Finding a weekday that suited all the PCs proved difficult however. One said: 'Wednesday is out – A-level maths all morning'. Another said: 'Tuesdays out: A-level science all morning'. Another said: 'Monday's OK – GCSE maths, I can give them something to be going on with'.

This highlighted the tension between teaching and managerial work. The programme coordinators on the one hand knew that they would be 'treated' to a day out and a free lunch by the college. On the other, they knew the day would generate large amounts of extra managerial work, as they would be made responsible for turning ideas and suggestions for courses into programmes and outlines which in turn would further 'intrude' on their 16 hours a week of teaching work, which does not include preparation and marking. The programme coordinators had been relieved of just three hours of teaching for their managerial work. Two and a half hours a week alone was taken up at meetings with the section manager either as a group or one-to-one. The seemingly obstructive comments above and the apparent difficulty of finding a day for the 'away day' reflect this ambivalence over these processes.

Management training: The PCs were told of their training days and that they had to attend two of them, 13 or 19 December and 8 or 10 January. 'The last two are Friday afternoons!', said one of the PCs. 'No industrial organization in the world has staff training time on a

Friday afternoon'. 'Would you care to support that statement?', said M challengingly.

This particular programme coordinator had previously held M's job in the 'old structure' but had decided against applying for a section manager's post in the new 'streamlined' organization. He was particularly vocal in his criticism of the new regime, particularly in relation to its cost. The new structure had been 'sold' to the college, he said, on the basis that it would save money. However, calculations he had done showed that such an argument did not stand up and that the new 'structure' cost the college more and diverted more energy into managerial work (and away from teaching), thus intensifying the requirements on teachers. M reported at interview that she and this programme coordinator worked well together and she often referred issues to him for advice. However, the last extract from the meeting illustrates tensions between them.

From the above it is possible to suggest that the meeting was used as a device for stationing programme coordinators as 'managers' of college activities. The multiple forms and form-filling practices seek to control programme coordinators by providing ways in which their activities and prospective actions can be translated into categories which are then available for accountability. Such processes as monitoring staff hours require them to almost continuously monitor and codify their time and their colleagues' time at work, ostensibly to maximize income. However, there is a sense in the duplication and intensification of these control processes that they are being extended because they *can* be extended. Imperializing power, as Fiske (1993) has shown, is engaged in a continuous processes of seeking to know and control identities, relations and socio-political space and time. The 'meeting' is a crucial site for the extension and distribution of this control out across the college. It is here that the programme coordinators are intensively stationed, not just directly through the section manager's work of control of verbal, physical and spatial elements at the meeting, but also discursively through the overlapping positionings embedded in the monitoring, strategic planning and bidding forms that distribute and disperse the appropriate managerial identities and relations into related sites and spaces.

Managing, then, relies on the regularized confinement of bodies in meetings (small groups, as above, or individual meetings with one's manager). It is at the same time a systemic exercise carried out through a cascade of paper-based discursive practices which seek to codify, report, categorize and prompt the programme coordinators to make particular remarks upon which they will be made accountable – upon which they can be judged.

However, while there was little overt challenge made to this stationing in this *particular* forum, there are elements at work that suggest that such events only partially succeed in stationing section managers and programme coordinators in this, and other colleges, as continuously 'managing'. There *were* points of contest, highlighted by the grimacing and mock head banging, particularly over the duplication and 'overloading' of programme coordinators. Chapter 7 addresses this in the context of the problems, tensions and partiality of constructing the managerial station in FE. However, in the next two chapters I turn to explore the managerial station in universities.

Notes

1. College names are fictitious. Brief profiles of the colleges and universities can be found the Appendix.
2. Interviews with each of the principals were returned to them along with a request that they read the texts and forward any further comments that they might like to make. Just one of the four returned a comment. The principal quoted here advised caution in using these last sentences as he said they 'sound like witches milling round a cauldron'.
3. All four universities in the sample have appointed new directors or vice-chancellors since 1990. Three were internal appointments.
4. It is worth adding that the college board sets aside a sum each year for distribution through the PMS system, and this is divided up according to one's 'phase' or level. The senior management team in this college, for instance, gets three 'shares' for an 'outstanding' PMS score while their subordinates (section managers) get two and *their* subordinates (programme managers) get one.
5. To put this in a national perspective, the lecturers' union's (NATFHE) monitoring of job loss across FE suggests that upwards of 15,000 lecturing posts have gone mostly through early retirement schemes since incorporation in 1993 (Berryman, 1997).

5

Making Managers in Universities

But the innovation that has given me the greatest personal pleasure was undoubtedly the decision by the Kangaroo Court of Academic Development to close down the grossly underperforming Philosophy Department and replace it with a brand new Department of Quality Assurance. As many of you will know no other area, apart from the call centres, has shown such a significant growth in the last two years.

(Taylor 1998b: 52)

Turning to HE, a similar set of nationally orchestrated and locally devolved practices and knowledges to those found in FE colleges have come to form the managerial station in universities. Also in line with the argument here, the university senior post-holder is not 'told' his or her place, but takes her or his place in such practices and knowledges: through multiple reporting and review practices often carried out in small-group 'management teams' which problematize established identities and station the former professional colleague as a 'manager' of others' performance.

In order to establish this in relation to the university sector, particularly the aspect of the senior post-holder taking her or his position in the new practices and knowledges, I begin this chapter with an analysis of vice-chancellor statements from annual reports from the early 1990s. I then provide a sketch of some of the key aspects of the managerial station in universities drawn from interviews with university senior post-holders. I then move to material from one of the post-1992 universities in my sample, City University. The narrative in this section describes how, far from being a neat clinical transformation, the emplacement of the managerial station has involved a 'night of the long knives', as Urban College's principal described it – or in this case, a 'morning of the long knives'. The example illustrates how the dispersal of the managerial station often involves painful and bitter political battles. Through this narrative, entitled 'From charisma to managerialism via an "execution"', I also develop a more focused account of the 'body topography' of managers in post-compulsory education.

Stationing the university: identities, relations and knowledges

If the 'manager' is a stationing constituted institutionally by nationally orchestrated and locally devolved practices then clearly the way in which the 'university' itself is 'put into discourse' (Fiske, 1993) contextualizes the construction of the manager in these settings. Understanding the 'university' or the 'college' as, for example, a small- to medium-sized public enterprise sets the tone by which managerial knowledges and practices come to reconstruct senior post-holders as managers. In order to draw this out, I offer here analysis of public statements from vice-chancellors found in the 1991/2 annual reports of one pre-1992 and two post-1992 universities. The use of these particular reports is significant. As Chapter 3 outlined, the early 1990s marked the 'high water mark' in terms of expansion of HE and the progressive reduction in unit income. This was alongside the introduction of quality assurance and audit processes. The years 1991 to 1993 thus represent the high point in the progressive managerialization of HE, while 1994 to 1996 represent a similar period for FE colleges – where 'independence', expansion, cost reduction and audit processes come together to strengthen the FE managerial station.

Annual reports and vice-chancellor statements: some background

What is of interest here is that such statements by vice-chancellors, if we explore them intensely, outline key aspects of the reconstruction of the 'university' as a more intensively managed institution, and of the development of 'managers' or the managerial station in these organizations. Of course annual reports are promotional public relations vehicles distributed by institutions to various audiences. They, alongside prospectuses, are the 'glossy magazines' of the marketized post-binary education environment. By tradition the introductory statements to these public relations packages are not written by an institution's most ardent internal critic or most jaded, disaffected student. They are written to recommend the university to various audiences – that is, to various subject positions embedded in other knowledges. At the same time however such statements carry with them certain sets of authority relations between particular subject positions (e.g. vice-chancellor as chief executive officer, academics and administrators as 'staff'). While the 'university' is a mix of discourses, those articulated through the vice-chancellor statements might be said to be either dominant or at least in ascendancy at a particular time. However, the way in which authority relations are embedded in vice-chancellor statements is *not* immediately obvious. There is a particular convention, or discursive practice, at work. All three texts examined below follow this convention to some degree. This involves the authority figure broadly *congratulating* all those involved with the institution for their efforts. This establishes the hierarchical relations in such a way as to seemingly deny direct authority relations. The addressee is *not directly* called upon to support the institution but is thanked or congratulated for doing so. The authority relations become clear if, for example, we hypothetically turn the exercise on its head and try to imagine the circumstances which would allow or encourage the people of the organization to congratulate the vice-chancellor for that person's good work. Also, while the message of the vice-chancellor statements is ostensibly one of turning the 'spotlight' on the university, the implicit process is the production and reproduction of existing relations of power. In this we can see how particular stationings are attempted. Such statements thus provide material for the mimetic inscription of particular subjectivities which reproduce 'appropriate' authority relations. Again this links to statements at the beginning of the previous chapter which suggest that power involves us not by directing us to be a particular subject but through our taking up positions within particular knowledges. The vice-chancellor does not directly tell organizational subjects how to be, but congratulates them on being a particular organizational subject, thus providing materials by which subjects can mimetically inscribe themselves into organizational subjection. Obviously, this is particularly the case for those 'closer' to the centre of institutions – namely, senior postholders who rely to varying degrees on the positive evaluation of vice-chancellors and principals for their positions. Of course such statements cannot in any way be assumed to constitute organizational subjectivity. One must assume that a vice-chancellor's statement is but one discursive practice engaged in producing and reproducing relations of power.

The three statements are from: Keith Thompson, vice-chancellor of Staffordshire University until his retirement in September 1995; Sir Kenneth Green, vice-chancellor of Manchester Metropolitan University until his retirement in September 1997; and Professor Sir Gareth Roberts, vice-chancellor of the University of Sheffield and chair of the CVCP until September 1997.

Staffordshire University director's statement

Higher Education, paradoxically has experienced another boom year at a time of deep economic depression. This Review is both a very broad overview and a number of snapshots. It aims to give accurate impressions but not comprehensive coverage. We hope that it is stimulating. We want it to be enjoyable to read. It is a picture of success, success at Staffordshire University in a context of success in Higher Education generally, success which is to be welcomed and celebrated. This success has been bought at the price of enormous efforts by both teaching and support staff in the context of a steadily declining unit of resource, namely with student numbers rising faster than resources and, consequently, than staff numbers. Our work is central to the investment in the knowledge and skills which are crucial to the future economic well-being of the UK. We are delivering. But we shall need continued and increased support if the devotion and enthusiasm of our staff is fully to be realised.

(Staffordshire University, 1993)

General features: contents and relations

The key rationale for undertaking close textual analysis is to recover and highlight features which might be said to have social effects. Thompson's heavy use of neo-classical economic discourse to describe HE (for instance 'boom year', 'investment', 'unit of resource', 'economic well-being') can be read as part of a process of positioning the university within government-sanctioned neo-liberal understandings of the public sector. One possible social effect of this is the construction of a new relation to oneself for those engaged in HE. For example, senior post-holders might be provided with languages and practices which position them as the managers of firms in an expanding education service industry. The dominant metaphor for the university, which Thompson drives home in his crisp categorical statement 'We are delivering', is that of a production process which produces 'goods' for consumption. In this construction the university does not spend public funds on education but 'invests' them in the production of valuable objectifiable goods – in this case skills and knowledges. In order to achieve this rewriting of HE as a factory-like production process, a number of textual tactics are employed. One is that the people involved in this production process to some extent 'disappear'. Decisions over the rate of increase in student numbers for instance 'disappear' into a machine-like production process. The agency of people is nominalized and abstracted into nouns like 'skills' and 'knowledge'. Also the state's role as an agent in this process is obscured through the sentence construction: 'but we shall need continued and increased support'.

There is, one could argue, quite profound 'stationing' work under way in Thompson's statement. The key features of this would first be the downgrading of the state's role in funding HE in favour of a position where the state provides support for it. The second feature would be the elaboration of HE as a production process which 'delivers' agent-free commodities (skills and knowledge) which are sold in a market and owned in a broad sense by UK plc (Winter, 1995). Both these constructions reflect and, one might argue, are engaged in contributing to the highly contentious processes of the privatization, commodification and managerialization of HE. The link between the knowledge of these processes and their actual elaboration is through the construction of 'new' identities or subject positions for people through discourse.

Identities

Thompson's statement makes available for readers certain subject positions. Students, according to Thompson's rendering, are on the one hand little more than the bearers of funds and some aggregate of resource (e.g. 'steadily declining unit of resource, namely with student numbers rising'), and on the other hand a vessel which somehow receives 'investment in the knowledge and skills'. 'Staff', meanwhile, are positioned in different ways. 'Staff' are an aggregate ('staff numbers') on the one hand, but also the providers of 'enormous efforts' who may or may not, depending on whether further support (funding) is forthcoming, provide further realizable 'devotion and enthusiasm'. What we have here is the process noted above of 'congratu-lating' staff. This reinforces and reproduces the positioning of the 'staff' and the vice-chancellor and other senior post-holders. But what subject positions does the speaker take up himself in the text?

First, Thompson establishes himself as an authoritative voice in the text through the use of categorical modalities of which 'We are delivering' is perhaps the most direct example. However, there are variations in the positioning of this authoritative voice and its relation to others in the text. Thompson begins by adopting a position as a kind of observer of HE, then shifts to that of an insider, and then on to a position where he is one of a group of overseers of staff. For instance, he moves from 'higher education has experienced' to 'Our work is central' and 'We are delivering' and on to 'we shall need' (here the speaker is positioned as an authority on the 'needs' of staff) 'continued and increased support if the devotion and enthusiasm of *our staff* is fully to be realised'. The use of 'our staff' positions the speaker as a member of a managerial élite in a somewhat paternalistic positioning to employees of this education corporation. This positions the speaker as someone who is directly involved in realizing the value of labour power – as a manager in other words. In short it is through statements such as this, and their articulation in multiple documents and practices, that the managerial station is produced and dispersed.

Manchester Metropolitan University vice-chancellor's statement: general features

What is striking about the Manchester Metropolitan University text in Fig. 5.1 is that it is not until the last paragraph, and specifically the last ten words ('it can only thank those who made it all possible') that any hint of agency in the events described is provided. Up until this point the statement relies heavily on the use of nominalizations as the subjects of sentences (e.g. 'approaches', 'initiatives', 'planning', 'relocation', 'enhancement', 'progress', 'management'), and on passive agent-less sentences (e.g. '1991/2 ... was by any account'). By relying on nominalizations the statement effectively removes the actors from the processes narrated. In other words, it creates a 'world of thing-like abstract beings', as Hodge and Kress describe them (1993: 24), which seem to 'float' above the everyday world of social rela-tions. Even in the last sentence the agency is vague, as it is not clear just how 'those who made it all possible' actually went about doing so.

I wish to highlight a small number of other features which pervade this text and which, I suggest, render it as possibly the strongest example among the three statements explored here of the way strategic managerial

Figure 5.1   Statement of the Vice-Chancellor of Manchester Metropolitan University

---

INTRODUCTION BY THE VICE-CHANCELLOR

1991/2, the end, and the beginning of an era, was by any account the most significant year in the University's history.

Inevitably the spotlight was on issues relating to the change to university status, the creation of a new Funding Council, and new approaches to the funding of teaching, quality assessment and research.

Nevertheless, developments in the mainstream academic activities continued – with growth in student numbers, the introduction of new courses and generation of new research initiatives. Substantial increases in outstanding quality ratings of a variety of subject areas were particularly gratifying.

The most comprehensive planning exercise ever undertaken within the institution resulted in the production of the Strategic Plan 1991–2000, supported by plans relating to Accommodation, Support Services and other facets of its activities.

The benefits were reflected in the further enhancement of teaching accommodation and the relocation of certain departments, bringing nearer the coterminous siting of faculties and campuses. The student/staff ratio was maintained for the third year running, and new appointments made accordingly. Progress in implementing the Strategic Plan was also reflected in increased expenditure in real terms and enhancement of the staff base in the Library, Computing, Educational and Student Services, which should lead to further improvement in the quality of services provided for students and staff.

None of this would have been possible without the prudent approach to financial management which has transformed the institution since incorporation.

Towards the end of the academic year, merger with the Crewe+Alsager College of Higher Education extended the University's influence and visibility in South Cheshire, thereby enhancing its regional role.

Thus it was, in September 1992, that Manchester Polytechnic, established in 1970 with 7,500 full-time and part-time students, became Manchester Metropolitan University. Over those 22 years its student population has grown to over 25,000, its academic character increasingly broadened and enriched, and it has matured into an institution of higher education of high repute with the potential to become one of the country's great universities.

In that endeavour it is fortunate to be able to call on the pride and support it engenders amongst its students, members of staff, Governors and many outside friends. At the end, and the beginning, of an era it can only thank those who made it all possible.

Sir Kenneth Green

Source: Manchester Metropolitan University 1993 Annual Report

knowledges work to reproduce the 'university' in new ways. It is also as an example of what Hall (1993) described as the 'metallic managerialism' in HE.

The Manchester sample is heavily loaded with words that attempt to carry positive expressive values ('most significant year', 'most comprehensive', 'further enhancement', 'progress', 'further improvements', 'broadened', 'enriched', 'high repute'). Overwording and categorical modality are evident throughout (e.g. 'was by any account the most significant year', 'developments . . . continued', 'the benefits [of the most comprehensive planning exercise ever undertaken] were reflected', 'none of this would have been possible without the prudent approach to financial management which has transformed the institution since incorporation', 'merger . . . extended the University's influence'. How can these features be interpreted?

Firstly, as Fairclough (1992) notes, heavy overwording suggests that the contents of a text are the subject of ideological struggle – that is, struggle between differing ways of being, relating and knowing others and the world. It seems likely that the changes outlined by the vice-chancellor and their rendering as positive events are contested by other participants in 'the university'. One way in which they might be contested is that the vice-chancellor is involved in what Fairclough denotes as the commodification of educational discourse (1992: 210) through the inclusion of advertising discourses. In Green's statement events seem to be part of the 'business of constructing an image' (Fairclough, 1992: 210) or a representation of the university. Fiske (1993) argues that imperializing knowledge relies exclusively on *representational culture*, while localized knowledge engages *cultures of practice*. The contrast between the Staffordshire and Manchester texts highlights this difference. Of course Thompson's text draws on economic discourse: however, it engages with the participants at various points by constructing subject positions for both the writer and the other members of the university. The Manchester text is concerned almost exclusively with the subject position of the university itself. By looking back at the Staffordshire piece, then, it is possible to see Thompson's text not simply as productionist, but as reflecting the tension between imperializing knowledges and the localized practices of 'staff'. Green's text, however, is largely representational and disengaged from knowledges of practices.

Identities: the university

How is the university evoked? Just as the entire introduction to the annual report might be seen as part of a process of commodifying the university through an advertising discourse, I consider that the university itself is commodified within Green's text not as a production process, as in the Staffordshire text, but as a provider of services to users, consumers or customers. One way to 'hear' this is to introduce an alternative discourse. Universities are, traditionally, constituted as students and teachers/lecturers involved in a process of learning and teaching. Or to use a more traditional description, what students do is 'read' particular academic discourses, taking up their truth claims and their identities. Presumably academic staff are involved in speaking and rewriting these discourses. In the Green text this process has been largely erased. In its place the university is said to have growing student numbers, to have introduced new courses and to have generated new research initiatives. It has produced a strategic plan and it has quality services (computing, library, educational, and student) for students and staff. What has occurred is that in rewriting the university in an instrumental advertising discourse, Green has been forced to rewrite what the university actually does in terms of what it has and what it does for its users, rather than in terms of what happens there. It is this recourse to representational discourse which works to station the 'university' and to provide a basis for constructing the activities or practices of the 'university' as a site for the managerial station.

University of Sheffield vice-chancellor's 'foreword': general features

The first element worth noting from the Sheffield text in Fig. 5.2 is its length and title. It contains twice the number of words found in the Staffordshire and Manchester equivalents. It is also titled 'A foreword' whereas the two previous examples are 'introductions'. These differences suggest a more detailed, more discursive and more communicative (in Habermasian terms) text than those of the post-1992 universities. The Sheffield text appears to be less a piece of advertising copy and more a communicative tract. However, with that said, similar discourse types are found. The differences suggest that the pre-1992 university vice-chancellor mixes discourse types in a way not found in the other two statements. In other words the vice-chancellor has dipped into several 'pots' of discourse types as he attempts to paint various aspects of the university in particular ways.

Evidence that Professor Roberts' statement is seeking to incorporate textual features from governmental discourses is found throughout the text. The text includes the word 'standards' three times (once in paragraph 1, twice in paragraph 6). This could be seen as a link to the discourse types circulated by the Major government, perhaps to its charter programme for improvements in public sector service standards. The statement also resonates with a traditionally Conservative discourse on education standards, which the pre-1992 universities might see themselves as maintaining during a period when former polytechnic HE enrolment surpassed numbers in the 'old' university sector (Pratt, 1996). Yet the concern with standards also arises as a defence against falling standards due to increasing student numbers and declining funding.

There is also a series of terms and statements which can be traced to a wider public sector managerialist discourse. These include: 'responsibility and accountability' (e.g. 'devolve responsibility to departments . . . within an accountable framework', paragraph 3); 'efficiency and productivity' (paragraph 8); the emphasis on commitment to postgraduate research (paragraph 4) (again something that the post-1992 universities were considered to be less committed to); 'to the highest possible standards' (paragraph 6); and 'finding ways of providing additional teaching, research and social

Figure 5.2 Statement of the Vice-Chancellor of Sheffield University

A FOREWORD BY THE VICE-CHANCELLOR

By any standards, the development of the University of Sheffield intellectually and physically during the past year has been impressive. Such achievements are all the more noteworthy when set against a background of the major national restructuring of the higher education system in the UK. This has been necessary in order to accommodate the enormous growth in the participation of the conventional age group and the conversion of the polytechnics to university status. The United Kingdom now has nearly a hundred universities and there are few significant areas of population without a higher education institution close by. Sheffield is fortunate in having two, and we wish our sister university, the former Sheffield City Polytechnic, a bright and successful future.

It seems inevitable that an even more diverse system of universities will emerge during the nineties. The University of Sheffield can expect to be in the top echelon of institutions that combine teaching and research in almost equal measure. This belief is based on our established reputation for world-class research; the quality, relevance and distinction of our teaching; our eminence abroad; and the economic and cultural contributions we have made, both regionally and nationally, for nearly a century.

Future developments in the University of Sheffield will be determined by a judicious mixture of evolution, devolution and revolution! The majority of changes will inevitably lie in the first category, with staff building systematically on existing teaching initiatives and recent research discoveries. The separation by the new Higher Education Funding Council for England (HEFCE) of funds for teaching and research provides us with an opportunity to devolve responsibility to departments and give them more freedom to decide on their priorities within an accountable framework.

Two years ago we embarked upon a major programme of expansion to bring exciting, innovative and relevant degree programmes to an increasing and diverse population of undergraduate students. The favourable grant allocation we received in 1991 for funded student places confirmed our high standing with the former Universities Funding Council. Now that the University's plans for the development of undergraduate teaching are well in hand, our priority for the remainder of the decade will be to build on our reputation as a major research-led university. Accordingly, we plan to double our numbers of postgraduate students and to continue recruiting distinguished academic staff with an international reputation in research. Our commitment to postgraduate research is evidenced by a new scheme which the University is funding, involving the establishment of 200 new research studentships.

Several examples of our 'revolutionary' initiatives in the educational sector are contained in this report. These include our Early Outreach Scheme, which is designed to enhance the prospects of underprivileged schoolchildren in the local community; extensive franchising arrangements with further education colleges nationally; and a specially designed MEd in Teaching and Learning for our own staff.

The rapid expansion of undergraduate numbers, changes in school curricula and the lowering of the unit of resource raise questions of crucial

Figure 5.2   *(cont'd)*

importance concerning standards and quality. This University received an excellent report from the Committee of Vice-Chancellors and Principals' Academic Audit Unit when it visited Sheffield in June 1991. I am confident that we will be equally highly regarded by the HEFCE quality assessment units when they begin their visits in 1993. Their input will help us to identify distinguished teaching and to reward staff appropriately. At the heart of all our work is a commitment to maintain the highest possible standards in teaching and learning. We are, for example, already carrying out a rigorous review of our academic processes and administrative services.

In our local region, we continue to play a leading role in economic, social and environmental regeneration. One of the most ambitious projects in the higher education sector involves the University of Sheffield producing a development plan for a new University College in the Dearne Valley, an area twelve miles to the north of Sheffield which has suffered greatly from the collapse of the mining industry. We were delighted to be selected for this exciting project by the Dearne Valley Partnership, which is a joint venture between the private sector, Barnsley, Doncaster and Rotherham Councils, and central government. For the first time in this country we are exploring with them the ambitious concept that a new university college could act as a catalyst for regeneration. Another significant development this year has been the opening of the University of Sheffield Regional Office, which will provide a focal point for the establishment of partnerships with local private and public sector organisations. Central to the Regional Office's remit is the need to harness the intellectual skills of our students and staff for the benefit of the local community.

This annual report shows that we are a vibrant University, responding in a positive fashion to the many challenges that we face. I should like, however, to comment on two areas of concern. First, that the recession has had a deleterious effect on graduate employment, with little prospect of an improvement in 1992/93. Second, that it is a matter of great regret that the new funding arrangements and govenrment pressures have forced pay settlements in universities downwards in comparison with other occupations, despite the obvious progress that has been made in improving efficiency and productivity in both teaching and research.

Although the higher education sector is seriously under-capitalised, we are committed to finding ways of providing additional teaching, research and social facilities for the increasing numbers of students and staff who wish to come to the University. In this regard, buildings costing £18 million were opened during the 1991/92 session, with major developments focussed on St George's Square and on new student accommodation.

A university, though, is really much more about people than facilities. Its reputation and the quality of the contributions it can make to society depend on the achievements of its students and staff. Therefore, I should like to express my gratitude for the dedication, industry and creativity of all who are part of this marvellous University.

Professor Gareth Roberts

facilities for the increasing numbers of students and staff' (paragraph 9). Also highly managerial is the statement's support for the controversial performance-related pay programme which at the time was sweeping through the public sector. It also suggests that the information provided by the HEFCE's quality assessment units will help 'us' (clearly management) 'reward staff appropriately'. Both these elements point to the construction of the senior post-holder as a manager.

Subjects and relations

In terms of the subject positions which the text provides, Professor Roberts' foreword uses the first person plural pronouns 'we' and 'us' throughout the text to refer to the university. Their use, together with the authoritative categorical modality (e.g. 'future developments *will* be determined by'), attempts to establish the writer's subject position as a spokesman for the university as a collective. While the use of 'we' attempts to collapse social distance between the writer as a male authority figure and other members of the university, there is some ambiguity in the use of this pronoun. It points to the construction of the manager. While Professor Roberts' statement on the one hand attempts through the use of 'we' to eliminate overt authority markers, it also re-establishes social distance at other points in the text.

There are two key examples. At one point the statement notes in relation to funding that 'the separation . . . of funds for teaching and research provides us with an opportunity to devolve responsibility to departments and *give them more freedom*'. As noted above, 'devolution' is a key practice in the construction of the senior post-holder as responsible for performance and resources (Meadmore *et al.*, 1995; Thomas, 1997). The use of the word 'us', however, recovers the distance, hierarchy and control exercised between the receiver and the giver of freedom – between the managers and the managed, in other words. Later there is a degree of ambivalence in the comment 'we are . . . carrying out a rigorous review of our academic processes and administrative services'. I say this because these processes and services do not happen automatically. They are enacted by people. Therefore potential exists for one of these enactors to recover their ambiguous positionings in such a statement. There is in a sense a choice in the positioning for an interpreter. However, one subject position requires more effort to read than the other. On the one hand, the reader might be drawn to the 'we' in 'we are carrying out'. On the other, a reader is forced to recover their subject position in the nominalizations 'administrative services' and 'academic processes'. A reader who does this would likely find they were not a reviewer but one of the reviewed and hence positioned within a power relation as the object to be known, rather than the knower – particularly as the managed (including the 'middle manager') and not the manager (clearly 'very' senior post-holders in this case). I suggest this rendering of the university's review processes serves to 'hide' the power relations involved. The vice-chancellor's comments on these processes and those concerning the giving of freedom to departments suggest the move to constitute the 'university', as Parker and Jary suggest, as a 'legally constituted web of corporate surveillance mechanisms' (1995: 327). Clearly these practices suggest a new relation to the self for those to whom 'freedom' is offered. Thus the text has embedded within it the managerial stationing, which includes new practices, new identities (glossed as new freedoms), and thus new forms of subjection. This new subject – the managed manager for instance – may experience the power relations embedded in such processes of review and devolution as an intensified hierarchical visibility (the statement's 'rigorous review'). Alternatively they may be experienced as a new way of being oneself at work – for instance, being free to manage staff as human resources in an education industry.

Yet compared with the 'metallic managerialism' (Hall, 1993: 15) of the Manchester statement and overt productionism of the Staffordshire statement, Professor Roberts' text attempts to place the collegial and collective 'we' beside traces of a managerialist discourse ('rigorous review', 'efficiency and productivity', 'accountable framework'). The test would be whether a member of the 'we' (academic or services staff at Sheffield) would be able to identify with the text. I would argue that some sections of the text might not fit well with the discursive resources of some members of the 'university'. For instance, some could find the statement 'we are committed to finding ways of providing additional teaching' highly provocative. They might suggest that the foreword highlights the university's acceptance of the intensifying quasi-market environment and the enterprise discourse established by the Conservative government across the public sector in the 1980s and 1990s (the aim of which is seen by many as being to drive down the cost and arguably the quality of HE provision). Yet Professor Roberts' text does *not* surrender to this discourse. It does not include economic jargon nor does it overwrite students and staff with the nouns 'consumer', 'customer' or 'service user'. The statement also does not position the university as a thing-like provider of goods. In fact Professor Roberts' text uses the last paragraph to centre resistance against this discourse. He writes: 'A university, though, is really much more about people than facilities. Its reputation and quality of the contributions it can make to society depend on the achievements of its students and staff'. From this we can see that Roberts' text is trying to recover a community/society discourse which is denied by the consumerist. The use of the term 'quality', which is a word that has become synonymous with the government's programme for monitoring and managing HE, is a deliberate attempt, I would argue, to rewrite it into a different discourse.

Summary

This brief analysis of three statements suggests that the Sheffield text is intertextually more creative and complex and attempts to mix traditional educational discourse (with its concern for education as a situated social space containing students and staff) with some elements of a managerialist discourse. In contrast, the Manchester text relies on an advertising discourse to present itself while positioning students and staff as users (possibly customers and consumers) of services. The Staffordshire text evokes a productionist model for the university and tends to place students and staff in this process. The analysis suggests that it is the post-1992 universities (who found some favour with the UK government during this period) (Middlehurst and Elton, 1992), with their willingness to engage with market discourse, who have more overtly and completely imbibed the discourses of the market and the factory and have more firmly established the managerial station as the mode by which they are ordered and organized. Meanwhile in the statement from the pre-1992 university (Sheffield), the attempt is made to navigate a course between the existing educative discourse and that of the market. In order to do so a good deal more discursive work is needed. So while the Staffordshire and Manchester statements could be said to be engaging the 'new' order – an order of commodified knowledge and managerial privilege – the Sheffield statement, while constructive of the managerial stations through review and devolutionary practices, also reflects the need for older certainties about knowledge and academic prerogative to be protected from a radicalized state and a competitive post-1992 university sector.

The managerial station in pre-1992 universities

Yet despite the suggestion that the pre-1992 university to varying degrees resisted the managerial and market discourses, it is clear from interviews and documentary sources that the demands of the HEFCE in the case of England have played a major part, together with the declining unit of resource, in provoking pre-1992 universities into deploying managerial practices – even if the label 'manager' was not attached to these processes. For example, one of the 'new breed' of vice-chancellor outlined in a published account the many aspects to this, and the very real difficulties:

> The process of strategic planning was certainly helped by being forced by the UFC to produce a plan. It was agreed that the planning process should be simultaneously top-down and bottom-up . . . being forced to answer some difficult questions by the funding council helped us to articulate a clearer vision of our academic role. We were, in effect, being asked what our niche was, which disciplines constituted our distinctiveness and strength.
>
> (Wilson, 1994: 100)

The paper from which this extract is drawn offers a direct account of the attempt to suffuse one particular pre-1992 university with the managerial station. Alongside a new strategic planning process, which Professor Wilson translates here into a questioning of the university's 'niche', this university was at the time in the process of:

- introducing a devolved budget system;
- introducing internal audit procedures (which anticipated the teaching quality assessment of university departments);
- introducing the modularization of courses;
- reorganizing academic areas to maximize their response to the then 1996 research assessment exercise; and
- restructuring its central administration.

In reflecting on this broad agenda, Professor Wilson (1994: 103) recognized the problems of such a campaign. He noted the problem of overloading ('our staff were under tremendous pressure from the sheer pace of reform'), of wide variability in relation to the reform agenda ('uneven performance across departments') and also the key problem of attempting to 'reach in' and change the daily work habits of the people the programme sought to address – that is, replacing locales with stations. Professor Wilson's text explicitly identifies this. What was required was 'articulat[ing] the management agenda in some detail to change the direction of individual work programmes towards institutional priorities. There is a tendency otherwise for all of us to go on doing what we most like doing' (Wilson, 1994: 104).

While he suggests that it would be a mistake to introduce line management in a university context, he nevertheless emphasizes the importance of 'management competences' so that more 'developmental rather than administrative thinking' (1994: 101) could occur. While I return in the next chapter to the issue of the problems of and resistance to the replacement of locales with stations, it is clear that such an 'agenda' (this formation of multiple practices whose directionalities work to establish the managerial station in universities) was at work throughout the pre-1992 and post-1992 university sector.

Meanwhile at pre-1992 Middletown University,[1] the vice-chancellor emphasized during interview the importance of retaining elements of the 'committee structure', and the problems of instituting a 'corporate university'. Nevertheless he welcomed and was working to strengthen centralized management and auditing processes: 'the whole quality assessment/quality audit is useful. [Through it] we discover things that are going wrong and we sort them out. This is very useful and it is very valuable'.

In terms of strategy, Middletown's pro vice-chancellor outlined the programme:

CP: You talked about action plans and strategically looking at the research work that goes on: is that a different way of looking at the university than three or four years ago?

It was never done before, there was no strategic direction about research ... now of course we all sink or swim together, this department has to make a return to the research selectivity exercise and if we have got someone whom we are carrying then instead of getting 32 times whatever the unit of resource is, we only get 31 times, we have got to carry this guy.

Here the managerial station is at work. Department heads, through audit practices tied to funding, together with devolved budgeting, were being made acutely aware of the source of their funds, the level of department perform- ance and implicitly what steps might be required to improve this. Yet iron- ically this 'devolution' and the construction of stations in the university's 44 academic departments created problems of its own. One key issue at Middletown was the variety of departmental performance across this large departmental university. The university had a devolved budget framework, introduced by the previous vice-chancellor, but this had led to problems which the univer- sity's personnel officer identified as lying with the variety of responses by heads of department to the demands of managing – i.e. being constituted as managers: 'You have a mixture of those who don't particularly want to do it, but accept that they will do it for a period of time, and others who are enthusiastic about it and manage in the truest sense of the word'.

In response to this the vice-chancellor was developing a new post of 'executive dean', which would control one of six core university budgets. The aim was to try to address the imbalances that a competitive framework produced. So while the managerial station had been established to varying degrees, and in some cases heads of department sought to work as 'managers of small businesses' (as one head described himself), this created institutional conflict between the centre and the 'periphery'. The pro vice-chancellor addressed this as follows:

> We are trying very hard to use the funding rules that the funding council use as a guide rather than as a straight formula for funding within the university. Otherwise we will find ourselves in very severe straits and collegiality would just disappear . . . so we do have a judgemental ele- ment in our own funding mechanism which enables us to put money where it is our perception that it is needed. I must say that a lot of people don't like that, they want the winners, want the mechanism that gives them the greatest money.

Middletown's vice-chancellor meanwhile was at the time very aware of *not* being seen to introduce a 'corporate' managerialism (for instance through a new layer of executive deans), or adopt what he and some of his senior colleagues regarded as the 'worse' directorate-style managerial practices exhib- ited by the post-1992 university 'down the road'. What was known as the 'vice- chancellor's group' sought to maintain at least a semblance of 'consensus' across the institution by working with the university council and senate while at the same time reducing the number of alternative decision arenas – i.e. 'committees' – and strengthening central control through executive deans.

The managerial station in post-1992 universities

It is this issue of strong central control worked out through the dictatorial practices of senior post-holders and 'their' deans which many argue has become the hallmark of the post-1992 universities since incorporation in 1989 (e.g. Pratt, 1991; Middlehurst and Elton, 1992; McVicar, 1993). As Malcolm McVicar (1993: 203), now vice-chancellor of the University of Central Lancashire argues: 'Turning to further and higher education, we observe that heads of department and those above are now described explicitly as managers . . . The collegial model has been replaced by a more hierarchical model'.

Yet the development and dispersal of the managerial station across post-1992 institutions, and the tensions around this, are more politically problematic than this quotation suggests. The next section of this chapter offers a telling example of this, and the next chapter devotes itself to the question directly. However, before giving this account it is important to illustrate the full array of practices and knowledges, and not just changed contracts of employment, that are involved in constructing the managerial station in post-1992 institutions.

To do this I draw on the text of an interview with the head of chemistry at City University. This offers an impassioned description of practices but also of the effect that such practices have as they produce the managerial station: 'As a head of department the job is principally managerial, one is supposed to be, to use the vice-chancellor's phrase, "managing an outcome" rather than administering a process'. Here the managerial agenda might be said to have 'leaked' into the text of this head of department. It works directly at this point in the text to frame the context in which the head of department works. Yet, as might be expected, the vice-chancellor's phrase is used ironically. The space of action or scope for 'managing the outcome' is severely constrained. The head of department went on: 'to some extent I do think that at my level I am administering a process which is being managed higher up. When I get the chance I am also managing my own processes within the department, trying to take it where I think it would be best going'.

The head went on to outline the multiple processes which elaborate the managerial station. He suggested that 'the bureaucracy has multiplied. It started off bloody awful and it got worse'. He said his work involved: completing a yearly government-demanded appraisal process with all department staff (18 members); conducting a university prescribed research student review, producing an annual research report; producing a staff development activities report; drawing up the department's yearly and five-yearly academic plan; organizing the faculty quality audit of the department; and the 'full-blown' university-based quality assessment process modelled on the funding council's programme.

Alongside all this was the department's devolved budget which in a science department involved a 'substantial sum'. The university at the time was also adjusting its modularization programme, and this required that the head be involved in what he described as the 'administrative nightmare of validation and revalidation' of courses. Yet besides this the key issue for the head was the problem of departmental 'survival'. The effect of these multiple reporting processes, which formed the managerial station, was that the department head regarded himself as responsible for contextual issues far outside his control.

Recruitment and the quality of student intake were crucial issues in this chemistry department. This was set against a diminishing unit of resource, increasing costs of consumables, maintenance of safe facilities and the tense relations with staff whose rates of pay had been slowly diminished along with a steep increase in workload during the four previous years of university expansion. Student numbers had increased from 250 to 337 in the four years prior to the interview. The head outlined the overall effect of this succinctly:

> So it's going to be difficult to recruit, it is going to be difficult to provide quality student experience given the limited unit of resource and against this background staff who want to work and want to give a good quality service are getting very frustrated, annoyed, and depressed and the morale is low because they are not able to. The space isn't there, the money isn't there, and the quality of the students is so low they are having to dip below their normal level of teaching . . . *managing that is going to be a challenge if not to say an impossibility.*

Here we can read how the managerial station produces an identity which takes responsibility for 'managing' these issues; someone who is divided off from former colleagues and made directly accountable for the department's performance in the face of broad political and economic processes. Of course, as the account in the next chapter drawn from City University illustrates, such stationings are challenged from time to time, and their success is partial and variable. Also the installation of the managerial station – that collection of practices – across an institution involves bitter political battles 'at the top', as the next section shows.

The coming of the manager in post-1992 HE

This section develops an institutional narrative that depicts the intense political battles involved in establishing the managerial – and some would say intensively bureaucratic – station in one particular post-1992 university. The section also addresses specifically the embodied aspects of the construction of managerial stations in HE. It argues, drawing on the body topography framework put forward above, that the shift to a more managed post-compulsory sector involves new ways in which bodies are positioned, covered, talked about and 'experienced' (in the sense used here). As I have already argued, the concepts 'station' and 'locale' include the reconstruction of the body-subject by imperializing and localizing knowledges. The construction of more managed universities and colleges is not just about changed funding mechanisms, new measurement techniques, new languages, new reporting and review process. It involves the 'enfleshment' of these processes, to use Peter McLaren's (1995) term, or, to use the phrase of the personnel officer at Tower College, putting 'flesh on the bones of the new structure'. It involves attempting to change the somatic construction of bodies at work. It involves changing the spatial, verbal and physical embodiment as well as changing investments of desire (bodily energy). I will now illustrate this with material drawn from interviews with senior post-holders from City University.

Example: charisma to managerialism via an 'execution'

In the late 1980s the high profile director of a polytechnic in the north of England was forced to resign following what was described by the trade press as a 'colonels' revolt' against him. The event can be broadly read in two directions using interview material from those involved. First, it can be understood as a response by senior staff to what they saw as the director's erratic, vindictive and overbearing 'style' of management. Second, it can be read as the ascendancy of a corporate/bureaucratic mode of managing (see McNay, 1995).

In relation to the first reading one of former director's early supporters, a head of department, had this to say: 'We felt at the time [of his appointment, *circa* 1980], that what this polytechnic lacked was a public figure. We needed someone who was going to project us into the sector. [The director] was someone who could do it'.

The director was said to have 'flair', be 'charismatic', 'a brilliant speaker and a bit of a cowboy'. This era is remembered as exciting and entrepreneurial. Alongside the director a so-called 'rat pack' of senior staff were said to 'virtually run the institution' outside of formal committee structures. The 'rat pack' had nicknames. For example, one was called 'the fat controller'. They also had their particular language. Entry was through 'initiation'. One dean who joined the former polytechnic at the end of the 1980s, and who became known to the 'rat pack' as 'Huey', told me that he gained his credibility through his 'hard-man antics' at a three-day senior staff conference in France (which latterly came to represent the excesses of the former director's era): 'I wasn't part of the rat pack or any other pack. I think the rat pack wanted me in . . . in rat pack terminology I demonstrated through the initiation ceremony, I "went through the due processes" that gave me credibility. It was an interesting time for me as an observer of this saying "where do I fit in?" '.

The 'rat pack' represents a group of senior staff whose ethos broadly supported and was supported by the former director himself. In part this was done by 'getting rid of certain people'. Yet membership of the 'elect' inner circle created tensions. Towards the end of his tenure, the director was said to have 'got rid of all the people he didn't like' and started to turn on 'those that were good'. One or two maintained that he was 'mentally ill'. All of these issues created what one senior manager called a 'seething mass' of tensions and conflict. As to the cause of this: 'I actually think it was the director, it was the old director. I don't know, we were changing so rapidly. Certainly the old director had a great deal of involvement in it because we all started . . .'

At this point in the interview this senior post-holder abruptly paused and gave an interesting description of how the practices developing among people in the institution spilled over into his home life: 'There was this occasion when my wife said to me, "Don't bring any of those practices back from that polytechnic into this house. If you want to play like that when you are at work, you play like that, but don't bring it back into this house". I thought, "What is happening to me?". Now it wasn't just me, it was a whole host of people who felt like that'.

Not long afterwards, as the story goes, the 'charismatic/vindictive' director was toppled by an alliance of the senior managers and deans. They met secretly at the former polytechnic's conference centre one Tuesday morning and then presented the director and the polytechnic governors with a vote of no confidence. A few days later the director was publicly challenged at an academic board meeting over the veracity of statements he was making, and many of those present on whom he might have counted for support turned against him. What followed was an 'independent' inquiry by the governors and then the director's formal resignation. A pay-off of some kind was made which included an agreement that the departing director would not discuss the events in a public forum.

The alternative reading of the director's removal concerns the ascendancy of the 'accountable' managerial station. The previous director had been challenged by a corporate or bureaucratic 'style' of managing – strong on conformity, accountability and responsibility, much in the mould set out in the National Advisory Body for Public Higher Education's publication *Management for a Purpose* (NAB, 1987). The incoming director, in contrast to the 'charismatic' former director, was known as a 'safe pair of hands'. There was respect for his financial conservatism and attention to detail, even if this meant what one close colleague described as 'pathetic arguments in management teams about names: "we can't have that person called a manager or that person called a head". It was conformity down almost to boredom'. A head of department had this to say: '[The new director] is a managerialist, everything is in its place. It upsets or threatens his sense of law and order if a group forms and it's not in his organizational chart'.

Other things changed. While the former director was known to frequently walk about the campus, the new director was distant and out of touch with the day-to-day rhythms of the institution. He was seen by some as 'hidden' away in 'mahogany row' with his organizational charts, funding spreadsheets and the institution's growing 'library' of policies. Behind the closed doors people were being intimidated and bullied along by the new 'managerialists' (who were compared to Stalinists by some). This created a 'grapevine' of stories which directly questioned the new senior post-holder's public commitments to an open information policy. As one head of department outlined:

I think there is a lot of hypocrisy in this place and the higher up you go the more hypocrisy there is. It's about people doing the opposite of what they say. For instance, 'Openness OK' [raises his eyebrows – the university has an official open information policy]. At the heads conference around the bar someone says 'Have you heard what happened to [former head of personnel]?' 'No.' 'Oh we're not meant to talk about it. Shall we go for a pint up the road?' Turns out he'd been suspended for some impropriety. It's this knock at the door at 4 a.m. stuff. You realize that this isn't a very open society.

Another head (a member of the so-called 'rat pack') said:

[The vice chancellor] is very rigid in his approach and extremely inflexible. The [deputy vice-chancellor] is a very difficult character to deal with. He will not allow conversation and unfortunately I don't even think he is aware of it. He makes very pejorative remarks and statements like 'You are all academic heads so I'll explain this to you twice'. You know, is that supposed to be funny?

Teaching and administrative staff resented the secrecy and control that this corporate 'style' produced. A staff newspaper sprang up, saying in its first editorial that it was 'a response to the information and consultation gap ... It takes as its premise the idea that a polytechnic is primarily about people and ideas, not management and products'. Even new heads of department, whose appointments were either made or closely vetted by the director, were critical of the centralizing, controlling practices:

It's amazing in a small institution that it is so much more centralized. I had more responsibility for staff as a course leader in Birmingham (polytechnic), than I do now as a head of department. It makes us feel disempowered. Far too much is being churned out by the directorate in terms of policy but it's down to the paperwork on your desk; you wonder if they are trying to *tie you to your desk* ... it maybe looks as if we're puppets on a string'.

In opposition to a ban on any mention of the former director, people started to talk about this period in relation to the current regime. One dean recalled the discussion at the three-day senior staff conference two years after the 'execution': 'People felt that they were able to talk about [the former director] and mention his name. People were saying things like, "I haven't been able to mention his name since he went", and "he was a right bastard, but he was good and we miss him now". People were saying "yeah, well, we probably are managed better, but we miss that vision"'.

Discussion

A body topographical analysis of the managerial station at work in this example highlights how bodily desire (physical energy/sensuality) is unstable, open, and on the move. The competing stories in the above account are not simply the work of discourses which somehow suffuse a domain of language practice. The competing stories are effects of variable processes of investment of desire in different modes of practice, various discourses and particularly in other bodies themselves. These can be mapped through the changing spatial, verbal and physical presence of bodies.

During the former director's tenure people invested in the practices, discourses and body of the charismatic. For the 'elect' these were passionate, exciting, 'playful' times. There were 'crusades' in the discourses of access, student-centred learning and cross-disciplinarity. There was the bending and breaking of rules, the doing of deals. Doors were open, bodies moved about and made their own groupings which enlivened some and ostracized others. One highly symbolic aspect was the fact that the director did not have a desk in his office. 'What do I need one of those for? I pay you to do the writing', he is remembered as saying. Instead of a desk he simply had, according to one of his acolytes, an 'old wobbly chair' he had bought from his former college. The desk is an important marker in the construction of a managerial station; it is a key symbol of the due process of bureaucracy. In effect, this denial of the 'desk' reinforces the 'due process' of groups like the 'rat pack' and contempt for bureaucratic due process. Yet at the same time there was alleged to have been favouritism, vindictiveness and a 'seething mass' of disputes and conflicts among the 'followers' and with the former director. For bodies whose investment was in due process, order and control, the 'party' of the mid-1980s had to stop! The symbolic 'execution' of the former director, publicly embodied in his humiliation at an academic board meeting, and carried out with weighted symbolism in secret behind closed doors by the polytechnic's board, marks the shift to an investment in order and security. Bodies invested in the 'safe pair of hands' and *his* tools of order: policies, budgets, targets, appraisals. Slowly and as a counterweight to the entrepreneurial culture of the past, there was a shift towards the notion of being a 'manager', not freewheeling and dealing 'academic heads'.

The price of order, however, was the intensified stationing of bodies. This was through their increased confinement to desks (like 'puppets on a string') and behind closed doors huddled together in vertically integrated 'teams' (faculty management team, university management team, executive team) with other similarly clothed and practising bodies in the controlled spaces of small rooms and executive offices. Here control could be more easily exercised, instructions given and accountabilities more closely monitored than in large committees or the loose informal mate-like groupings. This required the increased codification of bodies in charts, through budgets, audits and a huge increase in paperwork. The price of an investment in security is secrecy, double-talk and masculine authoritarianism. A positive assessment of this would be that people became more responsible and accountable for resources and the institution was 'better managed'. Yet the shift to a bodily investment in the corporate order, signalled by the term 'better managed', is itself an ongoing unstable process. The managerial station's body topography is always a partial process. The new topography of corporate order, in spite of a ban on official discussion of the past surrounding the former director, was challenged by a *remembering* of the investment in the exciting entrepreneurial order he embodied. The comments above such as 'I haven't been able to mention his name', represent both the official ban and the individual bracketing of turbulent practices and emotionality associated with the 'charismatic order' and the 'execution'. The recovery of the investment in the charismatic order/leader, from what many remember as the 'seething mass' of emotionality and conflict, represents a challenge to the investment in the practices, discourses, and symbolic bodies of the corporate accountable managerial ordering.

In summary then the body topography of the managerial station might be said to have the following features. Spatially there is the shift from large committees to small teams in vertically integrated line management structures through which control is potentially more easily and efficiently achieved. Instructions and accountabilities can be more closely monitored, and conformity with the organization/department's 'strategic direction' can be exercised. Alongside this is the creation of more intensive one-to-one relations between the 'manager' and members of staff (through appraisal, review and audit processes), and the more intensive pressure to station post-holders in offices, at desks, within particular confines, away from teaching and collective spaces.

Symbolically or verbally there is the increased codification and commodification of bodies and labour in charts, budgets, spreadsheets and audit documents, and the huge increase of 'audit-able' paperwork. Physically the body's coverings do change. There is the shift to more formalized attire for senior post-holders. For men the extreme is the shift from 'woolly jumper to suits' together with attempts to lose weight. For women the shift is to more executive dress. And in relation to the investments of desire, there is the investment in the discourses of the private sector business manager, perhaps to the extent to which education managers come to understand themselves as small business people with a portfolio of products sold onto a market. Yet this investment is unstable, as is the recourse to managerial language, practices and relations – as the next chapter discusses.

Note

1. As the reader will note, I have up to this point drawn on material from other universities. The four universities in this study have been given fictitious names in order to conceal their identity and that of the senior post-holders who were interviewed. Middletown and Harbourside universities are pre-1992 universities – that is, chartered universities, while City University and Southern University are post-1992 universities, created by the Further and Higher Education Act 1992.

6
Just how Managed is the New Higher Education?

Ah, Dr Piercemuller. Professor Lapping will see you now.
Thank you Maureen. Piercemuller. There you are. Do come in. Sorry to bother you on your research term but I wanted to make certain you were fully up to date with the next departmental phase of TQM.
TQM?
Total Quality Managment.
What else?
Quality in every area of Quality and continue the cycle of the never-ending improvement of Quality. That couldn't be clearer could it, Dr Piercemuller?
Only if you removed the waste paper basket from your head and put down the bunch of flowers.

(Taylor, 1994: 127)

The 'manager', according to the discussion so far is constructed through imperializing management knowledges and practices. These attempt to establish managerial stations in universities and colleges. These comprise particular embodied practices (e.g. small-scale, closely controlled meetings) and bodies of knowledge which attempt to reshape social relations and identities. In both FE and HE it is overlapping budgets, planning and audit processes[1] which are substantially engaged in constructing these stations. Through these, senior academics and administrators are rendered more explicitly accountable as supervisors and organizers of academic and administrative labour and responsible for its 'performance' measured in largely quantitative terms (e.g. research income, cost reductions, surpluses from income-generation work). Yet while the *strategic intent* of such processes can be identified, their *actual implementation* and elaboration out across the social terrain of FHE is often highly problematic.

This chapter explores these problems, arguing that during the research period (between 1993 and 1997) a constant and ubiquitous state of hostilities existed between the managerial station and the professional and administrative 'stations', which were rendered progressively as locales in FHE. There are, in other words, constant hostilities between the 'power bloc', in the form of imperializing knowledges intended to measure, reward and increase the productivity of FHE, and 'the people', comprising identities and relations located within academic and administrative locales in FHE which are the objects of these knowledges. This chapter discusses this 'state of hostilities' in universities, drawing examples from the chartered universities Harbourside and Middletown, and from the statutory 1992 universities City and Southern. The chapter discusses in some detail the tensions within and in some cases the resistance to the managerial station. It begins with problems at the 'core' of Habourside University, and then turns to discuss the tension between 'core' and 'periphery' at Middletown. I then discuss administrative identity before turning to explore how heads of department position themselves in relation to the imperializing measures. In this I discuss, for instance, efforts to constitute the measures as 'business as usual'.

However, before embarking on this I want to briefly note how the Dearing Report (National Committee of Inquiry into Higher Education, 1997) addressed this 'state of hostilities'. Unsurprisingly, the inquiry's major recommendation in this area was that it was managers themselves who need to be better equipped for their jobs, particularly in relation to making HE more cost-effective through the use of information technology. The report noted that 'too often, programme directors and heads of department have inadequate training and are not engaged sufficiently in the quest to achieve greater effectiveness in the use of resources' (Section 15.12). But in the detail of the committee's report there are clear tensions around this call for more effective management. The special report on academic staff noted that 'In conversation with academics we sometimes found scepticism about the need for the present scale of management activity in higher education' (Section 3.39). In a different way the report highlighted the tensions between administrative and support staff and 'managers': 'Staff often reported that their working lives were made considerably harder because management decision-making was ill-informed and unrealistic' (Section 4.53).

It is clear from this that management, managers and management activity are controversial and problematic in HE. Therefore, management's possible extension or enhancement, as recommended by the inquiry, is likely to be not just contentious but also fraught with difficulties.

Making it happen? The problems of making managers in HE

The key element in this state of hostilities in universities and colleges was succinctly put by a pro vice-chancellor at the pre-1992 Harbourside University: 'What is going on is the product of the need to change deeply rooted historical identities to manage very, very big business'.

Three points can be drawn from this. First, the categorical term 'need' is put to work. Through it, managing universities in new ways is made an imperative rather than a choice. Second, the speaker uses the term 'identities'. This may alert us to the way in which people's work is undertaken through historically conditioned ways (knowledges and practices) of being oneself. In particular, the pro vice-chancellor referred to the challenge of 'management' to traditional academic and administrative identities – 'Management language is certainly somewhat alien to traditional administrators', he said.

In this particular university, management knowledge practices were identified with both the reforms introduced by the new vice-chancellor, and with the vice-chancellor himself. A particular target of these reforms at the time of interview was the university's central administration, which had been the subject of a review of operations by management consultants promoting 'business process re-engineering' methods (see Grint, 1994 for critical review). The pro vice-chancellor noted that as a result 'It is not surprising that central administration would feel very strained. [They are] traditionally very conservative. [Staff] are not chosen for managerial abilities or expected to play managerial roles'. Meanwhile the vice-chancellor was said to 'read endless books on management and speak the managerial language'. This resulted in a powerful clash with traditional administrative and academic identities. The pro vice-chancellor suggested that for people who had 'grown up' in traditional line management particularly in finance and estates, 'thriving on chaos'[2] doesn't seem to make too much sense.

Third, the pro vice-chancellor's statement reconstructs the university as a 'very, very big business'. This particular institution he said enrolled '17,000 to 18,000 full-time equivalent students, employed more than 1000 academic staff and around 3000 other staff, operated more than 6000 residences and had an annual turnover of £160 million'. And yet, 'you have a very traditional way of managing it. The vice-chancellor and pro vice-chancellors are not professional managers. I'm a professor of philosophy and I still technically spend a quarter of my time in the department'. In this we can hear how constructing the institution through management discourse (note the construction of the university through quantification, in the above statement), problematizes 'historical identities', including that claimed by the speaker himself, at this point in the interview.

The vice-chancellor meanwhile identified the tension between what I term here the managerial station and established modes of practice (locales) as follows:

> If I have discovered anything in the last three years it is that the implementation is a lot harder than strategy. I think the difficulty of implementation at a departmental level is how to get beyond the likes of me making speeches, to action [which] will actually allow targets to be achieved on things like student numbers ... We have talked about implementation as though it is all neat. The other side of the coin is things going wrong all the time, *people won't take responsibility for it so it reaches up until it gets to me.*

One can sense the frustration, even anger, produced by the hostilities between competing identities. In effect the vice-chancellor could be influential in setting targets with which he sought to station the activities of his staff, but their implementation depended upon mobilizing or transforming the locales which maintained these competing identities. This involved reaching in and changing the day-to-day, week by week practices that made up the working lives of people in this strongly departmental university.

Yet it was clear from collected accounts of events at Harbourside that 'hostilities' between the knowledges and practices of the managerial station, and the locales, constructed as the targets of such knowledges, were at work within the vice-chancellor's group itself. The pro vice-chancellor confirmed this with the following description:

> The senior management team is a peculiar mixture of four pro vice-chancellors, who do get on very well with each other but don't necessarily see a lot of each other, never meet regularly with each other and in a way there are good reasons for this because we might start to behave like colonels you know . . . the other members are the vice-chancellor, the registrar and the director of planning and it would be rather invidious of me to give examples but it is not a very comfortable group. [The vice-chancellor] has a rather didactic, non-dialogical style and I think all the pro vice-chancellors have felt frustrated in some way; there is quite a lot of tension.

This didacticism could be read positively as a determination on the part of the university's top post-holder to give clear messages. Yet it is also clear from the vice-chancellor's interview that this didacticism was informed by the vice-chancellor's positioning in managerial discourse, of which he was a devotee, as the university's chief executive. At interview he commented: 'One of the things that complicates the vice-chancellor's role, certainly in the traditional universities, is that in the past it has been less executive than it is now'.

It was clear from discussion that this vice-chancellor used his visits to commercial firms of a similar size to Harbourside to learn more about managing large organizations, and this 'learning' was being directed primarily at the administative 'centre' of the university:

> Occasionally I go to other people's PR-type lunches with the board of directors somewhere or other. It happened to me recently with a major chemical company round here; it wasn't ICI, but it is still a £300–400 million turnover multinational, and you are [in a] dining room like this with three or four of the directors in their group headquarters. So I said 'How many people have you got in your group headquarters?', which is what I always ask, and the answer was 35, and you know that included the secretaries and the receptionist, so then we had a long talk about the systems that enable them to run this . . . and from my personal point of view I envisage an outcome where there is a kind of vice-chancellor's office which will actually take me nearer to the strategic shaping side . . . but it won't be what I do at the moment which is quite a lot of firefighting in terms of day-to-day management of the place because there are not enough people, you know, all the contemporary

jargon 'empowered to take decisions at the appropriate level where they should be taken', so too much filters back and people get nervous about that.

Interviewer:[3] Your managers are not managing?

Exactly. Well they are called administrators and you know only administrate if there is somebody telling them what to do basically.

But while the vice-chancellor was critical of the slow pace of change, the lack of responsiveness found in the 'administrative culture' and the highly problematic process of actually implementing strategic directions, it could be argued that he and his 'group' itself were caught in this state of tension between the managerial station and the academic and adminstrative locales. This was elaborated by the incoming pro vice-chancellor (pro vice-chancellors at Harbourside were at the time appointed for a four-year term) who was just about to join the vice-chancellor's group. He was well aware of these tensions between a vice-chancellor who saw himself as a chief executive and a group of four professorial pro vice-chancellors who brought with them to varying degrees their academic departmental identities. The new pro vice-chancellor saw his contribution to the vice-chancellor's group as restarting productive dialogue. He said: 'If you have got pro vice-chancellors who don't talk to one another, and a vice-chancellor who doesn't talk much with the group and a registrar, you might have as many as six people right in the middle who aren't much talking to one another. That might be difficult . . . I think that perhaps I can get people talking to one another a little bit more than they do'.

These tensions at the 'centre', and the attempt to reconstruct the university's central administration, explain the rapid departure (to a 'rival' university) of the university's registrar just six months after arrival. Yet there is in the comment from the pro vice-chancellor an interesting analytical point with regard to the different kinds of knowledge practices that make up the managerial station. The vice-chancellor's didacticism might be seen as an effect of his recourse to representational practices (e.g. plans and strategies), rather than to the dialogic practices which tend to provide the basis for locales.

A further aspect to the tensions that run through the very highest offices at Harbourside, and between the managerial station and academic and administrative locales, focused on the practices of the university's strategic planning office. This had been established as part of the vice-chancellor's 'reforms' and controversially the vice-chancellor had appointed a close woman colleague of his, from the department of which he was formerly head, as director of this unit. While the director of the planning office refused to be interviewed for this research, her reputation was for aloofness. Her close relationship with the vice-chancellor meant that many considered her to be out of reach of criticism. The head of a large university service department said:

What we lack is any sensible input into academic planning which is done by a planning office which is autonomous and rather dictatorial. It's headed by a person who is a very difficult personality to work with and sees no need to discuss things with people. In fact she doesn't like discussing, doesn't like 'talking shop' so I think that both myself and my financial colleagues have found this extremely difficult.

Clearly, there are a number of gendered dimensions at work in these comments (these are discussed in Chapter 9). It was clear that the 'planning office' threatened both traditional administrative and academic identities, particularly the latter as it directly challenged academic control over the direction of academic work in what one of the pro vice-chancellors described as a 'strongly departmental' university. The newly-elected pro vice-chancellor also mentioned the tensions around this: 'We have got a planning office, as well as everything else. If you listen to heads of department, one of the difficult issues is where pro vice-chancellors don't have control but planning [the planning office] does'.

While hostilities between the identities constructed by the managerial station and the traditional locales punctuated relations at the 'centre' of the university, they were also keenly felt in relations with departments. While 'out' among the departments there was some evidence of support for what was widely regarded as the vice-chancellor's strategy, there was also evidence of staff searching about for local tactics with which to resist the centre. A head of department said:

One of the present complaints is that heads of department are suffering from initiative fatigue. The vice-chancellor is issuing all these signals about yet another new thing and people are saying what the hell do we do to channel this, to limit it, to choose. Are we allowed to choose, *or are we going to be downgraded in the perception of performance* if we don't jump through every hoop that we are directed to?

As a result of this, the same head of department opined that the vice-chancellor's 'reforming' efforts had 'run into the sand, because it is too big an institution; there are too many entrenched positions for him to sort it'. The comment 'what the hell do *we* do to channel this' also suggests that relations between heads of department had been strengthened as the corporate centre has become more active. In this and one of the other universities included in the study, 'heads groups' had formed and met regularly. Interestingly, the vice-chancellors in both institutions saw these formations as forums for 'management development' (that is, as stations), while many heads themselves understood these groups in more subversive terms, as gatherings through which resistant practices could be coordinated; i.e. as locales. Yet in these universities, this desire for resistance was often splintered by the competitive relations between department heads (e.g. competition between heads for extra centrally distributed research funds or extra student numbers; there was also a tendency for heads to keep to themselves valuable information which might benefit 'their' department) and the individuating practices of the university itself. The key example of this from the post-1992 universities was the removal of heads from national bargaining and their 'placement' on individual, often very open-ended and locally negotiated contracts.

Nevertheless, at Harbourside and elsewhere it seemed that 'messages' from the centre were handled tactically and as a result muffled as they 'cascaded'. The diversity and the power of these departmental locales is well articulated in the observations of a pro vice-chancellor at Harbourside:

> Departments have amazingly different cultures and these seem to persist through thick and thin rather like family identities – you know, incredibly democratic or very hierarchic or rather anarchic, just competent . . . or angry or very polite. They seem to have persisted because it is a departmental university and university departments have a lot of power.

It is important to note here that despite the willingness of interviewees in the chartered universities to read the statutory universities as intensively managerial and executively driven, similar relations with the 'centre' were evident. A head of department in post-1992 City University noted for instance that 'Deans spend a lot of time with the vice-chancellor's group where they are definitely inferior. I think there is less mediation of instructions the further up you go. The deans get told in a fairly bloody minded way to do this by Tuesday; they mellow a bit as they tell us, ask us and so on down'. Thus strong managerial relations are problematic, particularly as information about departmental activities is often tactically handled. The head of department continued: 'He [the vice-chancellor] might be quite surprised to find out how we fund things like study leave [laughs] . . . I'm quite happy for [the vice-chancellor] to be very distant from it as long as he understands that he is distant from it which by and large he does [but he] does say silly things occasionally'. This illustrates how the dynamics of change are complex and contradictory and mediated by embedded and emergent localized knowledges about 'how' to change. These comments illustrate for instance how some senior academics understand their task as buffering and protecting their colleagues from what they see as the demands of managerialism – for example, increased auditing and planning. Of course, whether this neo-paternalism is intended to preserve and/or boost a research-centred culture, or whether it is regarded simply as a condition of improving levels of measured performance, is a matter of judgement. As Fiske (1993) suggests, the relations between locales and stations is not necessarily fixed nor respectively imperializing and defensive.

The head of a science department at Middletown went so far as to suggest that 'managing' amounted to protecting colleagues and their existing professional practices. He observed that:

> You have got to protect the institution . . . the HEFCE is a bully, the research councils are bullies, they know they have the whip hand and

they bully you. You have got to jump partly because your institution's jumping, so if your institution's jumping then it is passed down the line. What I tried to do since I wasn't going to be able to do much research anyway, was to actually act as a sort of barrier and of course the better I was at that the better known I became in the [academic] community and the university community, the more effective I could be as that barrier.

Rather than reading himself as a proselytizing manager, this head of department represented his actions at interview as protecting or ameliorating the distress of his colleagues. Instead of administering the blow of the 'bullying' HEFCE, he positioned himself as softening its impact by ensuring that his department was well equipped 'to jump'. By positioning the HEFCE as a 'bully', he was also able to suggest sympathy for rank-and-file academic staff, and at the same time potentially secure a degree of support for measures which enabled the institution to be responsive to the demands of the power bloc. However, a condition of taking this position was not so much the insidious weakening of the established (professional) practices but their active support. During the interview, this head of department gave numerous examples of the strengths of his professional locale. As a consequence of these protective actions, which he ascribed to himself, his department had adapted to the many changes demanded of it, which included semesterization and modularization in addition to the performance measures for research and teaching, without sacrificing the established culture of the department, which relied on field trips and close contact with students.[4]

This rosy picture of a department adapting successfully to new pressures, without any significant erosion of traditional identities, relations and practices needs to be complemented by a recognition of how the department's student numbers had been increased and how pressures on department members to maintain research ratings were intense. As the head observed:

> The department has been subjected to ever increasing pressure as a level 5 department to keep at level 5. The result is that I find that some of my staff are stressed far more than I was at their stage, especially the young people. They respond in different ways. Some of them become frenetic and overactive which is sometimes detrimental to their families, sometimes detrimental to their teaching, certainly detrimental to the minimum administration that I expect them to carry out. Others become rather sullen and take refuge in teaching or in other displacement activities like being on committees or computing, which is the biggest displacement activity I know. It is much easier because computing suggests that they are actually doing something which they could do with a pen far more efficiently very often.

Here the degree of internalization of imperializing pressures by many members of staff is recognized. The head of department said that the self-discipline of these staff made it unnecessary for him to intervene to ensure that levels of research productivity, as measured by the research assessment exercise, were sustained. This observation suggests the extent to which academics had 'invested in' the disciplines of the power bloc, assessing their 'excellence' in terms of the rating that they achieved rather than the value which they placed upon their activity.

But, of course, there is more to it than this. The rating received by the department influences the capacity of staff to attract research grants as well as their career prospects and the regard in which they are held by colleagues/competitors in their discipline. All these factors are relevant for explaining why academic staff are receptive and responsive to the imperializing discipline of the performance measures which, as the head of department's comments indicate, displace their effort from other activities, such as teaching and administration. As this head also observes, another important and overlooked effect of the pressures of the imperializing discipline is their divisive and potentially demoralizing influence upon a minority of staff (in highly rated departments) whose status and career prospects are weakened by such pressures and who, unlike the head, have no opportunity to move from research into administration-cum-management. Finally, this example again illustrates how imperializing management discourse is mediated by distinctive locales and, more specifically, how senior post-holders are 'made' (or destroyed) by these disciplines and how they represent their effects within and without the immediate locale.

Challenging administrative traditions

A further aspect is the differential positioning of senior administrative personnel by the managerial stations. Administrative senior post-holders also confront managerial knowledges and practices. As is clear from the pro vice-chancellor's comments from Harbourside, the reconstruction of the administrative/service senior post-holder as a manager meets the established practices that produce administrative identities. However, generally, but not exclusively, given their service-based activities and in some cases their background, senior administrative post-holders in the sample position themselves as managers. They understand themselves less as 'civil servants' to dominant academics, and more as managers of vital university services in their own right. Yet this repositioning, this investment in the discourses of the manager, produces tensions. While there are tensions in relations with academic senior post-holders who find administrative staff unwilling to take up the new practices (of not 'taking responsibility', as the vice-chancellor suggested above), it is more likely that these tensions run in the other direction where academic heads are challenged by the newly empowered service managers. The estates manager at Harbourside reflected on this:

> Given the age of this place, it has grown up with departments being very territorial. They actually consider the buildings that they occupy as *theirs*, that is completely contrary to the current ethos . . . some heads

are extremely vocal about these kinds of things. So when I go to talk to those people, they will immediately jump up in the air and if I was equally volatile we would quickly have a head to head, which is what I seek to avoid. So I let them get it out of their system, and at that point they will start to talk a bit more rationally.

The 'current ethos' is concerned with maximizing the use of space. The rationalities of increasing the efficiency of space use are in conflict with the investments of desire in the localized spatial practices that departments have constructed. Thus many academic heads of department find approaches from service managers on issues of space use intensely emotional. From a body topography perspective, the 'getting it out of their system' could be read as a response to the potential severing of the patternings of desire, built up over years of use, which link academic presence with physical space. Alongside this is the challenge from the administrative staff, traditionally subordinate to academic work, who through investment in the discourses of the manager present as equals of academic heads and come armed with, for example, the rationalities of corporate space use performance indicators but also the practices and knowledges of corporate finance, information technology and human resource management. This repositioning of the administrative officer as service manager can be highly problematic (particularly for women in such positions, given the inherently familial and heterosexual character of FHE institutions) (see Chapter 9). The academic secretary at Middletown commented that: 'As a manager I feel that it is my role to make things happen . . . to make sure that the policies handed down by the institution are actually implemented'. Yet he was particularly sensitive to the problems of taking this position in relation to academic departments. He outlined his approach thus:

> You push a bit here, you push a bit there and you work away with people who are likely to be enthusiasts and bring them into positions where they can exert some authority often through the committee structure and you begin to effect change in that way . . . it is also true to say that centrally directed initiatives in the academic area can sometimes come to grief if you can't get the reciprocal support from academic colleagues in the academic community.

What is clear is that the tensions and problems of conflict between the managerial station and academic locales are constantly in flow. The 'centre' and the 'periphery' for instance are not solid bases, but dynamic sites. At one point 'stations' are constructed, at other times and in other circumstances locales form. While the above suggests that departments operate tactically in relation to a radicalized 'centre', the extracts from the interview with the registrar at Middletown which appear in the next section suggest that the opposite is also likely to be the case, as embedded administrative identities are challenged. The registrar, a member of the vice-chancellor's 'management group', offers one of the strongest defences of traditional academic and administrative identities in the sudy. While the comments need to be read as a particular response to the interview in which they were recorded, they nevertheless are part of the flows of knowledges that make up these sites. A concluding comment from the academic secretary at Middletown suggested that more traditional administrative identities had been overturned by those embedded in the knowledge and practices of the managerial station: 'I think there has been a shift from the model of the university administrator as the civil servant, that kind of role, into the manager and certainly at the senior level one has to see oneself has having a managerial responsibility, without always having the managerial authority to carry some of the things forward'.

Challenging traditional identities

Middletown's registrar represents the imperializing discourse of management as directive and authoritarian, and sets this against what is seen as the natural collegiality of the university:

> The culture is not one which welcomes the concept of direction. The whole culture of the academic community, and I support all of this, is focused on individual excellence or team excellence [and] the right of the individual to pursue what they feel they want to pursue. That is why anything which smacks of management [that] starts to leak into, either emotionally or in reality, that very important freedom of the enquiring opportunity so that even if the management were to be of what one might call non-academic areas, it would still be seen as a beginning of a move to a different type of arrangement.

According to this registrar, moves that are corrosive of the local autonomy of universities pose a threat to an established 'culture' (or locales, in the terms used here). Thus excellence depends upon preserving 'the right of the individual to pursue what they feel they want to pursue'. The new measures, imposed from above, are understood to exert pressure upon academics to do what will be good for the ratings (e.g. engage in 'quick and dirty' types of research that have predictable but unexciting outcomes and which will be readily published and/or attract further research funding). The registrar continued, growing ever more engaged in the defence of collegiality:

> I don't want our senior academics, or any of our academics, to feel that they are working in an institution which is starting to relegate them to 'the workers'. Do you know what I mean? Because, in the folklore, the opposite to management is 'the workers' and I have been in academic institutions where bluntly I have heard senior management staff talk about 'the workers' and I find that intolerable. In a university, particularly like this one, the academic staff are not just employees, they are statutory members of a chartered corporation. And it's different. They

are different – they have a status in the institution which needs respecting. And I'm very sensitive to anything which overtly and unnecessarily disturbs what I think is the important theory amongst the staff that they still work in an institution which puts their activity first, not the management first, not the 'corporate' as necessarily first.

The concern expressed is that the new performance measures will radically change the ethos of universities so that their members relate less to each other 'horizontally', as colleagues within a chartered corporation, and more as 'managers' and 'managed'. As the new measures are applied, the worry is that corporate interests will come to take precedence in ways that subvert the activity of academics who, it is believed, must be free to pursue their agendas without interference. However, to make this point the registrar is obliged to undertake a considerable amount of discursive work just to re-establish something that only a few years earlier would have been largely taken for granted. The volume of the background 'hum' of management discourse has become so loud that the speaker is forced to deal directly with it. This requires an appeal to freedom, to good taste and finally to an argument about the legal status of academic employees in a pre-1992 university.

However, it is instructive to counter-pose the registrar's text with that of the head of a science department at the same university. This head had embraced the managerial stationing. As a consequence he understood the problems of his position as an effect of the university 'centre's' inability to extend to his post the 'tools' which would allow him to become that 'manager'. The responsibilities attached to his role, he observed, were not matched by authority: 'I don't have the ability to move as fast as the manager of a small business, but *that is what I am*'. He went on: 'There is a major disparity between the objectives they pass down and the tools that they pass down to carry them out. I have just written an extremely irate, not extremely irate, extremely measured but extremely lengthy and pithy letter to our personnel director pointing out the small influence a head of department has over promotion'. According to this head of department, the university had been complicit in increasing the degree of accountability shouldered by senior post-holders for departmental success, but had largely failed to provide sufficient support/tools to articulate senior post-holders' investment in the position of manager. This was, he said:

> endemic in the university system. It has tried to make middle managers, who are heads of department, accountable. It has tried to hold them responsible for the success or failure of their activity measured by research assessment rating, teaching assessment rating, our total grant income, numbers of students, so I'm responsible for the success of those things, but none of the devolved spending power has come down with that, so we have got a large can to carry without any of the power to do anything about it . . . if this department takes getting on to £2 million to run, I think I should have a say over 90 per cent of that or whatever fraction is appropriate, a high fraction of it, and the centre

should retain that bit which is necessary, which it can sell to me as a service that I require.

In relation to this I am not arguing that these relations are fixed; that the 'centre' or 'departments' are either defensive or productive of the managerial station or the particular locales. These relations are dynamic and the outcome of the problematic and changing dissemination of management knowledge and practices across a terrain. The comments show that far from subordinating embedded academic and administrative identities, management priorities flow around these. There is a sense, for instance in the registrar's comments, that one way to support and confirm traditional administrative identities is to confirm academic identities. As well as defending academic freedom, he also highlighted the need to defend 'non-academic' areas from management as this would be 'seen as a beginning of a move to a different type of arrangement'.

These comments show the diversity of response to the issues. While some of the comments can be read as a confirmation that universities are being reconstituted as knowledge factories organized by managers whose aim is to intensify and commodify the production and distribution of knowledge and skills, the data suggest that this reconstitution is partial and is likely to remain so. This is because the stationing of senior post-holders as managers is subject in many cases to a personal and professional struggle between existing localized practices and knowledges and those of the new imperializing discourse. Thus a recurrent managerial problem and challenge for these post-holders, which is unlikely to go away, is to develop a sufficiently integrated 'performance'. Of course, this 'performance' is located within particular spaces and embedded within those discursive practices and conflicting knowledges that make up these sites, yet the challenge for senior post-holders is to enrol the support of 'the managed' by contriving to reconcile embedded, largely localized and tacit discourses with the imperializing discourses associated with the new performance measures.

Business as usual?

One way to attempt this 'reconciliation of locale and station' is to emphasize the continuity of 'old' with 'new' practices, arguing for instance that the new disciplines could be used to support and facilitate established practices. The presence of the managerial station is acknowledged but is seen as something of a puzzle precisely because it is deemed to be broadly congruent with an established ethos, particularly in techno-science areas where the rationalities of management resonate with the functionality of disciplinary knowledge bases. For example, a head of department at Harbourside said that 'we have introduced a system which frankly I think has helped very considerably to open up financial issues, but of course this has put much greater demands on the head of department as a manager of resources'. The need to introduce a 'system' which would 'open up financial issues' is a direct outcome of the introduction across the university of a devolved funding process, known in this institution as 'resource centre budgeting'. This, as the head said later, was 'designed to reflect what the UFC was then doing'.

In response to resource centre budgeting, the department's senior staff were reorganized into a 'management team':

> When I took over as head of department, because I had a number of other commitments which I couldn't relinquish at very short notice, I [took over] on the basis that I would set up a management team. My colleagues had already been thinking about structures in the department and ideas were developing which I pursued and implemented a couple of months after I took over, and that gives me a management team.

Through this, each member of the 'team' had responsibility for areas such as department finance, planning, particular programmes and quality. However, the head of department turned back to academic priorities when questioned about these processes:

> CP: Was it just about money in these two periods? Were there other issues as well?

> Surely. Let's step back a stage. We've all of us been producing departmental plans and statements of objectives and one of the things that I have tried to make abundantly clear in any statement of objectives that I've contributed to is that the objectives of the department are academic. They are there in terms of teaching and learning and research and dissemination and the development of the profession in our case, and finance is a constraint and really I see the finance objective as making sure that we have sufficient finance to allow us to carry out our other objectives.

Related to this issue of continuity is the question of whether or not senior post-holders spoke of, and enacted, themselves as managers. In other words, to what extent had they come to know themselves through an imperializing discourse of management? And thus, to what extent had the demands and stationing of the power bloc been uncritically embraced? Of course, I am not assuming a singular response to this, as clearly the 'kind of manager' one is shifts and changes in relation to the 'audience' (see Appendix for discussion). However while at *this* interview, *this* interviewee explicitly used the term 'manager' to describe himself. Others meanwhile agreed that they were effectively managers, but stressed the importance of *not* calling themselves or presenting themselves as such. For example, one of the pro vice-chancellors interviewed at Harbourside volunteered that: 'It matters very much that you have got, *we don't call ourselves this,* "managers", you've got a centre, a senior team that is in touch with what is going on and can give some suggestions as to developments'. For him the acceptable face of management within the context of universities was that of an adviser who is well informed about the problems and issues of local operations, and therefore cannot readily be 'fobbed off' by departmental heads. The favoured representation of such practice is being 'in touch' and offering advice rather than imposing requirements or controlling activity in an overt or explicitly managerial way.

His fellow pro vice-chancellor at Harbourside identified a similar approach:

> I'm told by [the vice-chancellor] that I'm the very model of a modern manager.[5] I find that puzzling because I don't think of myself as a manager. I haven't read most of the books. I have very little direct authority with respect to most of the people who would nominally work for me, except I am prepared to take responsibility and prepared to cover for them and certainly not to blame them publicly, which is an elementary thing. As far as I can see if you want to be a major research university you have got to have something like the traditional untidy structure of deans, councils and senates with a fair amount of departmental autonomy ... if you want to be a major research university you have to tolerate a certain amount of chaos and anarchy, you have to trust people.

Here, the view is expressed that 'a certain amount of chaos and anarchy' is a necessary condition of successful academic research activity. Since the research assessment exercises do not prescribe how performance is to be achieved, there is no direct pressure to change 'the traditional untidy structure' and, thus, this pro vice-chancellor reads his position as facilitating established practices rather than disrupting them. Later he referred to himself as 'One who tries to construct lots of internal and external networks and keeps trying to put them together'. However, the phrases 'people who would nominally *work for me*' and 'not to blame *them* publicly' suggest that, despite an avowed lack of formal authority, he nevertheless defines his relations managerially, and more broadly is willing to intervene 'privately' in ways that are tolerant of 'chaos' *as long as* they deliver the goods for the corporation.

Embracing the new measures

While in many cases the new practices and knowledges worked their way into some uneasy continuity with existing locales of practice, in other cases those interviewed readily identified themselves as 'empowered' by these imperializing measures, and ascribed to their actions rationales drawn from management knowledges. The following quotation is drawn from a head of school at pre-1992 Harbourside:

> I had long felt for years before taking on this role that things were too loose, that things were under-managed, and things were not properly evaluated. X said he was doing his research even if the annual list of

publications didn't seem to show any output. So what I was doing was picking up a school where its old residual staff were underperforming in terms of research with a lot of new people being brought in.

Here, output-based performance measures aimed at meeting funding council returns define people and their work in particular ways, and justify seemingly overdue change. The head went on to outline the steps that had been taken to raise the department's RAE rating:

> So in order to take us up in terms of research I had to set the kind of level that would be reasonable. One of the approaches was to set clear targets for performance. We set a very modest one. The normal expectation was that each member of staff should produce at least one article in a refereed journal each year and people who were not producing that were seen to be underperforming and were diagnosed for positive help. That has actually helped. The measure is crude but when I took over the school average per capita publication was about 0.4 or 0.6 of a unit per year which is treating each publication as the same – books, articles and anything else. In 1993 it was 3.8.

While acknowledging that average per capita publications presents a 'crude measure' of performance, this head of school suggested that 'an enormous cultural change' had been accomplished 'by making it clear that research really did mean producing stuff'. To achieve this performance improvement, the head said he had introduced a system in which 'people through the divisions and through the professoriate were going to set up little networks which would drive research forward'. This move was described as involving 'good man-management, good person-management'. By this was meant the requirement of senior members of the school to take 'a direct and close interest in the performance of their colleagues and help them to improve it, which had not [previously] happened':

> I started this when I first became head of school . . . during that year *I* arranged for myself with the relevant professor of the division to meet every single member of the non-professorial staff in the school to discuss teaching, research, life, work, everything. And actually several people in the long-standing staff said: 'I've been here 20 years and no one has ever talked to me about this before'. So in a sense that's management which had not been there. It was a very positive outcome.

This head of school, who's work might be described as either 'good person-management' or as 'increasing the degree of surveillance and visibility of academic output', suggests that it was managerial action, ascribed to himself, that brought about this cultural change. However, an arguably more compelling explanation for the increase in publications, and one to which the speaker only briefly alluded, was a massive change in the school's personnel brought on in part by a particularly bitter merger between smaller departments. This saw seven senior members of staff resign *en masse* and move to a 'rival' university. Reflecting on this the current head said:

> God knows why [the rival university] they took them, they weren't any good . . . I was delighted by this, after I got over the initial problem of coping with filling the posts the following autumn, and that means we have, I have, as head, been reconstructing the entire staff of the school in the new. It has been a great opportunity reconstructing the staff of the school.

Between 60 and 70 per cent of the academic staff had been appointed during this period and the professoriate had changed completely in that time. While it might appear that management in general, and the head of school in particular, had successfully mediated the imperializing discipline of the power bloc to raise the productivity of previously unproductive academic labour (e.g. through heightened surveillance and annual appraisal), the institution had recruited a large number of young, research-active academics. This is not to minimize the disciplining effects taking place, which of course included the strategic replacement of staff, but simply to note how claims about the effectiveness of local measures (e.g. close monitoring of individual research productivity) that directly parallel the imperializing disciplines need to be placed in a wider context.

Yet this head of department's investment in the 'manager' was not completely unproblematic. On the one hand, he identified the extra anxiety and insecurity induced by increased surveillance and discipline. He noted that: 'No one is aware of the pressure and the nature of the job until they actually *sit in this office*'. As well as highlighting the anxiety the head of department experienced in the job, this quotation illuminates how particular knowledges and practices produce the managerial station with a particular body topography. The head's office itself is dominated by these knowledges and practices. The desk and chair, particularly, act as devices for positioning the head of department's body in relation to the documents which carry the knowledges of budgets, strategic planning and audits. Through reading, reflecting and speaking about the relations of difference between particular norms and the department's performance embedded in these documents, these relations of difference become 'folded into' him as forms of reflexivity. Through repetitions of sitting 'in this office' these relations of difference become manifested in feelings of pressure and anxiety. Yet there are other, definitely subordinate, body topographies available to him in 'this office'. Away from the main desk and chair is a side desk, filing cabinet and shelves which display his published books. The filing cabinet contains lecture notes and research materials. The desk carries a collection of neat folders which contain details of ongoing research contracts and programmes. Here the body topography of the professional academic and subject specialist is available. While there are tensions between these two body topographies, it is the managerial station which dominates the office space and produces 'pressure'. The body topography of the professional academic can be understood as a locale in this space.

During the interview this head of department understood his work as 'managerial' and talked of how he was 'trying to produce the collective, to focus on the collective interests, but actually I'm leading it and directing it'. Here we hear how the positioning of academic manager is folded into him, in that he speaks of being and directing the collective. But this investment is problematic, not simply in terms of the tensions between the managerial station and the professionalized locale located in the office. The managerial station also clashed with the identities traditionally ascribed to heads of department at Harbourside. The head noted this in the following comment: 'In terms of a job description – there just isn't one. It's just institutional habit. The major problem I have had is getting people to be aware that this is not like being the head of the German department, of eight or ten people, you know, you actually are a business turning over £5 million a year with 100 staff – it's a very different kettle of fish'.

This 'pressure', induced by the individuating effects of the managerial station, was keenly felt by a dean at Southern University. Yet in response to this stationing, and as a way of countering its effect, he deliberately turned the offices around his own into teaching and research space which produced what he termed a 'freeway' of students and staff:

> When I moved in here it was quite deliberate to have a couple of teaching rooms and a research room there [next door] and a photocopier there to make it into a little freeway, a coffee machine and a common room down the hall and very often I can sit and chat with people there. If I'm not having a conversation like this [with researcher] and I'm not desperate to do something that requires my full concentration, then I keep the door open and people pop in and have a chat.

The dean here had introduced small physical changes to ameliorate the individuating effects of the topography of the managerial station. Others however simply felt divided. A head of department at Southern University for instance said: 'Half of me at least is completely identified with their [colleagues'] feelings, because I still am, I hope, a genuine subject leader . . . but there are times one has to say: "I'm wearing my associate dean's hat" . . . there is a sort of tension, sort of thing, that you have got to divide yourself in two'.

The head is a positioning – Janus-like – in two competing discursive practices, between managerial and professional modes of practice, between station and locale.

Selling the power bloc

In summary, many senior post-holders across all four universities noted their suspicion of managerial knowledges and practices, principally because they posed an obvious threat to the ethos and self-identity of professionalism. Yet it was clear that the *practices* of management had a seductive appeal in so far as they offer a way of addressing the pressure and anxiety being experienced by senior post-holders. They came to express the managerial positioning because it offered a way of addressing tensions and pressures but only as long as it was read as beneficial to fellow academics. As a dean at post-1992 Southern University observed:

> What you are about is creating structures which will make people's lives easier to bear. Everybody in higher education is increasingly stressed, is doing one and half or two jobs and what they want predominantly is *no longer just to be dismissive about management*, but if you have credibility as an academic and researcher and also you are fair, open, reasonable and friendly in your approach to staff, *then they see that as being efficient.*

In practice, forms of management are welcomed, this dean suggests, when they are shown to deal with issues that are of immediate, local concern. This depends of course on maintaining 'smooth' interpersonal relations where you are seen as 'fair, open, reasonable and friendly in your approach to staff'. What is counter-productive, the dean suggests, are more explicit manifestations of management in which changes are imposed rather than negotiated.

What staff 'don't buy', the dean observed, is 'hard management, hierarchical management, which is this "I am a hard manager, this is the most efficient way" kind of myth'. This 'industrial model' is said to 'carry no force': 'Basically what staff are most critical of is the kind of management rhetoric – business goals and so on – which is seen to be hierarchical and simultaneously no more competent, in fact, incompetent and inefficient in very real terms, and they will just not buy it'. Here there is an awareness of the tensions between locales that rely heavily upon cooperation and consent, and the imposition of objectives and the monopolizing and concealing of information, which is associated with 'the industrial model'. The dean commends the sharing of information and the selection of objectives for which there is widespread support. In other words, you:

> create a situation where you set certain kinds of objectives that they respect and endorse, like enabling individuals to do research, giving them access to budget figures, giv[ing] them access to staff funds, making clear in equal proportion (this is not necessarily in order of priority) that one of the things is to give the students the best deal we can in the circumstances.

Yet, what is clear from this is that while 'the industrial model' is criticized, and a more collegial and interpersonal approach recommended, this is done in terms of a productionist ethic. It is defended not because it is ethically more defensible, but because it is more likely to fulfil the demands of the imperializing disciplines: 'It seems to me to be a much more productive ethos to create [than one] which means that the next day they are going to find themselves at the top of a list of people who are non-people'.

In these extracts the dean offers a spirited justification for the me–them (manager/managed) split in terms of identity and relations *alongside* a neo-paternalist discourse which glosses management with notions of support, fairness and the collegial spirit of critique. In the process a 'nod' towards shared academic identity is made. Yet, however it is dressed up, the relation of manager to managed is dominant. This relation could be said to be constructed through a discourse of empowerment, skills and growth as identified by Watson (1994). The manager's job in this discourse is to create the environment in which people 'want to move in a constructive direction', as one of the interviewees put it.

In adopting this approach, it is less a matter of dissolving established traditions than recasting and reinforcing them in ways that can be shown to be 'good for the department and/or the university' rather than, or in addition to, being 'good for the discipline'. Where such traditions are established and respected, moves to introduce 'hard management' are likely to prove counter-productive. However, it is precisely the know-ledge or threat of such a 'hard' possibility that makes 'softer' forms of managerialism more acceptable and even benign as they are said to actu-ally deliver on the promise of improved 'output' by creating 'structures which will make people's lives easier to bear'. It is precisely this which pervaded many accounts of managing in the pre-1992 universities. Highly elaborate stories of bullying managerialism allegedly under way in nearby post-1992 institutions were often put to work by pre-1992 senior post-holders to support their, sometimes discursively complex, positioning as 'managers'.

A head of department at Harbourside University, for example, stressed the inclusive and consultative approach he took, and compared it favour-ably with the allegedly dictatorial approach at work 'down the road' at the local post-1992 university:

> Effectively I set a line, I set a lead and I expect people to talk it over. I expect people to challenge it, but I have set a sort of tone for the strategy of the school ... I think there is a significant cultural differ-ence between that kind of approach and the kind of approach, that obviously people moan like hell about, they get from the place down the road where their deans, who see themselves as very much associated with the deputy directors, are essentially implementing central policy outwards.

And similarly the vice-chancellor at Middletown had this to say:

> I know the flak which comes from the other university ... the staff are frightened as to what the hell is happening ... decisions are taken – bang – do this this week, two weeks later, change that, do this; now that really wouldn't happen here, and I would say that there is no decision that I wanted to take which hasn't gone through senate and been agreed.

Becoming the power bloc

As suggested in the previous section, the problems of the suffusion of the managerial station relate often to the relations between heads of department and 'very' senior post-holders. One of the deans at Southern University was keenly aware of being caught in the middle between the pressures upon him to be more of a manager, responsive to 'the executive', and to be a colleague responsive to the concerns of academic staff:

> There is a constant pressure I think from the executive to try and draw deans more into them. And that I think would automatically put a line between me and my colleagues which I don't want there. I think that the executive would like to see deans as both academic and resource managers. To be fair, our executive . . . have moved a considerable amount of resource authority to me. I mean I have a one-line budget really and there are certain things I can't do, but *there are a lot of things I can do that in the old days I couldn't do.* I think that they [the executive] are trying to shift the sort of academic [*sic*] and the resource decisions closer to the shop floor if you like, closer to the academic staff.

This dean's positive identification with the devolution of resources from the executive, which gave him a degree of power to fulfil his responsibilities, meant however that he was constituted more directly as an arm of the executive, with potentially negative consequences for his capacity to elicit support and cooperation from 'the managed'. The conflict between these aspects became apparent when he was asked to identify the issues that he was currently dealing with:

> The biggest problem really is maintaining an attachment to what we were sure about in the past; that what we were doing was of general national value and we had a sort of shared view about the worth of our work and colleagues. *Even though they really felt they were underpaid, they didn't blame the university for it.* It's a morale kind of thing really. I'm trying to succour a view amongst colleagues that we are professionals with skills. My own belief is that the government don't believe we are professionals with skills and they are consciously undermining us and trying to turn us into skilled shop-floor workers who can be bought and sold at will.

Once more, this interviewee highlights the importance of the traditional academic locale in which there was a taken for granted sense of 'the worth of our work' and the status of academics as professionals. The dean identifies erosion of these values as 'the biggest problem' – not just because it is demoralizing for staff but, arguably because in the absence of such values there is a resort to managerial forms of control which further corrode locales. While apparently critical of this development, and presenting himself as a defender of 'what we were sure about in the past', this dean positions himself as a resource manager who, effectively, does the bidding

of the power bloc. Institutional post-holders, such as this dean, are positioned by budget, audit and planning practices so as to accommodate the
demands of the power bloc. One effect is that they are likely to appeal to
certain aspects of the professional locale, and attempt to mould these into
the 'tools' of the managerial station.

Yet even if this highly problematic combination of elements were possible, efforts to achieve an accommodation with these demands become (even
more) problematic when long-established and often intimate relations with
small well-integrated departments are at stake. For instance, the dean said:

> It's more difficult to play the sort of jackboot Führer if you've known
> people for 20 years. I mean some of my staff I've known 27 years, and
> in the old days we would go off camping together and you know. With
> quite a few of the staff, I remember I was having my little babies and
> they were having their little babies and the wives know each other quite
> well. So there is a sort of network of human relationships that is very
> hard to pinpoint.

This shows how, despite the relative success achieved in stationing senior
post-holders as managers, extending the disciplines of the power bloc in
the local settings of academic work is fraught with difficulty.

Clearly, maintaining credibility – that is, being able to hold a certain view
of oneself in a variably hostile context of departments caught between
imperializing and localizing knowledge practices – is a key issue. The head
of department at Middletown, who compared himself with the manager of
a small business, identified his problem as follows:

> I have no sacking power. It is a constant bleat of heads of departments.
> I have actually no sanction over my staff. If they care to raise two
> fingers to me and go and do something else there is literally nothing
> . . . [pause] . . . I can do something about it. I can starve them of
> resources to some extent, not very helpful because they could also work
> to rule, give lousy lectures and do their administrative job badly . . . now
> I recognize that if I could sack people there would be a downside to it.
> I'm not saying [that] that is the panacea, just one of the tools which
> would enable me to be *taken more seriously as a manager* who could
> influence things.

Caught between the practices of the station and those of the locale, the
scope to actually do the bidding of the power bloc, apart from those times
when new staff are appointed, can seem limited – particularly given the
capacity of staff to subvert managerial programmes. A dean at Middletown
meanwhile reflected on the subtle combinations of inducements or 'carrots',
and 'sticks' available to improve staff performance:

> As with all these things, it's a mixture of carrot and stick. There are a
> few carrots that we still have available that one can give. Some of this is
> space, taking space away from people and giving it to others who will

be more likely to ... [pause] ... there are still some funds available
... we tend to keep a reserve back so we've got the odd few thousand
we can give to people who are being proactive and moving in the
direction we want, as a carrot.

Here, top-sliced funds awarded to those who are deemed be 'moving in the
direction we want' are used as a major means of control. For others these
funds can be withheld. Alternatively while the carrot is preferred, other
more coercive options were available, as this dean observed:

There are ways of making life slightly more difficult in terms of the
occasional public comment or message to heads of department and so
on. If they put in for particular things and [we] say well that is rather a
low priority. [However] I'm not the sort of individual who will sort of
stand up and say this department by and large achieves nothing. This
just creates enemies. I find it better by and large to try and encourage
people to work with members of teams. Those people who are being
difficult you sit down with, and if they are not prepared to work in that
team then perhaps there is another team they are prepared to work in
and I would say that by and large that has worked.

While acknowledging the limits of both sticks and carrots, this dean suggests
that the main form of control was a mix of the occasional public comment
(which is sufficiently understated to make its point without causing offence)
and peer pressure. Here recalcitrant staff worked with colleagues in teams
and peer pressure was used, rather than direct supervision, to discipline
those who were ineligible for, or indifferent towards, carrots. In summary
then, the above outlines how the management's imperializing measures were
addressed in the main by selectively mobilizing (through carrots, sticks and
peer pressure) the identities, histories and practices of the locale.

Challenging the managerial station: the case of a code for management

A key point from the above discussion is that managerial knowledges and
practices come to dominate particular spaces, thus constructing those spaces
as stations. Managerial knowledges and practices thus come to dominate
particular locations and prescribe particular identities, relations, embodied
practices and knowledges. Through the discursive practices of the managerial station, people are not so much forced to take up such positions, but
are drawn in and constitute themselves as the 'manager' or the 'managed'
by having to deal with these knowledges and practices. In these power-
invested, sometimes confessional-type arenas (appraisal for instance) it is
extremely difficult *not* to take up positions within dominant managerialist
discourses – that is, to make a sustained challenge to the incursion of
particular knowledges and practices (see Clegg, 1975; Mumby and Stol,

1991; Fairclough, 1993; Willmott, 1993 for examples). And, as Fairclough notes, even if the particular language and practice involved feels like rhetoric, it soon becomes 'part of one's professional identity' (1993: 153). However, this should not deny the possibility of questioning and challenging the ascendancy of a particular managerial station – especially among heads of department and services with a strong history of 'horizontal' relations and of dissent from dominant approaches. This was precisely the problem, of being forced to take a position within an alien discourse, in which heads of department and service found themselves in one of the two post-1992 universities in the sample.

The following is a short account of the intriguing political processes that surround both the construction of the managerial station at City University, and the challenge to this. This institution has a history of aggressive senior post-holders who were prepared to admit, in the privacy of the research interview, to being too 'heavy-handed' in their dealings with university personnel. In response to being positioned as managers within this context, some heads of department and service attempted to redefine and challenge the 'heavy-handed' application of management knowledges and practices. This drew in liberal notions of care and elements from the knowledges of professional locales. This redefinition surfaced in a document called the 'Code for Management'[6] (see Fig. 6.1). I will briefly outline how this code came into being, its effect, and then offer a brief summary.

Codifying the locale, challenging the managerial station

By 1991 this former polytechnic, now a 1992 university, was in the midst of a series of major changes. Student numbers were being increased so that the university would double in size in four years. The university's catalogue of courses was being rewritten in modular form. Heads of department and services had been 'forced' to sign new local management contracts which positioned them as 'accountable' managers within a strict line management framework. The carrot in this process was a salary increase of some several thousands of pounds a year. However, many heads felt that senior management's approach both to new contracts and to the range of other changes they sought to introduce was at best dictatorial. In response, heads of department suggested the 'Code for Management'. It is divided into two columns, one called 'responsibility', which might be seen as affirmation of the 'accountable' manager (discussed above), the other called 'respect' which draws notions from an idealized academic and administrative locale. It contains a series of liberal notions broadly along the lines of 'treat us as you would like to be treated'. At its inception, at a particular senior staff conference, the Code was an attempt by a group of heads to tie the *management*, which at the time referred to the then polytechnic's director and his assistants, to a particular code of practice. The senior staff meanwhile understood

Figure 6.1 Code for Management

The University is committed to quality management in pursuance of its Mission. The Code for Management demonstrates the shared values underpinning the managerial process.

Managers are committed to:

Acting with integrity, openness and respecting, without prejudice, the integrity, capabilities and individuality of other people

Appreciating and acknowledging the contributions of colleagues

Developing a friendly and satisfying working environment

Relating to colleagues in a courteous manner

Offering support, help and assistance to colleagues who seek it

Seeking, listening to and acting upon, as appropriate, the ideas and views of other people

Working to ensure that the expectations held of themselves and colleagues are reasonable

RESPECT

Managers are committed to:

Being accountable for the actions of themselves and of those for whom they are responsible

Fostering innovation, decisiveness, risk-taking and learning by doing

Promoting personal responsibility for decision making and the shared ownership of those decisions

Sharing information and giving feedback in a clear, constructive and timely manner to those affected by decisions and actions

Using a decision making process characterized by openness and the search for, and maintenance of, agreement

Using resources effectively, efficiently and in an equitable manner

Working for continuous personal and professional development

RESPONSIBILITY

the Code as a possible solution to a number of political problems they faced, such as improving relations with middle managers, but more importantly saw it as countering staff and particularly the polytechnic board's criticism of senior staff conferences. The year before, the three-day conference had been held in Montpellier in France. It is 'recorded' in the institution's unofficial mythology as an event of high entertainment, huge expense and expressive of a more extravagant era of the previous director who had recently been removed in a 'colonels' revolt' (discussed in the previous chapter). The Montpellier conference was organized by a largely self-appointed group of senior staff, known colloquially as the 'rat pack', who were closely associated with the previous director. The conference reportedly cost the institution in the region of £25,000. While some regarded it as a 'public relations success', others across the institution generally saw it as a 'self-indulgent jolly', as one head of department put it, without tangible 'outcomes'. As a result of the alleged 'excess' the conference had been investigated by the polytechnic's board, although nothing ever came of this. However, the new director was concerned a year later that a repeat 'performance' was unlikely to send the message to the board that he was now in control of the institution.

Yet during its history as a document, the Code for Management (very senior staff) became a code *for managers* – that is, all those on management contracts. This included those who suggested the Code in the first place and who were uncomfortable at being addressed as managers, preferring instead a head of department or service or senior academic title. What occurred, I think, is that the Code, while initially a form of resistance to the managerial station, became another means of stationing senior post-holders across the institution. Yet because the Code was associated with the challenge to and the attempt to rewrite the 'hard accountable' 'manager' in more socially reciprocal terms, this shift from 'management' to 'managers' was accepted as a compromise. Did it work? Well yes, and no.

At interview many heads of department and service considered that the senior management had 'failed to live up to their side of the bargain'. The *management* had continued to fail to abide by reasonable standards of conduct, they said. Very senior post-holders, meanwhile, almost in chorus voice, positioned the Code as being 'for the troops', as one said. This pro vice-chancellor suggested that 'the more pieces of paper you can have on your wall in times of rapid change the better'. Yet what was interesting was that both heads and very senior post-holders said that they found the Code 'useful'. It gave them a guide to relations with others. In other words, it offered them the rudiments of an identity, an identity that was not simply that of the 'manager' as embedded in the performance measures and strategic planning documents, but also linked with, and provided some continuity with, embedded practices. It thus provided an alternative discourse type, to use Fairclough's (1989) term, which we might call the 'respectful' manager. This is not to suggest that very senior post-holders were now operating in this way, far from it. But through challenging the bullying dogmatism of the 'accountable' manager discourse type, its continued distribution in relations between people was questioned and problematized. While the dominance of the 'accountable manager', as *the way* in which the 'managers' knew themselves and conceptualized their world had not necessarily been overturned, the 'respectful' manager discourse type broadened and diversified the discursive mix.

Another 'outcome' of the Code was that the voices of resistance were now more comfortable with referring to themselves as managers (from within the 'respectful manager' discourse type). Yet another was that those at work at senior levels who were resistant to managerialism positioned themselves in ways which ultimately supported the managerialist tide. A final 'outcome' was that the 'respectful' manager was drawn upon to add a 'respectful' gloss to potentially unpopular managerial manoeuvres.

This chapter has explored the tense and problematc relations between the managerial station, its auditing and planning and performance-based demands, and those of professional knowledge practices which the managerial station postions as a locale. It has highlighted how problematic, partial and uncomfortable these tensions become for those positioned by them, and shown how 'devices' such as the Code for Management may in some cases provide temporary relief from such problems.

Notes

1. Such as the research assessment exercise (which since the mid-1980s has ranked each department on a scale of 1 to 5 every 3–4 years), the teaching quality assessment process, and particularly the localized repetitions of these.
2. This refers to a big-selling management text by international management discourse circulator Tom Peters (1987), entitled *Thriving on Chaos*. The subtitle of the book is *A Handbook for a Management Revolution*.
3. This interview with Harbourside's vice-chancellor was conducted by the author and a colleague with an interest in this research.
4. On the other hand, this department had been a major beneficiary of the North Sea oil boom. In addition to providing equipment, oil companies had supported large numbers of doctoral and postdoctoral students whose presence and capacity to publish are critical for a '5' rating on the research assessment exercise. A virtuous circle had developed in which staff had been successful in obtaining research council grants and the head of department had become closely involved with major funding bodies through the presidency of his professional society.
5. The reference here is obviously to Gilbert and Sullivan's famously incompetent major-general in *The Pirates of Penzance*. Yet it is not clear whether the respondent himself or the vice-chancellor is aware of the irony underlying the latter's description of the former as 'the very model of a modern manager'. The comments could be read as strikingly subtle or strikingly naive, or both.
6. The 'Code for Management' is not the actual name given to the document at the particular institution. The name has been changed to protect the identity of the institution and those who provided material for the research work.

7

Just how Managed is the New Further Education?

> Once, managers all the way up to college principal saw a place for themselves in a union of educational professions. Now 'management' seems to start at the level of lance-corporal (should that read petty officer?). And that leads to hard choices of the 'them' and 'us' variety.
>
> (Jones, 1997b)

'Find a market, get into it, suck it, satisfy it and move on' – this is how one head of school at Urban College outlined his job. He described himself as one of the 'new breed' of industry-focused college managers. But he also had a problem. He called it the 'democracy problem'. He said it amounted to a tension between 'letting everybody have their say, and actually getting things done'.

This chapter draws out this and other tensions produced by the suffusion of the managerial station in FE colleges. Broadly there are two issues: the democracy problem, or the problem of taking up the uncomfortable 'place' between the power bloc and the people, and the problem of getting 'managers' to 'manage'. I begin with this first theme, move to discuss the second and then discuss both in the context of the contest between localizing and imperializing knowledge practices in colleges. But before that it is important to briefly situate FE in relation to HE, given the discussion in the last chapter.

There are significant differences in size, resources, expertise and status between FE and HE institutions in the UK. There are numerous ways of differentiating between institutions within the sectors, and of differentiating between the sectors on the basis of these criteria. However the key point here is that what I have termed the 'Thatcherite power bloc', in comparison with its engagement with polytechnics, colleges of HE and pre-1992 universities during the late 1980s and early 1990s, was probably at its most aggressive and capable when confronting the FE sector in the early 1990s. Equally the sector itself, where the average college is but a quarter the size of the average former polytechnic, and where colleges had long enjoyed in many cases 'cosy' relations with local authorities, was probably the least well prepared of the education sectors to deal with the energized and radicalized Thatcherite regime of the time. Furthermore, in relation to the first point, the techniques developed to achieve the 'nationalization' programme through quasi-market methods in public sector HE had been developed, tested and honed through the incorporation of HE by the same personnel who had engaged with FE. The key personnel were Sir William Stubbs, formerly PCFC chief, then FEFC chief, and Roger Ward, formerly Polytechnic and Colleges Employers Forum chief and then College Employers Forum chief. Sir William in retrospect regarded the FE sector as in the main 'less mature' than the former polytechnics and colleges of HE at the time of incorporation (private correspondence, 1997).

The imposition of the managerial station in HE, suffused of course through incorporation, new funding methodologies, intensified audit and performance review, has seen many senior post-holders take up the vocabularies and grammars of the business manager. Some come to read themselves as operators of small to medium-sized businesses with portfolios of products sold in an education market. The same has been the case in FE, as the head of school's comment above attests.

Caught in the middle between power bloc and people in FE

As with HE, FE colleges also have deeply embedded traditions of collegiality, professionalism and in many cases a commitment to liberal educational principles. Together these make up, through vocabularies and practices, locales which resist in varying and mobile ways top-down, imperializing knowledges and dispositions. The head of engineering at Tower College described these locales as a group of 'terrorists': 'If I'd have been Roger Ward, and I had my MBE for services to education, then I would have pushed the atomic button and got rid of everyone. He didn't so we have terrorists beavering away at the foundation who won't change'.

More specifically though, the tensions between locales and the managerial station, between collegial and managerial relations, come down to finely-grained differences in the knowledge used to 'see' and talk and be with others at work. They involve for instance the difficulties of 'seeing' colleagues as potential labour power which, it is assumed, needs to be transformed into actual labour, as in the following comment from a programme coordinator at Hillside College: 'I find it at times difficult to line-manage people that I've actually worked with on a same basis . . . I've now got to be aware of how many hours they are doing in terms of the 801 [per academic year] they should be doing. I've got to monitor their attendance. I've got to ask them to come in for different things . . . I had to tell [a colleague] that she had to do [some particular teaching]. She didn't want to but she had no choice'.

Here the programme coordinator is constituted as a 'manager' through the newly invigorated surveillance and enforcement practices of the college which address particularly the relationships between the teaching contract

and the work done. This involves a shifting back and forth between the
identities of locale and station. This proves uncomfortable and problematic.

Senior FE post-holders, in tandem with those in HE, have found themselves
caught between managerial and localizing knowledges and practices. A head
of school at Urban College offered the following account:

> We are in the middle, so, to put it bluntly, we get dumped on from
> above and we get dumped on from below. There is very little support
> for us in the middle, and this is confidential. Because above us my line
> manager has six other heads of school to line manage; he has a very
> big job now that there are only two vice-principals, a massive job. So I
> don't get much support from him.
>
> Below I'm supposed to be supporting my staff and helping them. I'm
> having to say to them, 'I want to look after you, I want to make sure
> that you are not stressed and not off work with stress-related illnesses,
> you are doing the right job in the classroom, your students are happy
> so that they stay with us' [but] then on the other hand, 'sorry but we've
> got to do this on a shoestring budget', you know, so 'I've got to ask
> you all to work up to the maximum hours and you've got to come in in
> the summer, you can't have a month off or five weeks off, you've got
> to come in'. It is that sort of balance. The pressure from above is to
> be economical and efficient, the pressure from below is not to give
> them an easy life; that is not what they want, they are all hard-working
> people, but to give them a reasonable standard of life which involves
> life outside the college.

Yet following this the speaker went on to distinguish different forms of
managing and to distinguish herself from the 'normalized' managerial identity prescribed by the managerial knowledges and practices of Urban College. She achieves this by accenting the term 'care'. The following quotation
also highlights how the stationing of the 'manager' is built first of all upon
contractual employment relations where the identities of senior post-holders
are linked to their exchange of labour for cash: 'I care about education, I
care about my staff, but I'm paid to care about the economic plight that
all FE colleges are in . . . it is difficult to be the sort of manager I want to be
because the manager that I want to be is not the manager that *I'm almost
being forced to be*'.

Embedded in this is a challenge to the managerial station. It is mounted
here, as it was with the post-holders in HE, by distinguishing different *types*
of manager, and privileging that which is subordinated. The pattern is
similar to the challenge mounted to the managerial station at City University
through the 'Code for Management' discussed in Chapter 6. It also links to
the subordinated formation in management discourse itself – that is 'human
relations' or 'people skills' (Hollway, 1991; Watson, 1994). As the following
quotation shows, the division between the professional locales and relations
with fellow teachers has been rewritten in management discourse as a division
between 'people skills' and 'balancing the budget'. While one could argue

that the former resonates with the head of school's identity as teacher and colleague (and also, one might suggest, with her as 'woman'), it is the ethos of 'people-centred management' which this head of school wants to promote: 'I see management as being about people skills. But I don't see that ethos as being within this college. Management is about efficiency, economies and balancing the budget. I would prefer to see it the other way around, but I think that is the nature of FE now'.

But how is this head of school being 'forced' to be a particular kind of manager, as she states in the previous quotation? Where does this force come from? It is 'done', I have argued, through the distributed discursive practices of audits, planning and budgets. Within these there are verbal/ symbolic processes which position bodies within a 'paper structure' of charts, budgets, and spreadsheets. These are embodied, spatially and physically, in the new vertically integrated management teams and in the one-to-one audits and performance appraisal processes. In the midst of this are investments of desire in the identities of the 'manager' as an agent in the education market-place, responsible, as Urban College's principal said: 'for delivering a volume of work on an annual contract at the right quality, set out in each area's business plan'.

However, subjectivity is, as I have argued, a disseminating and diffuse phenomenon. It is going on in a number of different spaces and places, in different discourses and practices, at the same time! Later in the interview, and arguably at different points in her working day, the same head of school who positioned herself as a 'manager' recovered her identification with the professional locale in her text. When reading this it is useful to identify the speaker's use of the pronouns 'I', 'you', 'we' and 'they'. These establish relations and identities whose sources are in both the knowledges and practices of the managerial station and the professional locale. However, the openness of the interview setting offers a chance to problematize the managerial relations and identities. The head uses snatches of dialogue to highlight and problematize these relations and position herself, somehow, between these different identities:

> I was a part-timer ten years ago, then assistant lecturer, then a main-grader then team leader. Then suddenly [at the time of incorporation] I'm head of school and this is all within ten years or so. I come out of that background and *I know what they are feeling and what they think.* It doesn't make it any easier for me because I think they now see me as having 'gone over', as it were, but I'm always trying to balance the two sides.

At this point in the interview the identification with colleagues made her uncomfortable.

> I'm always saying to staff when they come to me, 'How much does it cost?' You know, in a way I don't want to do that, but I have to. I have to make them aware. They don't want to know about the funding

methodology. They don't have to know that one student on a ten-hour course will bring you 14 units, something like that, but I do, I have to know how much that student costs me and how much income they are going to bring in and balance the two. If I don't my budget goes straight through the ceiling . . . So I must seem money-pinching and nitpicking all the time, whereas I want to say: 'Yes, I think that is a wonderful idea, go with it'.

Here the head of school has translated the subjectivity constructed by the managerial and professional stations, the different 'I's', into a dialogic situation. This translation allows her to reflect on the different ways she is positioned by the competing discourses. Note, also, how the embodied practices are drawn in. In the narrative 'they' (the teachers) come to 'her', rather than her going to them. The imagery here is of her being in her office, at her desk, embedded in the 'paper structure' and thus positioned by the body topography of the managerial station. Through this she is stationed within 'her' budget, within the funding methodology, which produces this 'I' – an 'I' that she finds troubling when she evokes herself as a lecturer.

Yet paradoxically at another point in the interview discussion, this head of school finds some interdependence between the 'I' of the managerial station and that of the professional locale. She said that performance appraisal for her was 'A very useful way to get to know your staff. We focus on our objectives. I'm very keen on objectives and targets and focusing'. Clearly the way 'she' comes to know 'her staff' in the latter comment is within the knowledges and practices prescribed by the managerial station – that is, within the imperializing knowledge practices of 'performance management'. So, in other words, particular aspects of these imperializing knowledge practices can be said to resonate, interconnect, and also reshape existing localized practices. This is the strategic objective, of course – to replace in the finest detail possible the locale with the station, and to form an *individuated* identity, where the *individualized* horizontal identity of the collegial locale had been formed.

Becoming the power bloc in FE?

For 'very' senior post-holders in FE the problems of this positioning, be-tween the power bloc and the people, tends to be read not as produced by the uncomfortable intersection of competing knowledges and practices, between conflicting identities, but as a problem with getting people to change, or 'getting managers to manage'. The vice-chancellor's antipathy at Harbourside for 'administrators' and 'administrative culture', discussed in Chapter 6, perhaps hides some of this discomfort in himself.

In colleges, as Randle and Brady (1997) point out, 'very' senior post-holders tend to assume that the problems of managing come down to the speed of reforms and a lack of expertise among academics now occupying management positions. Yet this largely denies the politics of expertise. It underplays the political problems of competing identities and the confrontation with professional locales, in which the senior post-holder, repositioned as 'manager', is also embedded. The following comment from the principal of Urban College is perhaps typical of this kind of response although the text is sophisticated in its approach. It draws on the prescriptions of management 'guru' theory, but at the same time distances itself from such theory. In doing this it presents the process of internalizing new processes as a series of seemingly natural progressive steps, and not as a political battle. The principal suggests that at the time of incorporation, it was

> unreasonable to expect middle managers to be the propagandists of change because they themselves have no experience to build on. They themselves didn't like it so later *you* bring people through these experiences, *you* bring facts to bear on it to demonstrate what is going on and *you* build back *your* processes of getting people to internalize that; so occasionally *you* do actually go through processes of upsetting an institution, an organization, and then rebuilding it in a sense. I don't like the phrase the Americans coined, the phrase 're-engineering', I don't like the phrase. But there is something in that. One has got to accept that some of those changes are traumatic.

In this text the principal uses the pronoun 'you' in a series of phrases which suggest some kind of naturalized formulaic way in which people internalize a particular 'change'. But he also uses the term 'your processes'. This suggests that such methods are aimed at wresting control of people from other processes. The quotation thus highlights the hostilities involved but denies these through its insistence on the seemingly unproblematic method by which people can be 're-engineered'.

Yet such 're-engineering' is partial. Far from being reconstructed, many senior post-holders talked of simply coping with being 'caught in the middle'. In Tower College a section manager found this highly problematic: 'I find I'm constantly caught between supporting the staff and thanking them and encouraging them and then some memo comes around and it's like snakes and ladders, you are right back at the bottom again. I have them all worked up and then someone in SMT [senior management team] sends a thoughtless memo around and you are back on step one'. At the time of the interviews these memos frequently addressed issues surrounding the monitoring and 'appropriate' use of staff time. These can be read as the attempt to confine and intensify the work practices of lecturers. Yet the close and long history of relations between the section manager and lecturers problematized this attempt to reconstruct professional practices. The section manager said that the 'paper structure' of monitoring forms carried

> an assumption that everyone is a skiver; that is not the way that I would look at people. I can't understand that way of thinking at all. The

thinking is, 'If they are not here what are they up to?'; that kind of thinking, it's hard to articulate. The personal performance review is fine, but the annual leave and classroom time [is not], it's just the way it's tackled. I have not had a problem with self-directed time, it's from the top that time is not being used properly. I know my staff do hours of prep at home that have to be taken into account.

This clearly outlines the tensions and problems of actually managing. The section manager does not have a problem with self-directed time – senior management have. The section manager is required to work *with* the embedded practices of the professional locale, around these issues, while top-down management practices attempt to more intensively station academic workers with regard to self-directed time. This leads to senior post-holders 'bending' and tactically resisting certain stationing practices, like monitoring forms and staff hours.

A senior official in the lecturer's union NATFHE, interviewed during the study, argued that the FE college locales were particularly difficult to manage:

The FE lecturers are a particularly difficult group of people to manage. There is a strong tradition of independence and autonomy and they don't take kindly to being told what to do. And these other people who are on management spine [contracts] identify with that. You can get [the lecturers] on the contract [the employers' contracts], but to actually get them to do the things that you want them to do when you want them to do it is quite hard really.

As a result, she argued, the newly 'empowered' managers have only very limited 'success' in reconstructing locales, outside of redundancy and dismissal, and end up relying on the 'workhorses' of institutions:

They pile more and more stuff on those sorts of people who largely do things that you give them to do . . . but it doesn't help with groups of people that have always been quite difficult to manage and motivate, and to deal with if things go wrong. None of this is proving quite as easy as they might have thought at the excitement of incorporation, aside from the fact that they [the new 'managers'] were getting new posts and promotions.

The need to work with and transform locales was highlighted by a head of school at Urban College. The story he tells here is very reminiscent of that told by the dean of post-1992 Southern University. What makes it particularly interesting here is how he presents the locale as being undermined by the top-down pressures, in which he is implicated, but also presents himself as defending and seeking to maintain aspects of locales which are productive of work relations:

When I joined the college there were three people in the school who all joined on the same day 26 years ago. So the thing is, they have gone to each others' christenings, and they have all been at the same age and they have all gone through the same phases, so the sort of thing was maybe 15 years ago when it came to the summer holidays 3 caravans went away from here because they had all bought caravans because they had all got young families and went away to be together. And that was the level of family-ness if you like that existed and the bonds that existed. So when I came it was exceedingly difficult to be part of that, it took a while to become part of the family. What has happened is, I got into that family, and we've introduced a few traditions that seem as though they were working well. What we try is to close the school from 9–10 a.m. on a Friday morning. In practice it has never happened. There are always one or two missing. We have the school meeting, we're now into cups of coffee and mince pies, but what we're finding is that the workload of the new members of staff is so great they exist in isolation. We try to bring the lecturers into this little clique, so I don't want us and them, I regret that. It means that we are going to miss out on a wider team spirit. I now don't know of any of my crew that meets socially, which is sad . . .

'Family-ness' can be read off as the practices and knowledges of the locale. The head's comment 'introduced a few traditions' highlights the importance for 'managers' to work within the practices of the locales, and the importance of locales to the running of the school. In this case it meant retaining aspects of past meeting practices in the new 'team' meetings. The head also outlines how such locales are being undermined by those practices and knowledges that produce the increasingly intensified, isolated and individuated FE lecturer. Intriguingly at this point in the text he denies any involvement in this process of undermining. Yet the following comment shows explicitly how this new 'manager' is deeply implicated in producing the individuated, intensified FE worker, which appears out of the loss of familial locales. He suggests that there were 'people' who *needed* to be 're-structured out': those who were both expensive and unlikely to contribute to the new performance objectives – unfortunately the same objectives which produced the isolated lecturer:

Some people we do need to restructure out, there are still people within this part of the world who came into education 20 years ago, they spent their first year learning the job and preparing their prep and if they were really good they spent the second year refining it and for the last 18 years they have been delivering the same old rubbish. [CP: Whereas in the regime now you have to be constantly changing?] Absolutely. And those people tend to be not only sucking the money in that area but sucking it in other areas as well. 'My timetable finishes at five and at one minute past five I will be gone'. We do need to be shut of that mentality, but just because people have been on old contracts here doesn't mean to say that they can't take on board the new requirements of *our enterprise*. But we've had the old sledgehammer: if you are over 50 you can go if you want, and everybody has gone and it has left some gaping holes.

Yet while this suggests that the deeply embedded locales are being slowly destroyed by the combined aspects of redundancy, increased workload and intensified surveillance, I want to argue in the remainder of this chapter that new locales are constantly being produced. New knowledges and practices aimed at the power bloc which tactically evade its directives, or undermine its discursive force, are constantly under production. As Rose (1996a) and Fiske (1993) suggest, people are multiple and discursive resources and practices are constantly being turned from one set of interests to another. For example, the resources provided by the power bloc are constantly being turned to other ends. This takes multiple forms. It might for instance take the form of simply 'forgetting'.

The finance officer at Hillside College discussed 'forgetting' in relation to 'cost-consciousness':

> People now are probably much more concerned about cost, but it's going to take time. We have a lot of problems trying to instil this in people. Last year the principal had to step in and freeze budgets in some areas. It may not be the person's fault. Very often it's about communication, but they still need educating in how to manage their own budgets. The main problem is that they just don't seem to be able to understand finance or they don't want to know anything about it, they just want to get on with educating people, they are not worried about the cost. Some people are very good but others just seem to forget about it.

A number of programme coordinators at Hillside offered examples of how this 'forgetting' was put to work. One recounted how much of the material she received from her section manager in 'little brown files with our names' was ignored. At the interview she pointed to a wire tray on her desk overflowing with such files: 'I don't read it; it's a good job this is confidential, no, you can't, and a lot of it is bumf . . . Some things you know you have got to do. And other things you feel, well, you will put them to one side and if nobody asks you in three months, what's the point?' And another said at a meeting: 'I'm sure we've all got memos on our desks that have been there for months and every time we look at them we think I wonder how long it will be before I can shred it?'

The construction of locales – that is the construction of spaces, knowledges and practices which tactically challenge imperializing knowledges and practices – takes numerous forms. The following examples of two 'training events' show how the space and time provided by the power bloc for 'management training' was turned by section managers and programme coordinators at Hillside College into space for the critique and challenge of top-down management knowledges and practices – that is, the managerial station. The accounts can be usefully counterposed with the observational account of the section manager's meeting with her programme coordinators discussed at the end of Chapter 4. As a simple demonstration of how localizing and imperializing knowledges produce 'people' in different ways, the two events involve the same people. The section manager in the meeting discussed in Chapter 4 turns out here to be a vocal contributor to the construction of the locale in the section managers' meeting. The event, while ostensibly set up to transmit imperializing knowledges and practices to the section managers, was effectively subverted, and used as a site for working through the group's tactical relation to the senior managers. And yet in the meeting discussed at the end of Chapter 4, the section manager drew on and reproduced the managerial station in terms of the managerial identity she ascribed to herself, and the managerial relations enacted. This difference shows how it is not the people but the discursive practices involved in particular events which are of key importance. These come to dominate particular spaces, configuring them, in the terms used here, as either stations or locales. These carry with them embedded identities, relations and knowledges. The two accounts presented here, of two separate but similar meetings, illustrate the way stations and locales contest one another *through* people, rather than being contested by people as agents. The accounts are written as narratives from an observer's point of view. Analytical statements are inserted in this text where appropriate to draw out particular points that relate to the discussion of locales and the managerial station. The main reason for including these examples here is that they effectively illustrate the instability and partiality of the managerial station, and how locales, which celebrate horizontal individualized, rather than individuated identities, are constantly 'breaking out'.

Section managers' training event

The 'set': a large committee room in the main office block of an East Midlands further education college (Hillside College). At one end of the room in front of a large oval table surrounded with chairs stands the college's staff development officer (L). Beside her is an overhead projector pointed at a large white screen. To one side is a folder containing overhead transparencies inscribed with lists of bullet points. These address issues like 'objective setting' and 'performance management'. It is 1.40 p.m. The staff development officer is waiting for the college's six section managers (M, C, R, S, G and T). They are ten minutes late for 'class'.[1] The staff training officer uses this time to tell me about how she is currently in dispute with the college over pay and contracts. Her job has been scaled back and she has been offered another contract with reduced hours at a lower grade (this helps explain to some extent her somewhat ambivalent approach to the management training event she is about to 'run'). By 1.45 p.m. five of the six have arrived. It is clear that if the meeting had been with the curriculum director they would have all been there on time.

By being late the senior managers were in effect signalling their position *over* the staff development officer. But they were also signalling that this meeting was to be constructed not as a management training event, where they would be stationed as 'manager', but as a meeting where other sub-ordinated identities could be articulated and affirmed.

> The meeting: it emerged that the section managers had already taken control of the agenda. L had given the group some topic options for the event. The group had all chosen 'performance management'. Yet they were all very familiar with the college's performance management approach. They had thus engineered this space to talk about other issues.

Indeed, L struggled all afternoon to take some control of the session – that is, to station the group as managers. For instance, the group were constantly diverting the session's activities into other issues. Alongside this were interruptions, high-spirited comments, jokes and teasing. Her presentation became more like a break between bouts of engagement with only tangentially related issues. The jokes and teasing drew material from the college's strategic planning and funding processes, but also involved stories about the senior managers which undermined their positioning as authority figures. In general the management training event provided a space where the section managers reaffirmed their identities as middle managers tactically responding to senior managers and 'their' demands on them.

Locales, as Fiske (1993) argues, are often highly pleasurable spaces where humour, joviality, teasing and general companionship are used to unravel dominant identities and relations. Yet this does not mean that the locale under construction here was unstructured. There was an excess of structuring discursive practices at work. In part the pleasure of this locale is found in this multiplicity and the possibility of moving through a number of discursive practices. As might be expected, discursive practices associated with gender and sexuality also provided pleasurable moments in the meeting:

> When L put a bullet-point list on the overhead M said: 'All the women have started writing it down' (there were three female and three male section managers). 'It's a sex thing', she said. 'Don't you mean a gender thing?' said T. 'It's a sex thing', she repeated, drawing attention simultaneously to the men's lack of courtesy shown to L, and the women's 'automatic' response to the teaching situation. Yet it was the women who interrupted and interjected most during the event with examples and issues. It was they who tended to maintain control of the verbal space and managed the boundary between the locale and the station – that is, between a support meeting for section managers, and a training event. M particularly mediated movement between the locale and the station. Often as comments, jokes and stories subsided she would say to L 'go on'.
>
> Later in the meeting it emerged that two of the male and two of the female section managers worked closely together (S and T were the odd ones out of these 'couples'). Later in the meeting these two 'couples' wanted to display the joviality and warmth of these relationships, and

the way they used these to alleviate the top-down processes. C and G worked closely together and relied on each other. G said: 'When I get in in the morning I'm on the phone to C [and say] "Have you done this?", and she says, "Oh my God", and then I say, that's OK it's not due until next month' – raucous laughter. M and R meanwhile share a large office. They related a similar story of their apparent ambivalence to the 'paper' structure'. M said: 'I'll say [to R], have you got that piece of paper that Sylvia gave us three months ago? He goes rummaging through this pile of paper on his desk, no. Was it important?' More laughter.

However, while the section managers worked to maintain the space as a locale, this was always going to be a fragile, temporary construction. While they berated, criticized, joked about and on occasion praised the senior managers, the senior managers on two occasions exercised 'their' control by 'reaching into' the locale and repositioning the group as 'managers'.

The telephone in the room rang a couple of times for G. The second time it was his secretary with a message that the curriculum director wanted to see him. She was in fact sitting in her office which was just two rooms away from the committee room where the meeting was being held. G got up and rushed out. He came straight back for his suit jacket. Someone said jokingly 'It must be one of *those* meetings'. 'G, you not suitably attired?', another one said, mimicking the curriculum director's voice. G came back two minutes later. He looked across at one of the other section managers. 'C, you too, to see F [the principal]'. They both hurried out. They came back in about 15 minutes. G was carrying a huge piece of computer paper with lists and figures on it. Nothing was said about this event.

One possible reading as to why nothing was said about this would be that it would have disrupted the locale with the knowledges and practices of the managerial station. Being called out demonstrated the individuating managerial station, while the locale was concerned with common, horizontal and also diverse identities, and not simply that of the 'manager'.

A central point of discussion at this 'management training' event however was the meeting that morning with the college accountant, which all the section managers had attended. At this meeting the college accountant was said to have 'opened up the books' to them and run through their budgets in detail. There were, as one of the group said, a lot of 'bombshells' in the presentation. The section managers had not as yet had time to discuss the 'bombshells' with each other. Yet discussion focused not on 'their own' budgets but on the senior management team's salaries, and particularly the senior management team's 'personal' budgets. These budgets had apparently not been included in the accountant's figures and, it was assumed, had been 'hidden away' in 'reserves'. A copy of the accountant's budget statement was tabled by one of the group and they proceeded to dissect this, looking for places where the senior manager's personal budgets could be located. These budgets were thought to be £16,000 and £18,000 respectively for the curriculum director and principal. They also discussed money that had been 'borrowed' from their own budgets. 'You won't get that back', said one.

Here the discourse of the beneficiary manager (as discussed in Chapter 3, is drawn upon). The senior managers were read as self-interested beneficiaries of the Thatcherite power bloc. They were also read as the most highly rewarded, the most out of touch with the difficulties of actually managing the college, and also as seemingly duplicit in their relations with section managers.

The section managers read themselves in this as 'charged with earning the college income and meeting particular targets on units earned', as one said. The 'hiding' of personal budgets showed that senior managers were unwilling to subject themselves to the same oppressive surveillance mechanisms that the section managers had to endure. In the midst of this the section managers challenged the competence of the senior managers. They wondered for instance whether the finance director/accountant really understood the FE funding mechanism. M said: 'I find [the accountant] very hard to follow' – everyone laughed in agreement. 'He doesn't finish his sentences'.

Budgets, along with a discussion of the disciplining practices of strategic management processes became key elements of the discussion. The section managers had all submitted their strategic plans with detailed operating statements to the curriculum director a couple of weeks before. However they criticized the senior post-holders' work on these. They suggested that senior managers could afford to set 'woolly', 'motherhood' and 'apple-pie' targets, because they were not involved in actually translating them into work on the ground. The group also admitted to 'filling boxes' with 'made up' targets and objectives simply to make sure that each of the boxes was filled. In relation to the first point M said: 'Take for instance the objective to work towards a "modular curriculum"? What do they know about a modular curriculum? Have they ever taught on a modular curriculum? When was the last time they ever taught? It looked to them like something that would add up to more student choice, but it has to be weighed again the costs'.

Sylvia, the curriculum director, had read each of the section managers' plans and sent them back some with 'revisions' marked on them. For instance, R found that the 1997/8 date he'd set alongside some objectives had been changed to 1996/7. He questioned why he was working on strategic plans for the year they were clearly in. Again this highlighted how the surveillance worked to produce plans which were designed simply for audit processes, rather than having any direct relation to actual college programmes.

The senior managers were also criticized for simply not knowing how hard it was to get staff to engage with things like the 'strategic plan', or 'individual operational plans'. R mentioned the engineers in 'his' section. He described them as: 'Cynics through and through; after they hear what I want from them, they find all the problems with it and reasons why it would not work. I have to be prepared for all this'. M suggested that she thought now (December 1996) was totally the wrong time to take the strategic plan to the staff. 'They are tired and looking forward to the Christmas break. They are like a sponge that will not take any more water. They will just say, "Oh yeah we'll do it", and not do it', she said.

At another point in the meeting G attacked the audit culture. 'I just about have to write down something about everything that is said to me or I say to others, so that it can be used in evidence for this or that'. The pendulum had swung too far the other way, he said. 'We used to work on a professional trust basis; now it is all justification and evidence, and the amount of time that goes into it is ridiculous'. He asked the question: 'What are we in business for?', quite unconscious of the use of the word 'business'. M replied: 'We are in business so that we can still be in business this time next year'.

Right through the session, however, the figure of Sylvia was very present in their talk. At one point when her name was mentioned, G began to force his pad down the back of his trousers saying, 'It wasn't me, miss'. At another point someone said, as G spontaneously got up to leave, 'If Sylvia were here she'd have said "Where do you think you're going?"'

Sylvia was positioned as the authoritarian school mistress, who enforced deadlines and required justifications if these were missed. But another construction was also drawn on.

M and S, who had been curriculum coordinators under the old structure, played the 'old lags' and told stories that compared Sylvia's approach to the previous curriculum director's approach. 'She's much better than we've had and we get along with her' said one of the group. 'I'm not saying that she's not doing her job or that I don't like her'. M, who had just been critical of Sylvia, was forced into a return that checked open criticism. M went on: 'I find it very hard to say no to her; there are not many people that I find it hard to say no to, but she is one of them. Every time I go in [to her office to see her] with one thing, "Can you tell me about this?", I come out with four other things to do'. R said: 'She's a very strong woman'.

In the first comment from M, there are elements of the charismatic subject discussed in Chapter 5. 'Sylvia' in this statement has special persuasive abilities. It is unclear whether gender is implicated here. The previous curriculum director, a man, was criticized by the section managers for using section manager meetings simply to 'report what senior management were doing'. The college's reorganization (introduction of the taught hour plan, a more disciplined strategic planning process and the appointment of Sylvia as curriculum director with her tight control over meetings and reporting) overlaid, and was intertwined with, Sylvia's gender. At interview Sylvia largely denied gender as a basis for explaining her 'style'. Yet R's reading of Sylvia as a 'very strong woman', rather than say a 'very strong person', or 'a very strong manager', highlights the importance of gender to the reconstruction of managing in the college (see Chapter 8 for further discussion). However, the dominant narrative of the afternoon was one of being in the middle and 'done unto', rather than as the 'doer'. While the curriculum director was respected and constructed in the familiar and feminized position of 'class teacher', 'the senior managers', as a group, were constructed as out of touch, variably incompetent and somewhat deceitful. The section managers read themselves as caught between this and a tired, somewhat recalcitrant staff. Yet, as the following illustrates, this narrative of the locale was potentially problematic outside the confines of the reconstructed 'management training event':

> When I left the meeting, just before it wound up, G was standing in the corridor outside the curriculum director's office. He was leaning on a radiator, talking to the curriculum director's secretary. 'It's more like a therapy session in there', he said to me as I went past. I smiled back.

G's use of this term, 'therapy', can be said to illustrate a number of aspects about the meeting. It could be interpreted as a way of distancing himself from the meeting – saying in effect 'I'm outside because I don't need therapy'. It could also be read as a way of protecting himself, the section managers and even the college from unfavourable assessments by an outsider (me, the researcher).

To name the meeting as 'therapy' is a way of drawing a line or setting a frame around a 'thing', thus creating that object and creating an inside and an outside. Thus the meeting is constructed as different from the outside, which is normalized. This framing allows the meeting to be read in such a way that it does not challenge the normalized outside, but is subordinated to it. It thus reaffirms and protects the normalized identities of G himself, the section managers (as 'managers') and even the college itself.[2]

'Therapy' also carries with it the possibility of a positive and legitimate reading of the meeting. G was suggesting that while the meeting might have seemed extreme to an outsider (me, the researcher), it was a chance for section managers to go through a sanctioned, psychologically necessary process of getting things 'off their chests', which would then reaffirm the normal. Using the term 'therapy' can be read as implying that the meeting had a functional relation to the health of the college. 'Therapy' suggests a planned controlled approach to healing or the alleviation of distress. The term suggests that the section managers' meeting was planned and executed either by senior managers or the section managers themselves as a way of alleviating the problems and dilemmas of managing. That is one reading. It glosses the event with the functional aims of the power bloc, in other words.

Another reading, the one suggested here, is that the meeting is a locale, a space where the individuated managerial identity, produced by the knowledges and discursive practices of managing, is challenged and undermined temporarily and pleasurably, where other identities can be articulated. The locale can be read as therapeutic but in a political sense, not a functionalist, medical one.

The second event I want to discuss in terms of the managerial stations and locales in FE colleges is set in the same room two weeks later. This time it is the turn of ten of the college's 30 programme coordinators for 'management training'. Programme coordinators in Hillside College represent the new layer of management in the college, created just six months prior to this training event in a reorganization. In the reorganization the college was divided into six sections which each comprised up to six programme areas. Each programme coordinator was made responsible for up to ten full-time staff and part-timers assigned to the programme area. In exchange the programme coordinators were given a new job description, but not a new contract: three hours per week 'off' the normal full-time teaching load of 801 hours (down to 753 hours per year) and a flat £750 per year salary increase.

Programme coordinators' training event

Despite involving a different group of 'managers', this event was very similar to that described above. The presentation by L, the staff development officer, was different, but the response from the group was similar. Broadly, the 'management training event' aimed at stationing the programme coordinators as managers was reconstructed as a locale in which the knowledges and practices of 'management' were challenged, and professional identities, among others, articulated and reaffirmed. Another difference was that the ten programme coordinators who had opted for this event all arrived on time.

The event began with L asking the group of ten programme coordinators (PCs) to split into two groups and construct a collage of what it was like to be a PC: 'What the role was about'. The groups spent about 20 minutes cutting, pasting and drawing and then regrouped to look at the two posters. Both collages were thematically identical. The words and images depicted doom, lack of time, falling quality. The detail of this emerged when each group was asked to comment on the posters. It is worth mentioning that this was the first time that many of the PCs had met and discussed their jobs together as a group. What arose from this was a two and a half hour discussion of a number of key issues. First, and centrally, all claimed that the three hours allotted to them to carry out their PC duties was grossly insufficient. This led to statements like: 'I'm either incompetent or the job is impossible', as one woman said. Others mentioned feelings of not wanting to come to work, not wanting to turn up on particular days (especially those days on which sections met, at which more work was unloaded on them by section managers). There was a tense moment immediately after the female PC said: 'I'm either incompetent or the job is impossible' when one of the very outspoken men in the group responded: 'It's probably both'. But neither speaker took this further and the group pursued the narrative of the 'impossible' job. It was 'impossible' principally because of lack of time, the PCs said. This lack of time, however, varied. Some of the PCs were acting as course team leaders, and personal tutors, while others were not.

It is worth noting here how the imposition of managerial knowledges and practices had the effect of questioning just what identity was to be articulated at work. The terms 'incompetent' or 'impossible' were used to articulate feelings of being between two identities, one professional and largely satisfying, the other managerial and oppressive. A second aspect, hinted at in the tension of the response to the 'incompetent/impossible' remark, was that the meeting was highly gendered. The men dominated the verbal space in a way quite unlike the section managers' meeting described above. The group was made up of six women and four men. Three men, S, J and B, were particularly dominating of the conversation while the women, particularly the group of middle-aged women from the business services section, made significantly less input. The women were, indeed, implicitly discouraged from speaking. Their comments were frequently left undeveloped, while the men 'egged' one another on, and in the process dominated the verbal space. The 'training session', however, was quite literally displaced. L went with this and tried to formulate what she termed 'achievable objectives' from the meeting. She suggested that the programme coordinators' concerns be codified and put to senior managers. In effect, she tried to translate the meeting into management discourse. However the group's discussion tended to 'stumble' over this and would quickly return to spirited discussion of the problems themselves. One response was put repeatedly: that a full meeting of programme coordinators, section managers and the curriculum director be held 'soon' to thrash out the 'role of the programme coordinator'. But this suggestion was not developed or taken forward. The meeting returned repeatedly to a number of core problems/issues:

> There were repeated calls for 'someone to define the [PC's] role', or to 'create a structure'. In general the meeting worked at constructing the position of the PC who had been 'conned' into a post that had turned out to be 'impossible'. PCs were required to run and organize courses, deal with paper systems and were said to be distrusted by senior managers who were never seen in person. But the biggest issue was that they did this while teaching just three hours short of a full timetable.

A key issue was excessive paperwork. This took PCs away from their teaching which, as a consequence, suffered. 'We are constantly pinching time from teaching to feed the paper system', said one. 'This paper system is leading to the demise of quality. Would you deliberately allow quality to slip on courses so that the students think they are rubbish and leave?' one asked. 'You wouldn't, you would continually improve them or work at doing things differently'. Another said: 'SMT [senior management team] need to know about this because the quality is slipping and the students are going to walk'. 'Things are at breaking point', said another. 'If you put this to senior managers they will say this is how it is in FE now', said another in response.

This was related to the college's drive for increased activity and reduced staff numbers. 'Eventually you reach a point where the thing collapses, the students realize what is going on and they walk, you can't meet your strategic plan targets and the whole thing collapses'. 'Staff are beginning to leave, students are beginning to catch on – if you take 20 minutes here and 20 minutes there, the quality of staff/student relations is going down'.

A number of PCs said they felt the squeeze on their time personally as the professional relations with students suffered. One said: 'I'm always two minutes late for everything. I go into a class, set them a task then I go out again to organize the photocopying for later in the session. In the past I would have been able to go around the class, chat to them and find out how they were getting on. And then there's always the telephone. You start to do something and then someone rings up from examinations or whatever and that's half an hour gone'. The 'paperwork' was frequently counterposed with the sanctuary of teaching: 'I don't think it's moaning, it's just the admin, not the teaching, I go into a teaching room and it's a sanctuary, and come out refreshed', said one. Another said: 'Just teaching is really refreshing, I come out of a class and think that was good, that's what I like doing, but after half a day of paperwork where I don't make any headway I go home frustrated, and don't want to come back the next day to more of the same. I feel sometimes that there has got to be more to life. I don't feel like coming to work, I don't enjoy it any more'.

One aspect frequently mentioned was the collecting of statistics on teaching, staffing and classes. It was unclear, the PCs said, whether these were 'really' needed to keep the college going. In some cases the PCs resented this because it led to strained relations with teaching colleagues in their curriculum areas. One said: 'I was in a meeting with my team the other day, there was an agenda but I said that there were things that I needed to deal with; I came out with form after form after form and someone said: "What is all this shit? Can't we get back to talking about students and progression?"'.

It was clear, however, that the PCs were not blindly following up all these requests for information and action via paper-based systems. They were prioritizing some and finding ways around others. 'I'm sure we've all got memos on our desks that have been there for months and every time we look at them we think I wonder how long it will be before I can shred it?' one said. 'Everything seems to be urgent and a priority, but it's not clear what is a priority'. It was the repetition of demands for the same information that infuriated some. 'We're also doing all this doubling up. Why should I fill in these absence forms? If I want to find out I ring up personnel and they tell me who's been absent. I even wanted to find out when I was absent so I rang up personnel and they told me which day it was' – laughter.

It was this that led the discussion to address the possibility of action: 'What we need to do is to decide what we [as a group] are going to do and what we are not going to do. Has anyone ever been pulled up before a disciplinary hearing for not doing the paperwork?' said one.

Yet despite these problems, two in the group highlighted the 'positives of the post'. In one case this was clearly at the expense of professional colleagues: 'I'd rather be in a position of having some control rather than have the shit always dumped on me'.

The above is an account of some of the key elements discussed at what was ostensibly to be a 'management training event' for new managers at Hillside College. In summary it, along with the account of the section managers' meeting, shows how locales which variably contest the managerial station are constantly at work in colleges. As in this case, they frequently take up the resources provided by the power bloc, turning management training, for instance, into a mutual support session and a critique of management. The imperializing knowledges are thus temporarily turned back on themselves, and the identities they produce are problematized while those identities, relations and knowledges subordinated by the imperializing formations are reaffirmed. The programme coordinators reaffirmed their subordinated identities as lecturers.

Yet despite these events, the knowledges and practices of the locale only briefly and temporarily hold the space available. In the meetings there was reluctance to take these knowledges outside the space in any coordinated way. The locales are fragile structures, which might be said to simply support the tactical response of senior post-holders to top-down pressures, but are generally subordinated to these. Yet this might not necessarily be the case. It is possible to identify ways in which such 'fragile structures' might come to take up dominant imperializing positions themselves. However, in the cases above, this seems unlikely given the dependence of the college on state funding and the suffusion of managerial stationing knowledges and practices at work in dispensing such funds.

Out across the college meanwhile the sentiments of the above locales are weakened and displaced by the pragmatics of compliance with the practices. This induces, as the following quotation shows, a sense of ambivalence and detachment. The following piece of dialogue is between myself, the researcher, and a newly-positioned 'manager', a programme coordinator, at Hillside College. It illustrates particularly how our multiplicity and fragmentation, inherent in our ability to live and work with different identities and relations, both provide the conditions by which locales can be produced and survive (thus underwriting points of contention and challenge to imperializing knowledge – those spaces where imperializing knowledge becomes slow moving and 'stodgy'), and also underwrite the suffusion of dominant practices and knowledges themselves. When we are confronted with the contradictions between the various positions we take up, however, one solution is to label our condition, as the speaker below does, as 'ambivalence'. This of course confirms a condition of multiplicity. Of course it may be that the 'interview' setting is one of the few where we might confront the contradictions between the different positions we take up. In other words, it is the interview process itself which works as a power–knowledge strategy to produce a coherent 'I', which in the normalized fragmentation of work we are seldom asked to produce or confront. As a final point in this chapter, I want to show through this quotation how it is *not* people that are at work, but discursive practices in the problematic suffusion of particular forms of knowledge – especially managerial knowledge in this case:

> CP: How do you match up these two aspects? On the one hand you identify with the teachers and the problems of the increased control over their work, and on the other you are engaged in keeping that control going.

> I guess it's just ambivalence [he said with a shrug]. There is a sort of ambivalence; on the one hand *I can see how they control my time. I spend more time filling in forms than I do actually teaching.* But then from a programme coordinator's position, people have signed a contract which says that they will do such and such and these forms are a significant way of following that through.

This senior post-holder's knowledge about himself (identity) and the teachers in the programme area (relations), and his use of time and space (the station), are constituted through the practices embedded in the 'forms'. His comment suggests an awareness of how, through this, 'they' (and by this he means the senior managers, but I might suggest the power bloc) come to constitute 'their' interests through control over 'his' time. In effect the programme coordinator is saying: 'I can see how they control my time; it's my time but they control it'. In this implied comment, the programme coordinator constructs himself as largely powerless to do otherwise. The pedagogical and professionally-orientated knowledges and practices which were drawn on to rebuff managerial knowledge at the programme coordinators' training event were unavailable as the managerial knowledge practices of form-filling and adherence to the new lecturer's contracts took their place. Comments such as the 'paper system is leading to a demise of quality', and the suggestion that programme coordinators should deliberately and as a group refrain from 'feeding the paper system' were not translated into this particular programme coordinator's work.

Yet this is not to suggest that currently subversive practice, such as ignoring paperwork or forgetting forms that need to be filled in, will not form the basis of alternative procedures at some future time. The section managers noted above that they were currently struggling to get programme coordinators to produce strategic planning document returns. In future the programme coordinators as a group may put their question, 'Has anyone ever been pulled up before a disciplinary hearing for not doing the paperwork?' to the test. Through this the rigidity of the managerial station will be challenged by the reinvigorated knowledges and practices whose identities the stationing processes have subordinated.

To conclude, this discussion has shown how 'managing' is far from smooth and productive. College 'management' is at its most simplified the distribution, completion and return of particular 'forms', through which bodies are stationed in time and space. Yet even this is a problematic and uncertain process which is confronted and challenged by other forms of knowledge and practice. What is involved is a constant state of 'hostilities', not, as management discourse so often suggests, in relation to intransigent people, but in relation to the multiple and fragmented elements of embedded knowledge and practice.

Notes

1. Access to this meeting was organized through the staff development officer. At this point in the research programme I had already interviewed three of the section managers. They were happy for me to sit in on the meeting, my having already established a degree of trust with them. This reassured the other three section managers, although C quizzed me on whether I would be reporting back to senior managers prior to the arrival of the three whom I had already interviewed. I tried to reassure her over this. She did not mention it again. Perhaps she noted the familiarity with which I was greeted by the three section managers I had already interviewed.
2. As I mentioned, some of the section managers were a little unsure about my presence. While this uncertainty subsided, I still represented a possible threat to the locale. Despite my assurance to the contrary, I may have been about to make a report on the meeting to senior managers.

8

Man-aging or Wo-managing Colleges?

Is your University sufficiently like a further education college to win Government approval? **Teachers 'R' Us plc**, one of the leading providers of high-class teaching staff to the further education sector, is proud to offer ten key ways in which you can immediately set about effecting that transformation . . . Sack your present male Vice-Chancellor and replace him with a female principal.

(Taylor, 1998c: 56)

The discussion in the preceding chapter highlights how professionalized and traditional academic and administrative identities embedded in knowledges and practices which construct academic and administrative locales can be said to be engaged in a 'state of hostilities' with ascendant managerial identities. Managerial identities are embedded in and dispersed by imperializing knowledges and practices which attempt to construct managerial stations across the terrain of FHE.

Alongside this, the discussion has touched briefly on some more deeply embedded aspects of this 'state of hostilities'. While there are a number of 'axes of difference' (Fiske, 1993) which inform the construction of locales and stations in relation to FHE management, such as ethnicity (Davidson, 1997; Page, 1997) and disability, it is the issue of gender in relation to management in colleges and universities that I wish to address here. The key reason for making this move is that gender difference is a core factor in the 'doing of managing' (Mangham and Pye, 1991) in universities and colleges.

For example, when City University is described by a male head of department as a very '*man-managed*' institution with 'tough males running the place'; or when committee meetings at Southern University are described by the academic registrar as spaces men use to 'make statements about their own power'; or when the principal of Tower College is described by the college personnel officer as a 'brave man'; or when the curriculum director of Hillside College is described by a section manager as a 'strong woman', it is clear that gendered practices and management practices are deeply interdependent. Furthermore, current academic debate around the character of management, and education management in particular, makes it imperative that the problematic interconnections between gendered identities, relations and knowledges, and management knowledges and practices be explored (Blackmore, 1993, 1996; Ozga, 1993; Brodeth, 1995; Maile, 1995; Hall, 1997; Whitehead, 1997a).

As the review of this field in Chapter 1 indicated there is now a reasonably coherent body of work which addresses the gendered nature of HE institutions, particularly the gendered distribution of work in these sites (recent examples include Brooks, 1997; Clark *et al.*, 1997; Heward *et al.*, 1997). Following the trajectory developed in Chapter 2 and used to frame discussion in the last five chapters I adopt a poststructural approach to exploring the interconnections between the identities, relations and practices of gender (Weedon, 1987; Butler, 1990b; Flax, 1995; Calas and Smircich, 1996; Knights, 1997) and those of management.

Poststructuralism and gender: a brief overview

Before outlining how such a reading can be achieved using the analytical terms 'station' and 'locale', I need to briefly offer a poststructural reading of gender. This identifies that difference between men and women is not located in or reducible to biological sex. A poststructural account is concerned with how various knowledges and practices make biological sex *socially* significant. Put simply, gender is understood as various sets of practices and knowledges which constitute and ascribe male and female bodies as 'men' or 'women'. Gender, in this reading, is neither invariant nor interior to such bodies, but is performed through culturally and historically specific discourses (Butler, 1990a: 339). As Butler notes, gender is a series of 'acts' which 'create the idea of gender' (1990b: 140). Gender then, in this reading, is not 'natural' but the effect of differing sets of practices and knowledges which can be said to have histories of their own. Thus at any one time or in any particular space, 'to do one's gender right', as Butler (1990b: 140) argues, is a cultural and political production which works to 'humanize' individuals in that particular social context.

Such 'humanizing' processes are not simply productive, but are at the same time regulatory and political. Ann Game (1994) highlights the political character of gender in relation to management and HE when she recounts how, when she took up the position of head of her academic department she became aware of attempts to place her in feminine subject positions – for instance, as a 'secretary who cleans up the academic mess' (p. 48). She suggests that while 'father' and 'manager' are perhaps the dominant alliance, such feminine positionings as 'mother' are also likely to 'go quite smoothly in management' in work organizations (p. 48). This is discussed below. However, as Game notes, to refuse the position of 'mother' is 'unsettling: for many men, and I suspect for some women' (p. 49).

To refuse highly gendered positions, such as 'mother', is risking being excluded or challenged. Alternatively, in other sites bodies performing gendered practices which were previously excluded may be drawn in and put to work in the construction of particular stations. It is the tensions and problems that surround the drawing of the localizing practices of the feminine into managerial stations in FHE, at a time of major reconstruction, that are the subject of this chapter.

Gendered work organizations: gendered locales and stations

Work organizations draw on and reproduce dominant ways of 'doing men' and 'doing women'. The dominance of men in management posts can be said to be an effect of the alliance between dominant ways of 'doing men' and imperializing knowledges, particularly scientific knowledges. Traditionally, managerial stations have been produced as masculine by what Cockburn (1991), drawing on Pateman's (1988) analysis, describes as a 'fratriarchal compact' between men over women in work organizations.

Cockburn suggests that in detail this is accomplished through two strategies: women's work is partitioned off from, and awarded lower value than, men's work and where women achieve senior positions they supervise other women, or their executive management role is identified with the 'feminine' aspects of the organization's work, such as personnel management. One effect of this, as Coleman's study shows, is that women frequently experience themselves as being 'different' in their organizations from the prevailing male norm (1991: 47).

But this is not necessarily the case, and, as I argue below, the reconstruction of universities and colleges has challenged some of the fratriarchal practices which conspire to produce the managerial station as masculine, or done by men, who adopt particular ways of being 'men' (Collinson and Hearn, 1994). I want to suggest that as new management knowledges and practices have been introduced (those which require more intensified and competitive responses), the fratriarchal compact, articulated as it has been through a paternalistic masculinity (Collinson and Hearn, 1994), has been challenged. In part it has been replaced, as Whitehead (1996b) argues in relation to FE, by a form of masculinity which emphasizes competitive, instrumental and rationalistic knowledges and practices. However, I want to suggest that the practices and knowledges of the feminine locale, traditionally subordinate to the managerial station, have also been drawn in both as a way of challenging the fratriarchal practices, and as a way of strengthening imperializing management knowledges and practices as these seek to construct stations. The argument here is that relations between localizing and imperializing knowledges and practices are not necessarily antagonistic. As Fiske suggests, localized practices which enlarge workers' terrain of control in the workplace may, at times, be complicit with corporate aims (1993: 81). Thus, the highly gendered practices and knowledges which have traditionally been drawn upon to resist dominant masculinities may at different points and in different circumstances be drawn upon to both challenge traditional managerial knowledges and practices and to increase the control and dispersal of managerial stations.

Front-runners and 'people' persons: conflict, reconstruction and women managers in colleges

Drawing on empirical material from four colleges in this chapter (and four universities in the following chapter), I want to explore what seem to be two particular issues in the relations between gendered locales and dominant masculine stations. The first involves the repositioning of women in highly masculinized social spaces as part of the distribution and dispersal of the managerial station. The second involves the problems and tensions that surround the positions of 'woman' and 'manager'.

The first issue has been highlighted by Yeatman (1995) in relation to HE management when she argues that women's relative outsider positioning – their lack of loyalty to the 'established ways of doing things' – means that they 'become highly valued managers for change in a new environment' (1995: 201). Thus the feminized dispositions that women bring may challenge the deeply embedded fratriarchal compact of masculine identities, relations and embodied practices which make up organizational sites. Yeatman suggests, drawing on her research of the 'femocrats' of the Australian public sector, and her experiences at Waikato University in New Zealand, that women are likely to be used by established male élites as 'front runners' in attempts to change these organizations, to call attention to 'all the fustian, patriarchal inefficiencies of the old institutional culture' (1995: 200). Yeatman argues that in the contemporary managerialist, competitive, results-based environment, which is ascendant in contemporary FHE, opportunities are and have opened up for women to take up these change-agent positions in education management. Men, of course, are not simply defending their traditional privileges, but, as Yeatman outlines, 'their fratriarchal loyalties [lead] them to deny how entrenched the sexual contract is in organizations' (1995: 204).

It is this aspect of 'loyalty' to the élite men and to the new FE which has been a significant aspect of the recruitment of more women into senior posts. In the four colleges in the sample there had been significant recruitment of women to senior positions following incorporation. City College had recruited a woman principal who in turn had been instrumental in appointing a number of women in senior curriculum and service areas. The new principal at Tower College had positioned two women in the two vice-principal posts. At Hillside College 'Sylvia' had been appointed as curriculum director as part of a restructuring exercise, and three of the six new heads of section were women. At Urban College four of the seven heads of school were women. To explore these issue further I shall draw below on material from Hillside College.

Wo-man aging FE at Hillside College

The case of 'Big Sylvia', as she was colloquially known at Hillside College, offers perhaps a 'successful' example of the way women have been drawn into senior posts in FHE to challenge and overturn not just traditional knowledges and practices but also the gendered knowledges and practices which support them.

In April 1996 Hillside finalized a major restructuring programme. As noted in Chapter 7, 30 programme coordinator positions were created in this restructuring. The job descriptions for these posts made the post-holders responsible to six section managers. These managers were in turn contracted as responsible to the new curriculum director. Prior to this the previous 'structure' had contained 12 programme coordinators, responsible to one male curriculum director. One of the new section managers described the former group as riven with factions: 'As long as this continued to exist we would not be going forward', he said. The former curriculum director was understood to be unable to coordinate this group. A faction, in the terms used here, would be a locale. The identities, practices and knowledges of these factions or locales would likely preclude 'going forward', as the section manager suggested. 'Going forward' here means increasing efficiency and reducing costs.

'Big Sylvia' had a reputation for being keenly efficient, 'impatient with time-wasters' and opposed to 'talking shop'. 'Sylvia's' positioning as curriculum director, and the depth of the reorganization into a more hierarchical 'structure' meant she did not have to face or directly challenge localizing powers in the way that the director of planning at Harbourside University was required to do. 'Sylvia' is a white middle-class woman in her late forties who has a long history of work as a teacher in the college, but also in recent times experience as a senior post-holder in charge of access and student recruitment.

Like Ainley and Bailey's description of the 'old FE' management as being a 'perpetual war of the roses' (1997: 40–1) between feudal barons, 'Sylvia' described the 'old FE management model' as 'all drawbridge and defences':

> It was a complete waste of time, as it neglected the client and the strategic direction. In terms of the old FE we had four people [senior post-holders at curriculum director 'level'] all doing their own thing, four different styles. It was difficult to move things in any timescale. It took three years to do anything and get it into action.

She suggested that one of the reasons why the new section managers worked well together (see 'Section managers' training event' in Chapter 7) was that they 'understood that this was the 'new FE', and they were not about spending time defending the 'old FE'. It has been agreed that the meetings [weekly section managers' meetings with the curriculum director] are about problem-solving, not whinging'.

Interestingly, when she was asked about the differences between her approach and that of the three other curriculum heads (all men) whose jobs had been collapsed into one (her new job) at the April restructuring, she said the key difference was that she was a 'people person': 'First and foremost it's about increasing the confidence and self-esteem of people.

I'm constantly working at valuing people, recognizing people's different contributions and getting on well with the team. If you haven't got your people behind you, you are not going anywhere'.

As is clear, the college's reorganization led to a significant change in personnel in senior posts. It shed a number of men from the middle manager positions and positioned a single woman, 'Sylvia', in place of this group. It also drew in four new section managers (two women and two men) to form the new section managers' group of 6 which replaced the larger and more factional programme coordinators' group of 12. A more hierarchical pyramid replaced a matrix pattern, in other words. Also, the selection of the new section managers appears to have been on the grounds of their loyalty to the 'new FE'. Alongside all this, of course, were the newly-invigorated strategic planning and monitoring practices, which 'Sylvia' was substantially responsible for dispersing across the college. It was clear from the interview with her that she was particularly engaged with these:

> The taught hour plan allows two aspects of the job – curriculum and resources – to be given to staff. Staff know where they stand. In the old system there was a lot of slippage between available hours and total hours used. We wanted to make that part of the normal activities of programme coordinators and section managers. The aim is to get optimal performance, so that I can report to senior management team the difference between hours used and hours available. Obviously I'd like there to be no difference.

In sum, this shows that 'Sylvia' was deeply involved in dispersing and elaborating the managerial station across the college. She and the section managers were effectively stationed by these practices and knowledges and the surveillance embedded in the senior management team's reporting process. Thus it would be a mistake to overplay the importance of the particular discursive practices of being a 'people person' which the curriculum director said she had brought to her work in her new post. However, her identity as a 'people person' is clearly part of both the significant restructuring and the newly-intensified 'paper structure'. Compliance with the 'paper structure' was clearly enhanced by those discursive practices 'Sylvia' identified as including 'constantly valuing people' and 'increasing the confidence and self-esteem of people'. This was confirmed by the story M told at the section managers' training event: 'I find it very hard to say no to her; there are not many people that I find it hard to say no to, but she is one of them. Every time I go in [to her office to see her] with one thing, "Can you tell me about this?", I come out with four other things to do'. This story attributes assertiveness and strength of character to M and *greater* assertiveness to 'Sylvia'. It also identifies 'her' as a tactically skilled 'manager' of people. It is here that the knowledges and practices of feminized locales, I want to argue, are being drawn into managing (at some cost, as discussed below). Of course, these practices are not simply attributable to women, but such practices are often highly prized elements in women's locales (Ferguson,

1994). The ability to establish mutual, cooperative, broadly equalized relations while at the same time being able to get people to 'come out with four other things to do' is illustrative of this. It is instructive here that at the section managers' meeting R read 'Sylvia' not as a skilled tactical 'people person', a valued aspect of women's localizing processes, but as a 'strong woman' – that is, as masculinized and able to hold her own with men.

Again, it would be a mistake to overplay the tactical discursive practices which 'Sylvia' drew upon, and which I would argue are drawn from feminized locales both inside and outside the college. The importance of these is interdependent with the restructured college *and* the intensified 'paper structure'. This latter aspect shifts the emphasis away from the embodied 'manager' and embeds the 'manager' in the demands and requirements of, for instance, the spreadsheet technologies of taught hour plans, staff hour plans, budgets and audits.[1] As 'Sylvia' herself noted, 'the taught hour plan allows two aspects of the job – curriculum and resources – to be given back to staff'. What she leaves out is that when control over curriculum and resources is 'given', as she puts it, 'back to the staff', it comes framed, embedded and largely locked into a raft of guides for action, prompts and requirements, all of which are, to a large extent, monitored from the desk of the curriculum director or accountant. As Fiske (1993) suggests, the control may have been given back, but the knowledges and practices which constitute the 'staff' and the 'manager' to whom it is given back are very closely defined and controlled.

Such 'front runners' or 'wo-managers' (as Deem and Ozga 1996 describe them) at second-tier posts in FE colleges are in part made visible because they are set against a background of highly masculinized or remasculinizing management (Whitehead, 1996b; Stott and Lawson, 1997; Leonard, 1998). Yet as the next section outlines this should be linked to a broad 'feminization' of particularly subordinate third- and fourth-tier 'management' positions. What this suggests is that 'managerial work' (the responsibility for bearing down on teaching and administrative labour in the face of stringent nationalized control) is 'falling to' and being 'taken up' by women.

Managing colleges: is it still really men's work?

> Women are being used in this climate as managers in Further Education, that is something I would like to say. Quite a few women senior managers are being used to bulldoze the terrible changes because they're desperate to get on and they've never been offered promotion before, and because you don't recognise a poisoned chalice when it's offered to you.
>
> (Prichard *et al.*, 1998)

FE colleges, as the previous chapters have outlined, have been engaged in a broad reconstruction principally through the suffusion of the managerial station. This station is centred on new funding, planning and audit methods which articulate the state's pressure to 'do more for less'. This suffusion has the effect of positioning senior post-holders in colleges as responsible for the problematic process of increasing the level of education activity while funds to support such increases have been progressively reduced. One response to this is that the gendered character of FE colleges has shifted from an environment marked by 'gentlemanly paternalism' (Whitehead, 1997b) to one punctuated by an aggressive, competitive masculinity. Whitehead (1996b: 165) argues that FE management 'has become a more masculinized work environment' (see also Kerfoot and Whitehead, 1995; Whitehead, 1996a, 1997a, 1997b) where the positioning of men as 'managers' in a more in-secure and competitive work environment reinforces and validates men's sense of having to know themselves and become more competitive and instrumental 'men'. However, material from the four colleges in this sample and survey data from the Further Education Development Agency's (FEDA) flagship management training needs survey suggest that an equally present and inevitably interdependent process, that could be read as the possible feminization of management in FE, is under way.

The example of 'Sylvia' precisely illustrates this. Women's previous out-sider position in pre-incorporation linkages between management and masculinities potentially provides a breach through which positions in the 'new further education' (a term Sylvia herself used) management can be achieved. Data on men and women in senior college posts support this account.

In 1990, Department for Education figures reported just 13 female FE college principals compared with 394 men (Department for Education, 1994). By 1995, however, there were 63 female FE college principals (L. Ward, 1995) in a sector of 452 colleges – one in seven headed by a woman (Utley, 1994a, 1994b; L. Ward, 1995; Stott and Lawson, 1997). The dramatic shedding of principals through early retirement since 1993 (Ward, 1996) (more than a third) has opened up posts for women. Figures published by the FEFC in 1996 noted that one fifth of principalships were going to female candidates (Ward, 1996).

Yet more dramatic recruitment is occurring in the much expanded, first-line or third- and fourth-tier management posts. The FEDA's management training needs survey (Brownlow, 1997), which sampled more than 3000 'managers' in 250 of the 452 FE colleges in England and Wales (see Figs 8.1 and 8.2), found that women have taken up a significant number of these new management posts in colleges.

The bars in Fig. 8.1 show that men continue to hold disproportionately more of the 'very' senior posts in the survey colleges (which was more than half of all FE colleges). Women make up just 18 per cent of principals – 17 per cent across the whole sector (L. Ward, 1995, 1996; Stott and Lawson, 1997) – and 34 per cent of second-tier managers (assistant/deputy prin-cipals). However, in third-tier posts (section and department heads), 42 per cent of post-holders are women, and at the fourth-tier (programme coordin-

Figure 8.1 Males and females in management posts in UK FE colleges

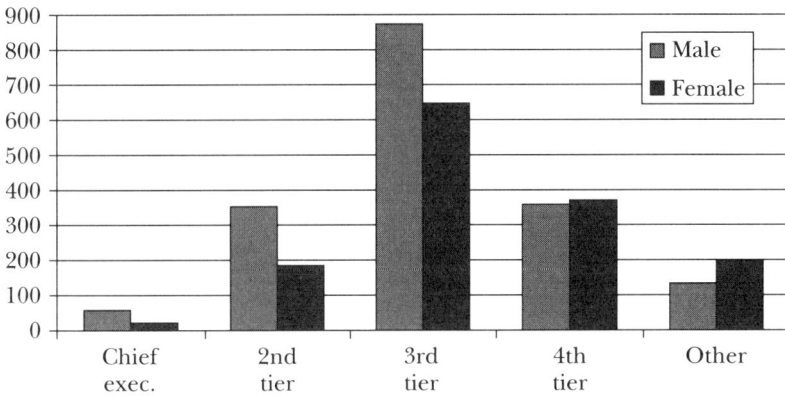

Source: FEDA, 1997

Figure 8.2 Number of years in management posts (*x*-axis) by male and female in UK FE colleges from a survey of 250 colleges

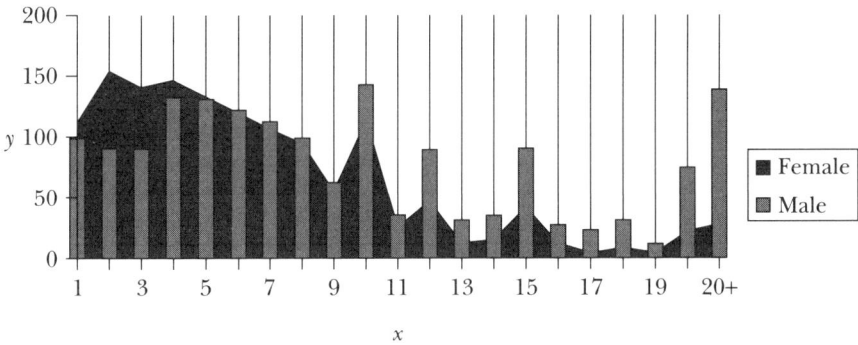

Source: FEDA, 1997

ators) women outnumber men, with just over half of these posts held by women (51 per cent). In total, women made up 44 per cent of managerial post-holders. However if this distribution is then laid against survey data that report the number of years in 'management posts', the survey shows a significant recruitment of women to management posts in FE over the last three years (Fig. 8.2).

In the survey, 554 women had been in a management post for four or fewer years compared with 410 men. In Fig. 8.2 the shaded area behind the bars shows the significant recruitment of women to such posts. Of course the validity of the survey results can be questioned. The agency relied on colleges to select respondents and it may be that women are more likely to become, or be selected as, respondents. Mick Fletcher, FEDA's head of training, commenting on the FEDA survey, said it showed that 'women are more heavily represented than men, in younger age groups and levels of management, and [are] more recent recruits to management posts'.[2]

This feminization is far from a coincidence. It provides a rich and elaborate example of the complex interdependence of connections between the knowledges and practices of gender and the managerialization of the public sector generally (Newman, 1994; Itzin and Newman, 1995) and public sector post-compulsory education specifically (Morley and Walsh, 1995; Deem and Ozga, 1996; Prichard, 1996b).

Of course it is at the post of 'programme manager' (where more women are now positioned) that the new demands on the sector are being translated, articulated and experienced. In particular, it is at this interface where the new disciplines of the FEFC in terms of funding, planning and auditing are engaged in attempting to 'reach in' and reconstruct the teaching and learning spaces of FE colleges. Thus it is at this interface that the complex patterns of embedded, localized practices and knowledges are being progressively challenged by the commodifying, standardizing, intensifying and deskilling processes that are potential outcomes of new top-down knowledges and practices. It is at this interface that the prolonged conflict over new lecturers' contracts has also been most keenly felt. Thus the 'feminization' of 'management' posts, significantly at 'first-line management' in FE, has a number of dynamic and elaborate characteristics. The following extracts from interviews with women in such positions highlight some of these characteristics. These texts elaborate something of how the problematic positioning of 'woman manager', at the interface between the top-down practices and the locales of colleges is articulated and thus experienced.

The female head of school from Urban College made the following comments: 'It really is more exciting now than it use to be because there is more chance of innovation and enterprise, whereas before, funded by the LEA, they just sort of went along . . . I feel it is more exciting being a manager than it was three years ago. I don't think I could go back to teaching to be quite honest'.

Here the head of school draws on the ever-present discourses of enterprise and innovation (du Gay, 1994) to articulate her new relations to the college and herself. Yet she also highlights how this development of the 'manager' involves problematizing relations and identities embedded in the deeply feminized locales of colleges. What appears to occur is that 'she' is required to take up more masculinized relations and identities, as 'she' is stationed by managerial knowledges and practices. This is articulated below in the shift from 'mothering' the staff to 'giving them the ability to think for themselves'. Being stationed as a manager induced her to rewrite what might be regarded as previously intimate and locally negotiated relations as unhealthy dependency and the 'mothering' of teaching staff:

I can remember going through with the change of contracts . . . I was anti, and lots of the staff were as well. It was fine if I was in control

of the management of my staff. It [was] open-ended if you like. I felt
that was fine as long as I could negotiate with my staff what we were
going to do, that was OK. But I always felt that that could come from
above; that they would put constraints on me; that I would have to say
to my staff, 'look I'm sorry I can't do that'. So I argued against the
contracts to start off with and it was put to me quite firmly [that I
should change my view] . . . but then you appreciate the need to do
this. I guess the explanation of it wasn't clear enough at the beginning.
I tried to not take it back to the school. I didn't want them to be
anti, because they were extremely cooperative and supportive, very
caring, too caring to the students, because we were in an annexe.
Because it was predominantly female it was [a] very very secure environment. I tended to coax them along. I didn't want them to feel
anything against the college. I did keep a lot from them and try and
protect them if you like and that wasn't good for them, because they
saw me then as the one to come to at all times. So I didn't give them
the ability to think for themselves, if you like, which is what I should
have done, it wasn't good for them and it wasn't good for me. We had
an excellent inspection report and the inspector said what a very nice
environment it was, how caring everybody was, and I never wanted to
take that away. Inevitably the times have changed and they had to
move on, and they are. I think they had a bad year last year. I wasn't
there for them to knock on the door because the person that took over
gave them the responsibility themselves. And of course I realized then
that I had not given them the space and had probably mothered them
too much. I feel that to a certain extent that was right at first; they
needed protecting.

This suggests that prior to the change of contracts, teaching duties, hours
and responsibilities were locally negotiated and subject to the localized
conditions of a highly feminized locale ('an annexe', separate geographic-
ally from the main college buildings). Being repositioned as a manager
and told 'quite firmly'[3] to change her position on the top-down contractual
processes required the head of school to reconstitute the complex and
supportive relations of the locale (the annexe).
   Meanwhile, as this head of school attempted to 'uncurl' her identity
from that of 'mother', other female senior post-holders *drew* on this positioning in an attempt to finesse a path between top-down pressures and
localized identities and practices. M, the section manager at Hillside College discussed earlier, drew on and half-heartedly rejected what Game has
referred to as the 'comfortable feminine position' of 'mother'(1994: 49).
One reading of this is that as more women are positioned as 'first line'
managers some of the traditional heterosexual nuclear family positionings
in colleges are being reinforced. As the reader may recall, at M's meeting with the programme managers in the section (see Chapter 4): 'when
another [programme coordinator] asked for something else and she quipped

back: "I'm not your mum!" "Yes you are", came the laughing pantomime-esque reply. "I don't want to be your mum, they don't pay me enough".' This shows how the shifting back and forth between the positionings of 'woman/mother' and 'manager' works to reproduce the managerial station. However, this relies on a certain ambivalence. The 'woman manager' is drawing on the practices of the locale to appease the requirements of top-down managerial practices. This suggest, and other research with women managers in FE colleges by Deem and Ozga (1997) confirms, that while the knowledges and practices of the feminized locale are drawn into the construction of the managerial station, they, like the paternalistic masculinities before them, quickly become expedient and productive aspects in the construction of particular historical constructions of the 'manager' in this sector. Thus the 'feminization' of, in particular, third- and fourth-tier management posts must be read critically.

Conclusions

The feminization of managerial work in FE colleges can be said to be a set of 'force' relations. These relations draw together the economic plight of colleges, more or less willing subjects (whose allegiance may be to the new order which provides these opportunities), and previously marginalized and subordinated subject positions found in the knowledges and practices of feminized or masculinized teaching locales, to finesse the introduction of an intensively marketized and managerialized FE. Thus rather than celebrate the influx of women to management work in this public sector as evidence of increasing equity or of determination on the part of women (Stott and Lawson, 1997), or as the resonances between different gendered practices and those demanded by the managerial mode/regime, it is important to suggest, based on the above, that the feminization of women, particularly to subordinate positions, is part of the reconstruction itself.

Feminization refers to the way the extra labour, particularly the extra emotional labour, required in actually managing crucial interfaces during reconstruction is supplied by women (Blackmore, 1996; Blackmore and Sachs, 1998). In FE and HE (Prichard, 1996b) the feminization of subordinate managerial posts has drawn in a raft of skills and knowledges, previously embedded in pedagogical and collegial practices, for application in organizational restructuring and survival, often with little or no recognition or reward. Thus it is possible to claim, as Blackmore (1996) suggests in relation to secondary education, and Deem and Ozga (1996) note in relation to HE, that responsibility for carrying the burden of this highly political and emotional transformation in many instances falls to a significant degree to women. And as Adkins and Lury (1998) argue, such resources are assumed to be part of women's identity, rather than occupational resources which are drawn on by what Blackmore (1996) identifies as the 'greedy' corporatized educational organizations of the late twentieth century.

Notes

1. See Meadmore *et al.* (1995) for an account of the interdependence of gendered practices and devolutionary practices in primary education management.
2. He suggests that while it is difficult to judge how representative this is of the sector as a whole, the overall number of respondents, the number of colleges participating and the congruence of the result with more impressionistic evidence about what is happening in FE give one confidence that it is not too far different.
3. In this case by a college principal with a reputation for an aggressive, competitive and macho approach to staffing issues.

9

University Management: Is it Men's Work?

Well that's your answer isn't it? Your computer doesn't recognise your new printer. Doesn't recognise? Doesn't recognise? Good God Maureen. I'm old and tired. I want to go back to the good old days when pens recognised paper and paper recognised envelopes. And you know what I'd like to do most of all, Maureen? Would you let me do it just this once? Just like you used to do? For old times sake. Please?
All right Professor Lapping. You just sit there and I'll be back in a moment with my pad and you can dictate your letter. And if you're very very good . . .
Yes?
I'll cross my legs. Just like I used to do.

(Taylor, 1999: 60)

The most obvious, but often unreported, feature of the management of universities in all three countries (Britain, Canada and Australia) is the sheer dominance of men and masculine styles.

(Miller, 1994: 30)

It is wholly unacceptable that the centres of modern academic teaching and excellence in Britain should remain bastions of male power and privilege.

(Hansard Society for Parliamentary Government, 1990: 11)

Yeatman (1995) argues persuasively in my view that fratriarchal loyalty mediates allegiance to professional locales *and* the elaboration of managerial stations in universities. Challenging locales thus involves challenging the masculinities which inform them. In three of the four universities in the sample women had, since the early 1990s, been appointed to very senior positions: in two cases as directors of strategic planning (in one pre-1992 and one post-1992 university) and in one case as a pro vice-chancellor (in a post-1992 university). Of course this should not be read as typical. As Lalage Bown points out (1999: 10) the picture in 1996/7 is one of strongly male-dominated leadership across the sector. Of the 146 UK HE colleges and universities, just 20 had more than one woman in a key post; 42 per cent of UK HE institutions had no women in any very senior post,[1] and there were no female senior post-holder at five of the ten universities who came top of the 1996 research assessment exercise. In terms of vice-chancellor positions, Bown suggests that 'a cynic might say that women are getting to the top in institutions which are smaller, financially weaker or slightly unorthodox, because these institutions are no longer attractive to men' (1999: 11).

In terms of the position of women in senior academic posts, from which senior post-holders are likely, but not inevitably, to be drawn, the *Times Higher Education Supplement*'s 'Women Professors League' (1997), drawn from Higher Education Statistics Agency data for 1996/7, shows a profession dominated by men. For instance, the percentage of female professors varies by institution from just 2.6 per cent at Heriot-Watt University to 29 per cent at South Bank University. The mean percentage of female professors is 9.2 (median 8 per cent) across 69 institutions with more than 40 professors. In terms of subject area (or 'cost centre' as it is identified in the statistics), the range varies from 33 per cent of professors in health and community studies being women (and 50 per cent of senior lecturers and researchers), to no women professors in civil engineering (3.4 per cent of civil engineering senior lecturers and researchers being women).

As might be expected the broader figures show that there is a strong gender distribution across academic subjects with men strongly clustered in engineering and science, and women in health, education and social studies. The percentage of female professors and senior lecturers reaches double figures in psychology and the behavioural sciences (14.5 per cent of professors and 25 per cent of senior lecturers and researchers), general sciences (14.3 per cent and 12.4 per cent), catering and hospitality management (22.2 per cent and 22.5 per cent), social studies (12.2 per cent and 23.1 per cent), language-based studies (14.9 per cent and 25 per cent), education (17.3 per cent and 32.2 per cent), design and creative arts (14.9 per cent and 22.4 per cent), and health and community studies (33.8 per cent and 50.5 per cent). Meanwhile the percentage of senior male academics surpasses 95 per cent in dentistry (99 per cent of professors and 79 per cent of senior lecturers and researchers), chemistry (99.7 per cent and 95.9 per cent), physics (99 per cent and 95.9 per cent), agriculture and forestry (96.4 per cent and 96.5 per cent) and mathematics (96.9 per cent and 91.2 per cent). In all engineering subjects men hold more than 95 per cent of both chair and senior posts. Men's presence is strong also in clinical medicine (91.2 per cent of professors and 76 per cent of senior lecturers and researchers), business and management (92.6 per cent and 77.1 per cent) and the humanities (91.9 per cent and 81.4 per cent) (*Times Higher Education Supplement*, 1997).

Given this broad distribution, it seems reasonable to suggest that women's relations with 'elite' men and men's relations with each other will be important in mediating women's recruitment to senior posts. In the cases of the new directors of planning at City and Harbourside Universities both women had close relations with the vice-chancellors involved. However, this apparent 'elevation' of a close female colleague evoked both explicit and implicit sexist criticism from some male members of staff. In post-1992 City University, the vice-chancellor was ridiculed by some senior men in the university. The vice-chancellor's close relationship with the director of planning and one or two other women who had taken up senior posts amounted to being 'henpecked', according to some senior male post-holders. The comment suggests that the vice-chancellor's masculinity was being compromised by the women he had positioned in senior posts. More seriously a number of respondents argued that women's close relationship with the vice-chancellor put these women beyond criticism and made them 'fireproof', as the male finance director suggested. These criticisms suggest that the vice-chancellor might be said to have breached fratriarchal relations which would be suspicious of close working relations with women.

In pre-1992 Harbourside University the fratriarchal problematizing of the 'elevation' of a close female colleague to a senior post was projected onto the particular woman herself, rather than directed at the vice-chancellor. It was her 'personality' which was identified as the problem for senior male service heads, and not, as I would suggest, the effect of her problematic positioning in a tense and highly masculinized environment.

At interview, the director of a major service department complained that 'we', meaning himself and his fellow service department heads who were almost exclusively male, 'lack[ed] any sensible input into academic planning which is done by a planning office which is autonomous and rather dictatorial'. In response to my query as to what he meant by 'dictatorial', the service head personalized, objectified and projected the new practices and knowledges of strategic planning, which the vice-chancellor had attempted to introduce at Harbourside, onto the new female head of the planning office: 'Yeah. It's headed by a person who is a very difficult personality to work with and sees no need to discuss things with people'. With this comment the service head by implication constructs himself and his colleagues as liberal, open and constructive, attempting to work with a difficult 'personality'. However, in the process he denies any suggestion that the way he and his colleagues work might be rigid, difficult and antagonistic towards different ways of working or relating to each other. There are therefore locales of fratriarchal practice which are antagonistic to women generally but to this woman in particular.

The head of planning was the only woman in the 'vice-chancellor's group', and one of only two women in the wider senior service post-holders group (the other woman was head of the university's personnel department). Relations among senior post-holders at Harbourside, as the previous chapter highlighted, were tense and 'difficult', a state of affairs brought on by the vice-chancellor's reforms which had identified the university's central administration (its central service departments) as in particular need of restructuring. At the time of the interviews many of the university's service departments were being prepared for a compulsory competitive tendering process, where they would become contractors to the university, and pit themselves against external competition to provide services to the university rather than be part of it. The university's strategic planning office was intimately involved in these reforms. It is unsurprising then that the senior service head's group was likely to have been a particularly difficult space for the head of planning, who was both a close confidante of the vice-chancellor and one of the architects of the 'reforms'. She also identified herself as a 'manager' rather than an administrator, had an academic rather than an administrative background, and was a woman among the men of this group. The effect of the conflict between these different knowledges and practices, including the fratriarchal loyalties among the group, was that the group 'lacked any sensible input into academic planning', as the service head suggested. He said that one of the problems with 'planning' was that its head 'doesn't like discussing, doesn't like "talking shops" so I think that both myself and my financial colleagues have found this extremely difficult'.

The discursive practices of 'discussing', as this book argues, are highly political. Discursive practices carry with them identities, relations and knowledges which position speakers in different ways. The locales identified by the service head in the last quotation as 'talking shops' were clearly repetitions of particular identities, relations and expert knowledges which, I would argue, positioned the new female head of planning, who was from an academic background and also identified herself as a manager, by definition as an outsider. She thus directly challenged in a number of ways knowledges and practices which reproduce sites such as the service department head's group. While the new head of planning, as the previous chapter suggested, represented the new management practices, the gendered aspects to this difference give this tension between managerial and administrative identities further 'edge', and highlight the fratriarchal elements found in such gatherings as this university's senior service heads' group. In summary, the tensions identified as an effect of the head of planning's 'personality' draw attention away from those practices and knowledges that are the targets of reform. But more importantly, the example illustrates also how women are positioned in some institutions as 'front runners' to challenge the embedded relations between entrenched academic and administrative knowledges and practices, and the fratriarchal compacts which support and reproduce them.

Stationing managers, stationing men in universities

The argument to date is that the intensification of strategic, imperializing knowledge practices – of 'management' – in universities does appear to have opened up in some cases space for women as senior post-holders. However it is important to emphasize the comparative rarity of women, the comparative rarity of challenges to male privilege, sexist and fratriarchal practices, and the hugely taken-for-granted nature of such practices among senior post-holders (de Groot, 1997; Deem, 1998; Hearn, 1998).

Hearn suggests this dominance and homosociability leads many who work in large sections of universities to present themselves as 'gender neutral', while universities can be said to be, in the main, very *man-managed* institutions.

This section explores this more directly. I want to begin however by drawing on the following accounts from Michael Roper's (1996) study of homosociability. This is followed by material from the HE institutions in the sample. Roper's work is of key interest here because not only is his empirical material drawn from a university setting (from an ethnography of an Australian university business school), but he discusses the importance of masculinized physical performance – Kanter's (1977) notion of homosocial desire – which could be seen to underpin the development of fratriarchies among senior post-holders.

In the following extract Roper's informants are discussing the performance of one junior manager who is the subject of Roper's discussion:

> In seminars he was a joy to watch. He used to command attention by showing his body off. He would walk up to the window, sit on the ledge, back straight, chalk in hand, making these expansive gestures . . . Then he would pace up and down at the front of the room, stop, put his hands on his hips like this [gestures] . . . Seeming to say all the time 'look at me, look at me'.
>
> (Roper, 1996: 216)

Roper goes on to describe how the seductive and erotic aspects of this performance influenced the head of department and other senior departmental members. They began to mimic the junior manager's gestures and body postures, thus 'confessing unconsciously in the process to their seduction' (1996: 217):

> Paul's sexually nuanced displays certainly do seem to have influenced senior staff. This is suggested by a story which both my informants told me about a meeting they had attended. Paul himself was absent, but halfway through it the head of department rose from his chair and began pacing up and down the room, moving and gesticulating in precisely the manner that Paul usually did. Soon his senior colleague – responding to this vigorous display – also got up from his chair, and began imitating the head of department.
>
> (Roper, 1996: 217)

Roper suggests that unspoken economies of homosocial desire, known colloquially as 'male bonding', work to form Yeatman's (1995) 'fustian patriarchal fabric' of university management. In the terms used here, such 'unspoken economies' are those localized masculine practices which support and produce the managerial stations and collegial or administrative locales. Roper's example also suggests that such stations are in the process of being reinvigorated by some of the new masculinized practices the junior manager has been, perhaps inadvertently, responsible for introducing.

An example of this, but one which arguably works to rebuff the managerial station, is suggested in the faculty dean's comments from Southern University in Chapter 6. He talked of how the close, long-term relations between himself and his colleagues made it largely impossible for him to be

an autocratic 'Führer' of a manager. This highlights just how deeply embedded relations are which revolve around homosociability, or the male
camaraderie of being 'mates'. The masculinity here is woven with a strong
egalitarian ethic between men which flattens overt institutional differences,
such as being a dean or a manager, and enforces an ethic where members
don't 'get above themselves'. What this suggests is that fratriarchal loyalties
are part of a 'cocktail' of resistances to the construction of the managerial
station.

Yet the effect of these 'unspoken economies' in establishing the dominance of men and particular masculinities in particular sites is that those
who do not share such knowledges and practices are excluded. The apparent refusal of the new female director of planning at Harbourside to join
the 'talking shop' of the senior service department heads, in ways that
would reproduce these locales, was just such an exclusion. The effect of this
is, as Walker (1998) suggests in her analysis of sexism in a South African
university, that while overt sexist practices have been removed, the exclu-
sionary character of relations between senior male post-holders remains.
The key point however is that the dominance of men in *management* in
organizations is not 'natural', but an effect of the interdependence between
imperializing political, historical processes and gendered relations and
identities. These suffuse managerial stations, in most cases, with masculinized
practices and knowledges. Yet as well as generalized homosocial exclu-
sions, aggressive and authoritarian practices are also likely to be present. A
head of department in City University suggested in the case of that institution the further 'up' the organization one went, the more aggressive and
compliant the masculinity at work became:

> The sort of brutalist approach gets more obvious at the top. What is
> very obvious is [that this is] a very *man-managed* institution.
>
> CP: What do you mean by *man-managed*?
>
> Well I mean whatever the pretence and actually whether we talk about
> men or women it is very much a traditional image of tough males
> running the place.

'Man-management' is used to suggest here that management in this university relies heavily on a mix of what Collinson and Hearn (1994) describe
as authoritarian and entrepreneurial masculinities. The head of department's comment suggests that masculinities at work among senior post-
holders, particularly in relations between deans and the senior team, are
based on aggressive and dictatorial relations overlaid with perhaps a concern for organization targets, performance levels and efficiency. This was
confirmed by comments from other heads in the institution. For instance, a
long-serving head of department suggested that:

> [The vice-chancellor] is very rigid in his approach and extremely
> inflexible. The [deputy vice-chancellor] is a very difficult character

to deal with. He will not allow conversation and unfortunately I don't even think he is aware of it. He makes very pejorative remarks and statements like 'You are all academic heads so I'll explain this to you twice'. You know, is that supposed to be funny?[The vice-chancellor's group] is very male dominated. They seem to be very task orientated people. Perhaps they are overworked, perhaps [the vice-chancellor's group] is insufficient [in number] but I think there is a definite need to have a more human relations-orientated type of person in at that level and we also need to have a team of deans who are stronger than the current team we have now.

Here, male managers can be said to exercise control through particular discursive practices. In contrast to 'Sylvia's' tactical discursive practices drawn from feminized locales (what this head of department might describe as a 'human relations-orientated type of person'), these include displays of inflexibility, unwillingness to listen, unwillingness to allow others to talk, patronizing humour and derogatory remarks. All these serve to organize and reproduce managerial stations in this organization through the medium of aggressive masculinities. This example from City University confirms Whitehead's (1997a) argument, for the post-1992 universities, that authoritarian, aggressive and competitive masculinities are engaged in challenging modes of practice which are more paternalistic or 'soft', to use Trow (1994) and Ainley's (1994) terms. Yet in some institutions this challenge to the paternalistic masculinity may also come from the practices of the feminized locale, as demonstrated in the next section.

Managing men and wo-managing universities: the case of Southern University

In spite of the above there are ruptures and points of reversal in these generalized and dominant practices. Southern University provides an example of a challenge to such practices. Southern University is a particular mix of historical conditions and embedded relations between men and women in senior positions. These inform and mediate the 'challenge'. In order to illuminate this case it is first necessary to note the following comment from a pro vice-chancellor at Southern University. In the statement he suggests that a paternalistic and heterosexual masculinity is at work among senior university post-holders. This positions men as breadwinners (academics in this case), women as housekeepers (administrators) and students as 'children'. This pro vice-chancellor said in relation to senior administrators, that:

> We are trying to treat them [the service heads] as equals, but they are unequal. The service people provide services and are therefore subservient in that way. They are not initiators or developers of the institution. They may develop new systems of finance or academic registry, but they don't see themselves as leading the institution. The deans

meanwhile, leading the schools, certainly do and should do because everyone else is dependent on them bringing in the students.

One vital piece of information left out of the foregoing statement is that all the deans at this institution are men, and the service heads have among them a high profile group of women. One of these women had this to say about relations between these groups:

> Two or three years ago the heads of service felt that they were on the periphery and were not being taken seriously. It is such a contrast that we are now just mainstream management. We are all affected by this and it has been quite a 'sea change'. [CP: In whose eyes?] I think both, you know, the heads of service now have much more confidence in themselves. If you feel inferior you tend to act in that way and I think the deans recognize the importance now of the infrastructure.

Clearly there is some contradiction between this and the comment from the male pro vice-chancellor at the same university. The two comments reveal a struggle over positioning in ways of knowledging the relations between university personnel. The first statement places academics, who are largely men, over service heads and service department workers, who are in this case women. This view reflects and reinforces assumptions about a traditional nuclear family which are 'close to the surface' here. The second, competing way of knowledging relations found in the service head's text draws on management discourse to challenge the traditional arrangement. The generalizing and equalizing aspects of management knowledge (highlighted here by the service head in the comment 'we are now just mainstream management') are drawn upon to help reposition this group of female senior post-holders in an equal relation to the dominant group of male academic heads. This also attempts to rewrite the assumptions of the paternalistic nuclear family narrative of the organization. The pro vice-chancellor's comment on the other hand suggests that he is both struggling with and ultimately resistant to this rewriting. He begins his comment by firstly 'flagging up' this equalizing aspect of management knowledge – for example 'We are trying to treat them as equals'. But he then quickly repositions service heads as unequal by returning to the notion of the academics as the 'natural' leaders of the institution and ascribing to administration a subservient position.

Meanwhile, the service heads were clear that they were challenging not just the way management meetings were done, but also the masculinized, fratriarchal practices in which meetings were embedded. A senior service head said for instance:

> The deans are all men at the moment. The interesting thing is probably that [the difference between them] depends on their academic background. The dean of arts and the dean of the business school, which has the professional women's development unit in it, are the

softies if you like. And then you've got sciences, you know, real hard tough and yet he [dean of science] is in fact very good with his staff. And then you have got the mixture in between. But yes I think one of the problems is that because they are all men there is a tendency for them to sort of [be] the boys together, the gang, and you know we should all drink Newcastle Brown and pints.

The social spaces in which these masculinities were reproduced (of being 'the boys together') were senior post-holder committee meetings. It is no surprise that these sites became the 'battlefield' between these differing gendered knowledges of the institution. Another service head described how she saw these meetings:

It has to be said that deans dominate these meetings because they're the ones who are used to spouting off and they don't think twice about whether their point is valid. And once one has said something the other deans have got to say something . . . and heads of services tend to see that it is a game and think oh . . . I have got more important things to do back at base, you know.

Such comments reflect an, at times, overt conflict among senior post-holders over the way power relations are exercised across the institution. To some extent the arrival of a female pro vice-chancellor at the university in the late 1980s helped to clarify the gendered character of this conflict. A service head offered some background to this:

We have a woman pro vice-chancellor who has an academic background. I work very very closely with her and we just have different ways of doing things. I think until she came [here] I hadn't realized just how uncomfortable I felt about some of the ways the committees worked and hadn't really had an opportunity to look at other ways of working because there was nobody else to work with in that way . . . She has a very open way of chairing meetings and a very different kind of way. The first meeting she had she ordered sticky buns and things like that, you know, like people were just taken aback, didn't know what to do with it. It is sort of a very disarming kind of role a kind of leadership style which she has which is very interesting. It's very interesting seeing it work, much more relaxed and informal and yet still getting the work done.[2]

Here the service head is referring to how the normalized hierarchical formality of organizational practices was challenged to some extent by the pro vice-chancellor's more open, informal ways of operating. These more informal ways of operating allowed the service head to be more 'herself' as a woman in these settings and to experience how the previous practices operated to position her as subordinate. These helped to define and reinforce paternalistic managerial relations. In effect the university's traditional meeting practices positioned the service head as different. Yet the open, informal and deconstructing practices of the new pro vice-chancellor served to open up this space for some reflection, and later challenge.

Women's challenge to management masculinities

The discussion has noted how this seemingly more open and informal approach to chairing meetings brought by the arrival of a new pro vice-chancellor at Southern University helped to create the conditions for a challenge to the discursive practices surrounding the running of university committee meetings. These practices, it can be suggested, both excluded women and supported dominant masculinities. Part of the challenge to these practices was through the 'new' management discourse of teams or 'team ideology' (Sinclair, 1992). However, this came not from a coalition of male and female senior post-holders but from a group of women who numbered just 5 among the senior tier of 27 deans, heads of services and executives at Southern University. In early 1993 this group made a formal challenge to existing meeting practices. They proposed that committees in the university be replaced with task groups and special project teams. It was argued that these would be both more effective and more flexible ways of working at senior levels. They suggested that on a trial basis all regular committee meetings should be cancelled in the autumn term in favour of working groups and special project teams.

While this particular proposal was rejected by other members of the senior staff tier, since then the practice of questioning the existence of committees has become embedded at senior level. The new vice-chancellor said in a published account that 'it was always interesting to hear what was said when the question was put as to whether the committee should continue'.

At the time, one of the proposers of this trial project-team programme related: 'It was just thrown out. [They said they] "couldn't possibly entertain that suggestion"'. The female service head said:

> Interestingly, those who chaired the senior committees were totally against it. There was actually no way that they were going to allow that. You know 'What would we do? We would have half a week not in committees, oh dear me'.

> CP: There is a temptation to suggest that men have got their identities very much tied into the committee structures. The 'chairman' and that kind of thing, whereas the women in the institution are happier working in a looser more informal way. Is that fair?

> My experience is that men use committees more to make statements about their own power and their own power base and to make statements about themselves whereas I think women actually want to make

... you know perhaps we are just naive, I don't know. We [the women] tend to go there thinking this is the agenda, this is what we are going to talk about. I think often the senior management here have other agendas and they are trying to prove other things to other people and that is one of the problems with meetings. They don't actually talk about ... some of the agenda items just get sidetracked because somebody has got a personal agenda for that day and they are determined that whatever the meeting is about they are going to make their point about something and so lots of it is used very much as a power base.

It is clear from this that the female service heads could be said to be challenging not simply the meeting practices, but the masculine identities and relations which underwrote these. Ian McNay, professor of post-compulsory education management at the University of Greenwich, drew attention to this, though not directly, in his account of events at Southern University. He had been contracted to provide 'management training' for senior staff at this university at the time of these events. He notes:[3]

> In one former polytechnic with which I have worked a (female) pro vice-chancellor (PVC) described how a group of women set out to colonize the committee system believing the institution to be in quadrant B (bureaucratic); they found, when they succeeded, that like a mirage, power was still beyond them – in the senior management team in quadrant C (corporate). Decisions were effectively taken outside the formal arenas which simply endorsed them. One PVC (male) acknowledged this. He countered by claiming that the collegial democracy had been delegated to departmental level, but 'the heads of department couldn't manage democracy so there were two levels of corporate state, the greater and the lesser'.
>
> (McNay, 1995: 110)

McNay hints at the gendered aspects of the changing managerial relations and identities, but, like many others engaged in the management development 'market', seems unable or unwilling to address this directly (Middlehurst, 1993; Warner and Palfreyman, 1995). Yet in the reading provided here Southern University was very 'man-aged' through informal mateship practices at corporate level, as well as the embedded fratriarchies of the committee room. Challenging these was one thing, but as McNay suggests, the more important decision making was along fratriarchal lines outside the 'talk shops' of the committee meeting. Nevertheless if established in place of committees, the suggested 'informal task groups' and 'special project teams' would have challenged the overlap between masculinities and management, to some extent. The dominance of male chairpersons for instance would likely have been challenged. The committee meeting practices which allow academic men to speak more, and draw on off-agenda subjects (which work to maintain the link between masculine identities and control) would also likely have been challenged. In other words, the body topography of the committee meeting would be challenged.

Conclusions: university management – is it really men's work?

In the UK at the time of writing 10 of the 146 HE institutions have female vice-chancellors, principals or directors. These are: Queen Margaret College (Edinburgh), Cheltenham and Gloucester College of Higher Education, Keele University, three colleges of the University of London, the Universities of Bournemouth, Staffordshire and Sunderland, and Manchester Metropolitan University. This is of course a very small number of institutions, most of which are post-1992 universities and colleges. Heward and Taylor (1992) suggest that the rise of women to senior posts in the former polytechnics and colleges of HE is due to their conforming to early local authority equal opportunities policies. But perhaps alongside this is a more suggestive explanation which mirrors the discussion of the feminization of, particularly, first-line management posts in FE: that the suffusion of the managerial station in public sector HE, which in some cases challenges the links between paternalistic masculinities and managerial positions, has opened up space for women. In this vein, Brian Booth, former rector of the University of Central Lancashire (formerly Lancashire Polytechnic) noted in 1992 that:

> The style of management in the former polytechnics has changed radically over the past three years through specification, via the articles of government, of the responsibilities placed on the head of the institution. The delegation of these responsibilities through clear line management structures and, in some institutions, the use of permanent rather than rotating posts at middle and senior management levels, has enabled significant career development for both women and men, in particular for women, who do not seem to get elected or nominated to rotating posts.
>
> (Booth, 1992: 24)

Alongside this of course is the development of women's networks aimed at supporting women engaged in taking up senior posts. As King (1997) and Powney (1997) outline, these networks are not simply involved in helping women to 'get on' in institutions but attempt to create different patterns in the way these organizations are articulated and practised. The assertion here is that the UK's post-1992 institutions include groups of women engaged in challenging traditional masculine, particularly paternalistic, dispositions. Of course it is also possible to find men who are challenging these taken-for-granted dispositions as well. But I would argue that given the strength of the fratriarchal knowledges and practices, it is *around* these groups of women, in post-1992 universities particularly, that the challenges and patterns are being worked out (King 1993, 1997; Farish *et al.*, 1995).

Notes

1. Senior posts in this analysis included: vice-chancellor or principal; pro vice-chancellor or deputy principal; registrar (or senior academic adminstrator); bursar (or senior finance officer); and university librarian.
2. This quotation is used on page 45 in the discussion of locales and stations.
3. McNay draws on Weick's (1976) understanding of educational institutions as 'loosely coupled systems' and argues that universities can be described as: a 'collegium', 'bureaucracy', 'enterprise' or 'corporation' depending on the extent of control over 'policy definition' and 'implementation' of policies. This produces a two-by-two 'box' where each organizational type forms a quadrant.

Conclusion

INNER RING ROAD

The University of Poppleton's Free Voice

Bringing you all the news your very own management wants to hear.

WELL DONE to everyone in the Marketing Department Team. At last week's conference in Biarritz on 'Selling the Modern University', the guys and gals from Poppleton picked up the Bronze Medal in the Mission Statement Category for Poppleton's proud slogan: 'Working Together for a Brighter Future'. Now let's try and put those brave words into action . . .

AM I the only one who is sick to the back teeth of those so-called members of staff who spend their time moaning about lack of pay and resources, extra teaching hours, and this university's whole-hearted subscription to the principles of scientific management? R.S. Likker, Deputy Assistant Manager External Relations.

(Taylor, 1998d: 56)

Trowler (1998: 158) argues that education policy scholarship, which situates policy in the context of political and ideological struggles, may not appeal to university managers searching for organizational change levers. Its 'depiction of social reality is an extremely complex one which denies the possibility of controlled, predictable change'. This book, by taking up elements from postdualist or poststructural social theory, supports Trowler's point. But it also questions the assumption that one can unproblematically assume the existence of the 'manager'. It has extended this general questioning of coherency and the possibility of 'managing change' to those who, through conventional discourse, are charged with this task. The manager, as this book has argued, is a much less stable site of discursive articulation than is often assumed.

To recap, the aim has been to explore the nature of and the problems that surround the formation of the manager in universities and colleges in Britain. This involved questioning how and to what extent managerial knowledges have suffused the terrain of FHE in the UK. I have drawn on a conceptual framework (Fiske, 1993) where the ontological commitment is to *discursive practice* or *knowledge practice*. I have argued that such practices and knowledges are actively engaged in 'materializing' identities, relations and bodies, and are reproductive of broad social alliances. Knowledge practices are not, as some poststructuralist writers are prone to suggest, simply multiple and contradictory. They form and encode variably dominant and subordinated social, political and economic alliances. To signal this difference, and following the lead of post-Marxist scholars (Hall, 1981; Laclau and Mouffe, 1985), I have taken up Fiske's distinction between localizing and imperializing discursive practices. In order to articulate this distinction in a way which allows empirical material to be addressed I have further borrowed Fiske's concepts of 'station' and 'locale'. These are understood as differing ways in which particular sites are thought about, talked about and enacted via imperializing, or strategic, or localizing, or tactical forms of knowledge. However in order to explore aspects of embodiment, left undeveloped by Fiske's work, I have suggested that it is important to address 'station' and 'locale' through a further pair of concepts: 'surface' and 'depth'.

The effect of this framework is to read or 'map' universities or colleges in socially significant but divergent ways. If read as stationed by managerial knowledge practices, their myriad sites would be understood as:

- managed by a manager, rather than administered by elected representative;
- customer- rather than student-focused;
- reviewed by quality-assurance audit rather than by peer review;
- corporately rather than professionally orientated;
- strategically rather than tactically focused.

Through this framework, the 'evidence' assembled and presented suggests that managerial knowledge practices have been relatively successful in reordering *some* of the multiplicity of spaces which make up contemporary universities and colleges in the UK. Yet the character of this reordering is mediated by localized practices and knowledges.

I have argued that managerial knowledge practices have been relatively successful in constituting senior post-holders as managers. Of course it is possible to refute this. The registrar's comments at Middletown University and the tensions among the very senior post-holders at Harbourside University (see Chapter 6) suggest that this repositioning is, even at the most senior level in universities, a partial and problematic one. Similarly the cases of the 'Code for Management' at City University and the 'management training events' at Hillside College highlight how in post-1992 universities and FE colleges these knowledge practices are readily challenged and undermined when space and conditions are available.

Of course the durability of these forms of resistance is highly variable. The managerial station is constantly 'under threat' from the incursions of other knowledge practices, which carry with them different identities and relations. The managerial station is variably threatened, in part because in many sites it is the reproduction of these 'other' identities and relations, which have a crucial bearing on the relative success of the range of activities for which the senior post-holder is constructed as having responsibility. Improved performance paradoxically relies, to varying degrees, on the knowledges and practices of the subordinated professional locales.

Using a conceptual framework influenced by poststructuralist writing, I have argued that a 'state of hostilities' has tended to exist in this education sector (during the period of the study) between the ascendant managerial knowledge practices and those embedded and variably subordinated (but not erased) academic and administrative knowledge practices. This 'state of hostilities' takes on a number of forms given, as I have suggested, that knowledge practices are mobile and constantly in the processes of colonizing and constructing spaces, surfaces and depths (particularly the affective, sensuous and emotional 'depth' of human bodies). When one set of knowledge practices meets others there may be brief moments of tension before one or more are displaced – briefly perhaps. What appears to happen is that the displaced knowledge practices 'appear' elsewhere and re-inscribe other spaces. The accounts of the various meetings highlight how knowledge practices of the locale produced management training events which were significantly at odds with power bloc constructions of such events. Thus any answer to the question of the extent of the suffusion of the managerial station must consider the variably ambivalent, but also tactical, nature of relations between these competing knowledge practices.

At the core of this of course is the demonstrated point that at a more micro level, this 'state of hostilities' is embedded in the detailed practices that form the work of senior post-holders themselves. For instance, the reader may remember the dean who turned the offices around his own into a student 'freeway' to alleviate the individuating isolation of the body topography of the managerial station; or the head of department who maintains a side desk where the body topography of his subject specialism can be reproduced.

Yet, as the last two chapters have suggested, rather than being subordinated and displaced, *some* knowledge practices have been 'drawn in' and productively put to work to appease top-down pressures and to reproduce the managerial station. The female principal of highly successful City College, for example, whose 'style of management' was praised in the college's FEFC's inspection report, said she had 'done a lot to try and involve managers as much as possible. I tell them I want to share my problems with them. My excuse is that I want to share my problems. We've encouraged managers to think corporately'.

Here the micro practices of a locale – a feminine locale based around the practices of 'sharing my problems' – are drawn upon to make up and reproduce the managerial station, one which would see senior professionals identify with the college's corporate identity and strategic direction. Of course there are other aspects of the college's circumstances which contribute to the construction of corporately orientated dispositions. In such a relatively small institution (between a quarter and half the size of a small university) these micro practices (e.g. 'share my problems') appear to suffuse the managerial knowledge and practices.

Conventionally, the final 'Conclusion' chapter of academic texts assesses the weight of evidence for and against the particular hypothesis which is being advanced. The differing commitments and priorities taken up here mean that the aim has been to develop a qualitatively rich, narrative-based analysis of a particular issue. However, I should like to make a series of points which I hope sum up the position presented here:

- At a conceptual 'level', I consider that the study demonstrates the importance for studies of management and organizational work to reject strong epistemological commitments to *division* between 'objects' (e.g. managers, professionals, men–women, self–other), and to focus instead on an epistemology of multiple and competing discursive practices which have the effect of attempting to 'hold' these 'objects' in place, and subordinate others.
- At an empirical 'level' I consider that the 'evidence' presented demonstrates that the 'hold' that managerial discursive practices might be said to have on senior post-holders is unstable rather than inevitable. This 'hold' can be said to be the result of the repeated inscription of managerial identities by the knowledge practices of the managerial station. These practices produce managerial identities through the mimetic effects of positioning particular bodies in relations of difference between various norms and accounts of performance. Thus the extent of the suffusion of managerial practices is an effect of the relative salience of these relations of difference in particular institutional settings.
- At a political 'level' I consider the study demonstrates how important it is, with regard to challenging managerial relations and identities, that this challenge be articulated not at 'the people' themselves, but at the discursive practices that constitute managerial identities and relations and which inscribe particular spaces, surfaces and depths.

Possible managerial futures

Given these points it is important to ask what possible futures might be available regarding the 'manager' in colleges and universities. As Chapter 6 argues it is possible to see the development of the manager in FHE simply in terms of a response to changing funding conditions and mechanisms. At the time of writing, financial conditions seem to have eased for the great bulk of colleges and universities, however the introduction of student fees, together with other changing socio-economic circumstances, has meant that recruitment and quality have become key issues. This will inevitably intensify the problems for many senior post-holders, positioned between institutional demands for continuity or increased performance and departmental and localized constraints. Calls for better and more effective management of resources will inevitably continue to be made, as in the Dearing Inquiry of 1997. There will likely be further recourse to Taylorite 're-engineering' or 'knowledge management' solutions (Ford *et al.*, 1996), and new policy agendas which offer seductive solutions to underlying tensions are likely to be unveiled (Robertson, 1998; Department of Trade and Industry, 1999). The 'pressure' will inevitably be on senior post-holders to 'square the circle', predictably perhaps with recourse to increased casualization, techno-logical substitution and intensification of administrative and academic work. This may have the effect of further isolating senior post-holders from the identities and practices of their 'colleagues' and paradoxically solidify the identities produced by the managerial station. Of course this is locally con-ditioned by differing circumstances. So perhaps one somewhat pessimistic possible future would be the increasing distance and difference between those stationed as academic and service managers, and academics and admin-istrative staff.

Further research

I should like to suggest a number of possible directions for future research in this field. First, further research needs to be done to address relations between other 'axes of difference' apart from gender (race, ethnicity, sexu-ality, ability/disability, age) and the construction of the managerial station. I have I think demonstrated the importance of the interdependence of gender practices, and the development of managers, but in my view I have left a 'roaring silence' with the omission of accounts of other axes in the construction of the managerial station.

Second, I consider that in many ways I have been studying traditional academic and administrative sites. Funding pressures are likely to intensify the relative fragmentation and dispersal of FHE itself. Using the conceptual framework advanced above, future research might be directed at consider-ing the tensions and problems of the dispersal of managerial knowledges and practices and the construction of new organizational forms. The deputy vice-chancellor at Southern University highlighted this in an early interview for this study:

> If I was looking five years hence I would not expect those schools to exist. I would expect to have maybe broken them up into something like 30 school units, smaller units without another superstructure. In other words not breaking the schools into units and retaining the schools but actually breaking them down into much smaller self-managing units. One of the things that will happen to us is that we will move from the degree of specialist management structure that we have now, specialist financial advice, specialist personnel advice and so on, to embedding much more of that in operational small units with shared responsibilities.

Of course such a statement is not a neutral suggestion of possible futures but is made in the context of an institution under pressure to more effici-ently match funding against costs – labour costs, in the main. While raising the question of efficiencies and flexibilities of labour in HE in relation to organizational size, it steers away from the problems of actually instituting the kinds of knowledge practices which might constitute such organizational forms. Future research might deal with how the further dispersal of the managerial station dispenses with the, admittedly expensive, embodied manager altogether. If for instance the imperializing knowledges of 'lifelong learning' demand the continued dispersal and fragmentation of the university and the college, and by extension of the embodied managers of these organizational sites, then it is the tensions and problems that surround the construction of managerial identities in non-traditional spaces, surfaces and depths, which could be addressed. Substantively this might involve an exploration of the changing interface between FE and HE, the development of the 'universities' by major corporations, the development of HE's so-called global 'flying campus' (Bennell and Pearce, 1998), computer-based distance learning and research programmes. These will inevitably be sites where the discursive practices of managing meet the knowledge practices of variably unpredictable and problematic locales.

Appendix: Research Sites and Methods

This appendix briefly discusses the institutional sites, the research methods and methods of data analysis used in this study of the constitution of the manager in FHE. It briefly discusses how the research methods and methods of 'data' analysis support the conceptual framework advanced for this study.

Research sites

The study on which this book is based drew on interviews with more than 65 senior post-holders in four universities and four FE colleges. Along with this, observational data from one university and one college were gathered, together with documentation from all eight institutions and a number of other named universities and colleges. The HE interviews were conducted during 1994 and the FE interviews in 1996 and early 1997.

The four HE institutions consisted of two pre-1992 and two post-1992 institutions. The two pre-1992 institutions, with their roots in the nineteenth-century expansion of HE, are located in the north of England. These were chosen because they represent what Peter Scott (1995: 44) calls the 'heartland' of the 'old' university sector. They make up a quarter of this sector and according to Scott are the most comprehensive of British universities, ranging across all the arts and sciences and embracing education, law, medicine, engineering and other professional fields. Each of these two pre-1992 universities has an annual turnover in excess of £120 million, has close to 20,000 students and considers itself to be research led. The two post-1992 universities meanwhile are representative of the 30 poly-technics created in the late 1960s and early 1970s which, in Scott's opinion, have been at the forefront of growth and innovation in HE since the 1970s. Both the post-1992 universities were former technical colleges (or amalgamations of these) which, during the late 1980s, in particular, grew into institutions with more than 10,000 full-time equivalent student enrolments and a turnover of more than £50 million.

In order to achieve correspondence of data across each of these institutions similar profiles of about nine senior post-holders were interviewed. These included three very senior staff (typically, vice-chancellor, pro vice-chancellor and registrar or equivalent), three high grade administrative staff (e.g. head of accommodation, personnel, planning, etc.) and three senior academic post-holders (e.g. dean, head of school, head of department). Semi-structured interviews lasting between 40 and 90 minutes were held with these senior post-holders while in one of the post-1992 institutions a significantly larger sample was interviewed alongside attendance at meetings and other events. In general the interviews in all four institutions addressed the following issues: the interviewees' current experience of work; past experience of work; changes in their experience of work; the consequences of these changes; and anticipated future changes to their experience of work. In terms of access, in each case the vice-chancellor or principal of each institution was initially approached for permission to interview senior post-holders. Introductory letters were then sent to each potential interviewee and a follow-up telephone call made to confirm a willingness to participate and a convenient interview time and place. It is an indication of the familiarity of the research interview as a practice, and the willingness of people to take part in such work, that only three potential interviewees declined to take part in the research across the whole sample.

In the case of the FE colleges included in this study, a similar pattern of sampling and interviewing was followed. Four colleges were chosen from those in the Nottinghamshire and Derbyshire regions to represent in terms of size and specialisms the general pattern of the post-1993 FE sector. Three of the four colleges have average state sector incomes of around £6 million. The fourth college is twice this size with FEFCE income of around £13 million (1996/7 figures). In terms of levels of funding, two of the colleges have a relatively low AFL, of around £12 (1995/6). One college has an average AFL of around £15, and the fourth college has a relatively high AFL of nearly £19. In each college six senior post-holders were interviewed including the principal, two service directors and three academic section heads. This was supplemented with four observational visits and further interviews with four programme coordinators in one of the colleges. The same question format as that used in the HE institutions was used in the FE college interviews.

Research methods

The interview is the core research method used in this study. While it could be argued that the interview is removed from the actual discursive practices of managing it has a number of strengths as a method, not least of which is that it is a relatively unproblematic way to organize access to a relatively large number of people in a variety of institutions. Yet principally the semi-structured private interview between researcher and senior post-holders provides a means of exploring the discursivity of the tensions that surround their positioning in colleges and universities. The interview provides some means of exploring those identities which are likely to be engaged in or produced by particular discursive practices. Essentially the interview can provide evidence of how senior post-holders routinely navigate transitions between various subject positions (e.g. of manager and senior professional). It can also provide material for exploring the important discursive practices through which locales and stations might be reproduced (e.g. staff–student field trips, off-campus meetings, teaching audit processes).

However, in line with an interactionalist critique of a positivist orientation to the interview (Silverman, 1993) I am *not* assuming that what is said in the interview 'reflects' other situations. Neither am I arguing, as conversational analysts and ethnomethodologists tend to do, that the interview is a discrete event that can only be explained on the basis of the interaction between those involved. The interview *is* a particular accomplishment in its own right, but it is also an accomplishment achieved through and with the discursive resources available in these sites. Of course interviews are contrived settings for gathering 'data'. Also they are easily treated as a public relations 'vehicle' by senior post-holders. Nevertheless, while it is important to assume that each interview is a *particular display*, each includes, to use Silverman's (1993) terms, a display of the particulars, that is, of the vocabularies and discursive practices which are at work in a particular social terrain. For instance, a particular account given during an interview is potentially the actual account at work in other interactions, although this cannot be assumed.

I have however relied upon a mixture of methods and not simply the interview. The argument here is not that a reliance on a mixture of methods produces some form of 'truthful' knowledge, but simply that each of these methods, themselves discursive practices, offers different ways of drawing on the discursivity of work sites, which can then be woven into the overall research narrative.

Observation and participant observation, for example, allow the researcher the chance to 'listen in' and 'work within' the terrain that is being reconstructed by new discursive practices and their embedded positions. They also provide ways of 'listening in' not simply to the official and unofficial stories, but also to the actual embodied practices. Documentary sources are also extremely useful in that they provide accounts of the 'official' discourses at work in particular sites. As Fiske (1993) and Shotter (1993) highlight, stationing or strategic practices tend to rely on representational devices and a realist understanding of language, whereas localizing power is embedded in more dialogic forms of practice. Thus documentary sources (e.g. job descriptions, audit reports, contracts, strategic plans, senior post-holder reports and reviews) are important in that they illustrate the character of the kinds of subjects such practices attempt to constitute across a particular terrain.

Research methods as discursive practices

The methods of interview, observation and the collection of documentary material were those adopted for this study. However it is necessary to discuss further some of the implications of these.

Such methods *themselves* are discursive practices. They are in other words actively engaged in constituting power/knowledge relations which variably provide and may help constitute particular subject positions, and hence subjectivities. Interviews particularly are, as Foucault's work (1990) highlights, genealogically linked to and implicated in the suffusion of modern forms of power. Derived from the pastoral ritual of Christian confession, the interview has spread in the modern age to become, along with the examination, one of the key rituals of truth and power. Foucault (1990: 61–2) argues, drawing material from his discussion of sex, that the power of this discursive ritual derives from two elements: the speaking subject being taken to be the subject of the statement, and the statement being made in the presence or virtual presence of a 'partner who is not simply the interlocutor but the authority who requires confession, prescribes and appreciates it, and intervenes in order to judge, punish, forgive, console and reconcile'.

But more than this, Foucault (1990: 63) argues, the interview/confessional has become part of the processes of scientific discourse because of its centrality in the production of the discourses around sex. Of course, as a practice, the interview has spread and changed and been put to work for various purposes: 'The motivations and effects it is expected to produce have varied, as have the forms that it has taken: interrogations, consultations, autobiographical narratives, letters, they have been recorded, transcribed, assembled into dossiers, published and commented on'. Again, I want to stress that given the commitments of the study here, the statements made by senior post-holders in interview are conceptualized as produced *in part* by the discursive practice of the interview, as a particular display. Yet they also provide discursive materials produced by and through other embedded discursive practices (e.g. localized administrative practice, the research assessment exercise, the appraisal, the contract, the management team meeting, budget processes etc). What is crucially important is the dialogic aspects of interview discussion. The texts of interviews, I want to argue, are intertextually linked to other discursive practices. The texts and utterances of the interviews with senior post-holders are dialogically produced by the textuality of the college or university. These research-orientated conversations in general terms can be assumed to refer to, respond to and anticipate the narratives, texts and stories found in these sites (Fairclough, 1992: 101). The interview texts are not read as being *of* the interviewees, reflecting some inner world of thought or emotion – rather, the subject is produced by and through the textual practices of the interview (the texts in action) as it is by and through the numerous other textual practices that organize the college/university.

In line with this, the interviews themselves adopt a certain approach aimed at *reducing* the extent to which a particular subject is produced by the practice itself. This opens up further the possibility of discussion of the effects of the discursive practices of the college and the university in which the interviewee is involved.

In terms of the power relations of the interview itself, I accept that it is inevitably engaged in enjoining people to produce an account for their various selves, to confess, in other words, and thus mimetically (re)inscribe themselves within particular discourses. However, a number of practices were adopted to try to reduce the 'need' to 'confess' in a particular way. Open-ended and deliberately ambiguous questions were used. The researcher explicitly denied any position of authority, in general terms positioning himself as a student or naive investigator. Tactics of dress and conduct were used so as not to directly evoke particular discourses and subject positions (e.g. a business suit).

Of course I assume that the subtle mix of elements including the vocabularies used by the researcher to present the study, the forms of dress he used, and numerous other clues that he is likely to have inadvertently given off, *do impact* substantially on the texts themselves. Nevertheless, by tactically attempting to reduce this, I was able to open up the discussion to those positionings in which the interviewees were embedded. As has been noted, the key questions upon which this study turns are: what subject positions does the speaker take up for him/herself, and how is this done (e.g. what practices are embedded in this, and what are the problems that surround this)? The same set of questions was used in each interview and I broadly adopted the same approach to each interview.

However, this was not a positivist approach to interview questions. I did not set out to mechanically reproduce the same conditions. There was and is a good deal of flexibility, aimed at producing rich texts. This richness comes from engaging with the interviews as a *particular display*. To learn from them, one has to respond differently to each. Of course the general framework of starting with relatively non-threatening personalized questions and moving on to more difficult questions towards the end was used, but as the questions themselves were highly non-specific they were treated more as prompts to further discussion of the issues that were being raised than as breaks in the discussion where the interviewee was to be solicited for his/her attitude to a particular aspect of managerial work.

The variety of ways in which I, as researcher, was positioned during the interviews give an indication of the relative openness of the event. In some cases I was positioned as an accomplice, as someone invited to share and invest in the heroics or problems of the position of manager. On other occasions I was positioned as a subject who shared a distance from and possible questioning of the subject position of manager. In some cases I was positioned as a confidant with whom unofficial stories could be shared with impunity. For some interviewees, the interview seemed to be a 'slot' in the diary where a reasonably well-rehearsed account of the institution, the work and the self would be offered. Interviews with the four college principals and the four university vice-chancellors tended to be like this. I was positioned as an outsider to whom the strategic agenda of the college or university would be explained. There were points in each of these interviews where certain questions interrupted such narratives and other stories were told, but large sections of the discussion dealt with, and were clearly repetitions of, well-rehearsed strategic narratives. Again this shows how the researcher is not outside the practices that construct knowledge of some areas. Researchers are deeply implicated in this construction, particularly during those crucial moments early on in interviews and during observations.

Other elements were of course important, particularly the physical location of the interview. All the HE interviews took place in the private rooms of the respondents. In FE, apart from interviews with the principals, most interviews took place in empty teaching or administrative rooms over which the interviewee had some control. However, 8 of the 28 FE interviews were held in 'public space', for instance in the staff work rooms which many 'managers' in FE share with their lecturing and administrative colleagues. This inevitably changed the nature of the discussion. Speakers tended to present the publicly consumable version of changing conditions of work. However this was not the case for each, and on balance, each of these texts provided useful elements for the study.

In summary, the interview as a discursive practice has a number of advantages and disadvantages. In terms of advantages, it is a relatively open space. Almost all the more than 65 senior post-holders I spoke with seemed to find the experience relatively harmless, even pleasurable. In part this was aided by the familiarity for them of the confidential research interview in FHE, and the identity of 'researcher'. As a result, interviews frequently went well beyond the 40-minute limit I would initially agree with the interviewees. Yet this signals a key disadvantage. The interview is a contrived space. It is not, directly at least, engaged in the discursive practices through which the manager is an effect. While interviews with senior post-holders bring with them assumptions about the relative importance of these posts, the interview is a space removed from other sites where the problems that surround the practices of managing might be directly articulated. As a result one can expect the speakers, given the relative openness of the confidential interview, to perhaps overplay their positioning and perhaps overstate their relative power or powerlessness in relation to others. Thus the interview should be treated as a particular display where many of the normalized controls on such displays have been removed. It could be argued that the interview's 'removal' of people from direct practices means that the new managerial identity can be analysed and critiqued by the speaker from within other narratives (e.g. the educator or administrator). Thus while the interview could be said to provide a space via which the tensions around such competing subject positions can be explored, it is important that this not be taken itself as evidence that such tensions are invariably articulated at points when the managerial or educational or administrative subject is engaged through particular practices.

After all, one of the ontological assumptions for this study is that 'human being' is fragmented and an effect of discursive practices. One's investment in and allegiance to particular practices in the midst of others cannot be guaranteed. Also, as Fiske (1993) notes, the identities produced by locale and station are not necessarily in opposition to one another. Of course one's commitment to a relatively coherent narrative of self across these diverse practices might guarantee some sense of coherency, and this is the kind of assumption that the interview questions suggest, yet it is important to hear narrative practices as just that – practices – whose content (and thus the formation of subjectivity) is constantly developing and changing.

Analysing the research texts

As noted above, the key questions for the research were what subject positions does the speaker take up for him/herself and how are these produced (e.g. what practices are embedded in them and what are the problems that surround them).

There are a number of forms of discourse and narrative analyses available which could be used to address these questions in relation to interview material (van Dijk, 1985; Potter and Wetherell, 1987; Curt, 1991; Bal, 1993; Burman and Parker, 1993; Feldman, 1994). However, Norman Fairclough's critical discourse analysis offers a number of tools which aid particularly the exploration of the subject positions found in interview texts (Fairclough, 1989, 1992, 1993, 1995; Fairclough and Hardy, 1997).

While Fairclough's approach has much in common with other forms of discursive analysis (e.g. Potter and Wetherell's), its strength and difference is found in the positioning of linguistic analysis within a broad social science frame of reference. His approach has a three-dimensional analytical framework for the study of discourse comprising text, discursive practice and social practice. Fairclough situates the analysis of texts (i.e. their vocabulary, grammar, cohesion and structure) within a micro-sociological analysis of discursive practices or genres, which he understands as practices of production, consumption and distribution of texts (e.g. the interview can be understood as a genre of language use). Discursive practices are then set within the broad frame of social practice. Following Halliday (1985), Fairclough suggests that actual texts must be read as simultaneously engaged in the problems of attempting to represent 'reality', to (re)enact social relations and to (re)establish identities (1992: 9). What this means is that the formal aspects of language (vocabulary and grammar) are understood as actively productive of relational, experiential and expressive characteristics which make up particular identities, relations and systems of knowledge.

Fairclough's emphasis is on the analysis of language and discursive practices, but it is clear that he understands 'text' to refer not simply to language forms, but to all human practices, objects, signs or representations that carry meaning (1992: 72). So clearly the practices that organize buildings, rooms, seating positions, forms of body conduct and forms of dress (the whole ensemble which produces the 'workstation' for example) are textual in that they have embedded in them discursive and social practices and therefore signify differently, depending on the discourses or discourse types or devices that make them meaningful.

'Reporting results': narrative position in the research text

A key question raised by this methodological discussion is what narrative position or positions the researcher ought to take up or draw on in producing the research text. In this short section I shall discuss the dominant approach, some of the problems with this, the issue of narrative position in texts which draw on poststructural approaches, and some of the problems and tensions around this.

As Hatch (1996) argues there are four general narrative positions or voices used to construct social science writing: the main character tells the story (Kondo, 1990; Burrell, 1993; Game, 1994), the minor character tells the story (Geetz, 1972; Law, 1994a, 1994b; Watson, 1994), the narrator tells the story as observer (Middlehurst, 1993; Elliott, 1996a; Trowler, 1996; Ainley and Bailey, 1997) and the analytic or omniscient narrator tells the story (Foucault, 1980). While Hatch commends this latter position, the dominant convention tends to be that of narrator as seemingly neutral observer. As Hatch argues such a position tends to affirm a realist and dualist position with regard to social knowledge – i.e. the world is 'out there' and made of 'things' which can be described by an observer. Even qualitative research, which directly challenges these assumptions, tends to takes up this dominant position (du Gay, 1996; Halford *et al.*, 1997).

The key point arising from this is that just as the interview as a discursive practice is infused with power relations, similar issues are raised with regard to the 'voice' of the researcher in the research report. As Putnam (1996: 385) argues, narrative position is not simply an outcome of the choices which researchers make:

> Power infuses the production of knowledge through the way we gather and analyse data, as well as through the way we present our findings . . . power is also embedded in the way that academic practices shape the production of research texts. The ideology of the research report strongly influences how we write, what forms we use, and what outlets we seek . . . These politics of representation may supersede the role of narrative position in understanding organizational research.

What responses to these issues could be made in the research report? One would be to follow the novel examples of a number of authors from across the social sciences who have recently taken up the challenge induced by this poststructural reflexivity over the 'author' and produced highly innovative works (Stainton Rogers and Stainton Rogers, 1992; Curt, 1994; Burrell, 1996b; Maclure and Stonach, 1996). I have taken a more moderate approach. While a substantial amount of the discussion takes up the conventional tropes of the qualitative research report, I have attempted to address these issues (in an inevitably partial way) in segments of the text.

First I use a fictionalized account of my positioning within the discursive practices of the academic conference to establish a poststructuralist or postdualist account of the construction of identity. In this the speaker is a 'me' discussing the construction of 'me' as an academic through the discursive practices of a particular academic conference. The example is used to provide the basis for discussing the construction of the FHE manager. Through it I am also highlighting a reflexive stance in relation to the narrative position or 'voice'. The example highlights how narrative position is not simply an outcome of the choices which researchers make in reporting their results, but, more substantially, is an effect of particular relations of power embedded in the dominant discursive practices which produce academic knowledge. In the segment, the speaker, attributed with an awareness of this, can be read as speaking back to the dominant narrative position which pervades the book and which itself is engaged in the production of an academic identity.

Second, in less dramatic fashion, the accounts of the meetings I attended at Hillside College have been written in such a way as to highlight the tensions around narrative position. Ostensibly I attended these meetings as an observer; someone listening in on the 'work' of section managers and programme coordinators. In order to highlight the problems of assuming that one can simply listen and record discourse in some neutral and positivistic fashion, I have put my reports of these meetings in the same block quotation format. By adopting this approach I have attempted to highlight that these segments of text should not be read simply as accounts of the meetings *per se*, but as accounts of the meetings written through the narrative position of the observer. Such an approach helps to highlight the inherent selectivity and 'storied-ness' (Curt, 1994) of research writing and also the production of the subject position of 'researcher' through the discursive practices in which he or she is embedded. As is clear from this discussion, issues of narrative position and power, like those that relate to the interview as a discursive practice, present substantial dilemmas for researchers taking up a broad postdualist position. Yet to foreground these issues at every turn in the research process, to make them the focus of research, risks compromising the possibility of using the time and space made available by research programmes to engage with, in my view, the more substantial issues of organizational life.

Bibliography

Adkins, L. and Lury, C. (1998) Making people, making bodies, making work. Paper presented to the British Sociological Association Annual Conference, 'Making sense of the body', University of Edinburgh, April.

Ainley, P. (1994) *Degrees of Difference*. London: Lawrence & Wishart.

Ainley, P. and Bailey, B. (1997) *The Business of Learning: Staff and Student Experiences of Further Education in the 1990s*. London: Cassell.

Alvesson, M. and Willmott, H. (1996) *Making Sense of Management: A Critical Introduction*. London: Sage.

Ashton, E. (1995) 'Management of change in further education: some perceptions of college principals', unpublished PhD thesis. Loughborough University of Technology.

Audit Commission (1985) *Obtaining Better Value from Further Education*. London: Audit Commission.

Bal, M. (1993) First person, second person, same person: narrative as epistmology. *New Literary History*, 24: 293–320.

Bal, M. (1994) First person, second person, same person: narrative as epistemology. *New Literary History*, 24: 293–320.

Ball, S. (1994) *Education Reform: A Critical and Post-structural Approach*. Buckingham: Open University Press.

Barnett, R. (1997) *Higher Education: A Critical Business*. Buckingham: SRHE & Open University Press.

Baron, B. (1978) *The Managerial Approach to Tertiary Education; A Critical Analysis* (Studies in Education no. 7). London: University of London Institute of Education.

Barry, D. and Elmes, M. (1997) Strategy retold: toward a narrative view of strategic discourse. *Academy of Management Review*, 22(2): 429–52.

Becher, T. (1989) *Academic Tribes and Territories: Intellectual Enquiry and the Cultures of Disciplines*. Buckingham: SRHE & Open University Press.

Becker, T. and Kogan, M. (1992) *Process and Structure in Higher Education*, 2nd edn. London: Routledge.

Beckett, F. (1994) Learning new tricks, *Guardian* (Education): 5.

Bennell, P. and Pearce, T. (1998) *The Internalisation of Higher Education: Exploring Education to Developing and Transitional Economies*. Falmer: Institute of Development Studies, University of Sussex.

Berry, R. (1994) *Management Accounting in Universities*. London: CIMA.

Berryman, S. (1997) Raising an army with demoralised officers, *Times Higher Education Supplement*, 14 November.

Blackmore, J. (1993) In the shadow of men: 'the historical construction of administration as a "masculinist" enterprise', in J. Blackmore and J. Kenway (eds) *Gender Matters in Education Administration and Policy*, pp. 27–48. London: Falmer Press.

Blackmore, J. (1996) Doing 'emotional labour' in the education market-place: stories from the field of women in management. *Discourse: Studies in the Cultural Politics of Education*, 17(3): 337–49.

Blackmore, J. and Sachs, J. (1998) Performativity, passion and the making of the academic self: women leaders in the restructured and internationalised university. Paper presented at the Winds of Change Conference, University of Technology, Sydney, June.

Bloland, H.G. (1995) Postmodernism and higher education. *Journal of Higher Education*, 66(5): 521–59.

Bocock, J. and Watson, D. (1994) *Managing the University Curriculum*. Buckingham: SRHE & Open University Press.

Boje, D. (1995) Stories of the story-telling organization: a postmodern analysis of Disney as 'Tamara-Land'. *Academy of Management Journal*, 38(4): 997–1035.

Booth, B. (1992) More power to the ex-polys elbow, *Times Higher Education Supplement*, 2 October: 24.

Bourdieu, P. (1990) *The Logic of Practice*. Cambridge: Polity Press.

Bown, L. (1999) Beyond the degree: men and women at the decision-making levels in British higher education. *Gender and Education*, 10(1): 5–25.

Boyett, I. (1996) The public sector entrepreneur: a definition. *International Journal of Public Sector Management*, 9(2): 36–51.

Boyett, I. and Finlay, D. (1993) The emergence of the educational entrepeneur. *Long Range Planning*, 26(3): 114–22.

Bradley, D. (1996) Who dares wins: intended and unintended consequences of the FEFC funding methodology. *Education Management and Administration*, 24(4): 379–88.

Braverman, H. (1974) *Labour and Monopoly Capital*. New York: Monthly Review Press.

Brewis, J. (1996) The 'making' of the 'competent' manager: competence development, personal effectiveness and Foucault. *Management Learning*, 27(1): 65–86.

Brindle, D. (1994a) 'Grey suits' face cuts in NHS purge. *The Guardian*, 9 March: 3.

Brindle, D. (1994b) Welsh told to save on NHS management. *The Guardian*, 24 March: 3.

Brodeth, E. (1995) Changing the rules of the 'men's club': a woman's experience of senior management in higher education, in J. Bell and B. Harrison (eds) *Vision and Values in Managing Education*, pp. 118–27. London: David Fulton Publishers.

Brodie, D. and Partington, P. (1992) *HE Developmental Leadership/Management: An Exploration of Roles and Responsibilities* (Occasional Green Paper No. 3). London: CVCP.

Brooks, A. (1997) *Academic Women*. Buckingham: SRHE & Open University Press.

Brooks, A. (1998) Regulating the politics of inclusion: academic women, equity issues and the 'politics of restructuring'. *International Review of Women and Leadership*, 4(1): 29–60.

Browning, S. (1998) A narrative analysis of competive advantage: a case of linking the bottom line to the narrative line. Paper presented at the 3rd Organization Discourse Conference, Kings College, London, July.

Brownlow, S. (1997) Full speed ahead! *Inform*, Summer: 8–9.

Bryman, A., Haslam, C. and Webb, A.L. (1991) *University Staff Appraisal Project: Final Report.* Loughborough: Department of Social Sciences, University of Loughborough.

Buchbinder, H. and Newson, J. (1988) Managerial consequences of recent changes in university funding policies: a preliminary view of the British case. *European Journal of Education*, 23(1/2): 151–65.

Bull, J. (1994) Managing change or changing managers, in S. Weil (ed.) *Introducing Change from the Top in Universities and Colleges: 10 Personal Accounts*, pp. 81–93. London: Kogan Page.

Burchell, G. (1993) Liberal government and techniques of the self. *Economy and Society*, 22(3): 266–82.

Burchell, G., Gordon, C. and Miller, P. (1992) *The Foucault Effect: Studies in Governmentality.* London: Harvester.

Burman, E. and Parker, I. (eds) (1993) *Discourse Analytic Research.* London: Routledge.

Burrell, G. (1988) Modernism, post modernism and organizational analysis 2: the contribution of Michel Foucault. *Organization Studies*, 9(2): 221–35.

Burrell, G. (1992) The organization of pleasure, in M. Alvesson and H. Willmott (eds) *Critical Management Studies*, pp. 66–89. London: Sage.

Burrell, G. (1993) Eco and the Bunnymen, in J. Hassard and M. Parker (eds) *Postmodernism and Organizations*, pp. 71–82. London: Sage.

Burrell, G. (1996a) Normal science: paradigms, metaphors, discourses and genealogies of analysis, in S. Clegg, C. Hardy and W. Nord (eds) *Handbook of Organization Studies*, pp. 642–58. London: Sage.

Burrell, G. (1996b) *Pandemonium: Towards a Retro-organizational Theory.* London: Sage.

Burrell, G. and Cooper, R. (1988) Modernism, postmodernism and organizational analysis: an introduction. *Organization Studies*, 9(1): 91–112.

Burton, S. (1994) Factors affecting quality in the new FE principals' views'. *Coombe Lodge Report*, 24(5): 349–439.

Butler, J. (1990a) Gender trouble, feminist theory and psychoanalytic discourse, in L. Nicholson (ed.) *Feminism/Postmodernism*, pp. 324–40. London: Routledge.

Butler, J. (1990b) *Gender Trouble, Feminism and the Subversion of Identity.* New York: Routledge.

Calas, M. and Smircich, L. (1996) From 'the woman's' point of view: feminist approaches to organization studies, in S. Clegg, C. Hardy and W. Nord (eds) *Handbook of Organization Studies*, pp. 218–57. London: Sage.

Canter, L. and Roberts, I. (1986) *Further Education Today: A Critical Review*, 3rd edn. London: Routledge.

Canter, L., Roberts, I. and Pratley, B. (1995) *A Guide to Further Education in England and Wales.* London: Cassell.

Chandler, A. (1977) *The Visible Hand: The Managerial Revolution in American Business.* London: Belknap Press of Harvard University.

Charlesworth, J., Clarke, J. and Cochrane, A. (1996) Tangled Web? Managing local mixed economies of care. *Public Administration*, 74(1): 67–88.

Chia, R. (1994) The concept of decision: a deconstructive analysis. *Journal of Management Studies*, 31(6): 781–806.

Chia, R. (1995) From modern to postmodern organizational analysis. *Organization Studies*, 16(4): 579–604.

Clair, R. (1993) The bureaucratisation, commodification and privatisation of sexual harrassment through institutional discourse: a study of the big ten universities. *Management Communication Quarterly*, 7(2): 123–57.

Clark, H., Chandler, J. and Barry, J. (1997) Gender and managerial relations in the changing life of the university. Paper presented at the Gender and Education Conference 'Transitions in Gender and Education', University of Warwick, April.

Clark, I.A. (1996) 'Human resource management and the incorporation of further education colleges: a consideration of cultural shift', unpublished MSc dissertation. Anglia Polytechnic University.

Clarke, J. and Newman, J. (1993) The right to manage: a second managerial revolution? *Cultural Studies*, 7(3): 427–40.

Clarke, J. and Newman, J. (1997) *The Managerial State*. London: Sage.

Clarke, J., Cochrane, A. and McLaughlin, E. (eds) (1994) *Managing Social Policy*. London: Sage.

Clarke, K. (1993) I listen, I consult, I reform, etc., *Guardian*, 5 February.

Clegg, S. (1975) *Power, Rule and Domination: A Critical and Empirical Understanding of Power in Sociological Theory and Organizational Life*. London: Routledge.

Cockburn, C. (1991) *In the Way of Women: Men's Resistance to Sex Equality in Organisations*. Basingstoke: Macmillan.

Coleman, G. (1991) *Investigating Organisations: A Feminist Approach: Occasional Paper No. 37*. Bristol: University of Bristol School for Advanced Urban Studies.

Collinson, D. and Hearn, J. (1994) Naming men as men: implications for work, organisation and management. *Gender, Work and Organisation*, 1(1): 3–22.

Collinson, D. and Hearn, J. (eds) (1996) *Men as Managers, Managers as Men: Critical Perspectives on Men, Masculinities and Managements*. London: Sage.

Common, R., Flynn, N. and Mellon, E. (1991) *Managing Public Services*. London: Butterworth.

Conway, T., Mackay, S. and Yorke, D. (1994) Strategic planning in higher education: who are the customers? *International Journal of Educational Management*, 8(6): 29–36.

Cooper, R. and Burrell, G. (1988) Modernism, postmodernism and organization: an introduction. *Organization Studies*, 9(1): 91–112.

Cowham, T. (1995) Quality, chaos and the management of change in further education, in J. Bell and B. Harrison (eds) *Vision and Values in Managing Education* pp. 81–94. London: David Fulton Publishers.

Crequer, N. (1996) Spotlight falls on crisis-hit college, *Times Higher Education Supplement*, 6 December: 29.

Curt, B. (1994) *Textuality and Techtonics: Troubling Social and Psychological Science*. Buckingham: Open University Press.

Cuthbert, R. (1992) Under new management, in I. McNay (ed.) *Visions of Post-Compulsory Education*, pp. 152–60. Buckingham: SRHE & Open University Press.

Cuthbert, R. (ed.) (1996) *Working in Higher Education*. Buckingham: SRHE & Open University Press.

CVCP (Committee of Vice Chancellors and Principals) (1985) *Report of the Steering Committee of Efficiency Studies in Universities* (the 'Jarrett Report'). London: CVCP.

CVCP (Committee of Vice Chancellors and Principals) (1996) 'University financies take a nosedive', CVCP press release 445, 1 October (http://www.cvcp.ac.uk/pr/pr445.html).

CVCP (Committee of Vice Chancellors and Principals) (1997a) 'University challenge for new government', media release, 2 May.

CVCP (Committee of Vice Chancellors and Principals) (1997b) *Higher Education Productivity: A Study for the CVCP*. London: CVCP.

Davidson, M. (1997) *The Black and Ethnic Minority Manager: Cracking the Concrete Ceiling.* London: Chapman.

Davies, J. (1989) The training of academic heads of department in higher education institutions: an international overview. *Higher Education Management*, 1(2): 201–15.

de Groot, J. (1997) After the ivory tower: gender, commodification and the 'academic'. *Feminist Review*, 55(spring): 130–42.

Dearlove, J. (1995) The deadly dull issue of university 'administration'? Good governance, managerialism and organizing academic work. Paper presented at the 1995 SRHE Conference 'The Changing University', Heriot-Watt University, Edinburgh, December.

Deem, R. (1998) Managing the universities of the future: new managerialism, new public service management and femocracies. Paper presented to the 'Higher Education Close Up' Conference, University of Central Lancashire, Preston, July.

Deem, R. and Ozga, J. (1996) Coping with crises and changing engendered cultures: feminist academic managers in UK higher education. Paper presented at the 1996 SRHE Conference 'Working in Higher Education', Cardiff, December.

Deem, R. and Ozga, J. (1997) Carrying the burden of transformation: the experiences of women managers in UK higher education. Paper presented at the European Conference of Educational Research, University of Seville, September.

Deetz, S. (1992) Disciplinary power in the modern corporation, in M. Alvesson and H. Willmott (eds) *Critical Management Studies*, pp. 21–45. London: Sage.

Deleuze, G. (1988) *Foucault.* London: Athlone.

Deleuze, G. (1992) What is dispositif?, in T.J. Armstrong (ed.) *Michel Foucault*, pp. 159–67. London: Harvester Wheatsheaf.

Delmont, S. (1996) Just like the novels? Researching the occupational culture(s) of higher education, in R. Cuthbert (ed.) (1996) *Working in Higher Education*, pp. 145–56. Buckingham: SRHE & Open University Press.

DES (Department of Education and Science) (1991) *Higher Education: A New Framework.* London: HMSO.

DES (Department of Education and Science)/Council of Local Authorities (1987) *Managing Colleges Efficiently.* London: DES.

DfE (Department for Education) (1994) Table B21/91: *Full-time Teachers in Maintained, Assisted and Grant-Aided Establishments of Further Education.* London: DfE Analytical Services Branch.

DHSS (Department of Health and Social Security) (1983) *National Health Service Management Inquiry Report* ('The Griffiths Report'). London: Department of Health and Social Security.

Downing, S. (1998) A narrative analysis of competitive advantage: a case for linking the bottom line to the narrative line. Paper presented at the Organizational Discourse Conference, Kings College, London, July.

Drodge, S. and Cooper, N. (1996) Strategy and management in the further education sector, in M. Preedy, R. Glatter and R. Levačić (eds) *Educational Management: Strategies, Quality and Resources*, pp. 205–17. Buckingham: Open University Press.

DTI (Department of Trade and Industry) (1999) *Competitiveness* (White Paper). London: DTI (access at: http://www.dti.gov.uk/public/frame7.html as at April 19, 1999).

du Gay, P. (1994) Making up managers: bureaucracy, enterprise and the liberal art of separation. *British Journal of Sociology*, 45(4): 655–74.

du Gay, P. (1996) *Consumption and Identity at Work.* London: Sage.

du Gay, P., Salaman, G. and Rees, B. (1996) The conduct of management and the management of conduct: contemporary managerial discourse and the constitution of the competent manager. *Journal of Managment Studies*, 33(3): 263–81.

Eccles, R. and Nohria, N. (1992) *Beyond the Hype; Rediscovering the Essence of Management*. Cambridge, MA: Harvard Business School Press.

Elliott, G. (1994) Re-naming of parts: how lecturers respond to restructuring in an English further education college. Bristol papers in education, comparative and international studies 2, *Research Training and Educational Management International Perspectives*. Bristol: University of Bristol.

Elliott, G. (1995) 'Policy and practice in further education: managing the process of change', unpublished EdD thesis. University of Bristol.

Elliott, G. (1996a) *Crisis and Change in Vocational Education and Training*. London: Jessica Kingsley.

Elliott, G. (1996b) Education management and the crisis of reform in further education. *Journal of Vocational Education and Training*, 48(1): 5–23.

Elliott, G. and Crossley, M. (1994) Qualitative research, educational management and the incorporation of the further education sector. *Education Management and Administration*, 22(3): 188–97.

Elliott, G. and Crossley, M. (1997) Contested values in further education: findings from a case study of the management of change. *Education Management and Administration*, 25(1): 79–91.

Elliott, G. and Hall, V. (1994) FE Inc.: business orientation in further education and the introduction of human resource management. *School Organisation*, 14(1): 3–10.

Ezzamel, M. (1994) Organizational change and accounting: understanding the budgeting system in its organizational context. *Organization Studies*, 15(2): 213–40.

Ezzy, D. (1997) Subjectivity and the labour process: conceptualising 'good work'. *Sociology*, 31(3): 427–44.

Fairclough, N. (1989) *Language and Power*. London: Longman.

Fairclough, N. (1991) What might we mean by 'enterprise culture', in R. Keat and N. Abercrombie (eds) *Enterprise Culture*, pp. 38–57. London: Rouledge.

Fairclough, N. (1992) *Discourse and Social Change*. London: Polity Press.

Fairclough, N. (1993) Critical discourse analysis and the marketisation of public discourse: the universities. *Discourse and Society*, 4(2): 133–68.

Fairclough, N. (1995) *Critical Discourse Analysis*. London: Longman.

Fairclough, N. and Hardy, G. (1997) Management learning as discourse, in J. Burgoyne and M. Reynolds (eds) *Management Learning: Intergrating Perspectives in Theory and Practice*, pp. 141–61. London: Sage.

Farish, M., McPake, J., Powney, J. and Weiner, G. (1995) *Equal Opportunities in Colleges and Universities: Towards Better Practices*. Buckingham: SRHE & Open University Press.

Farnham, D. (1991) From model employer to private sector model: the PCFC sector. *Higher Education Review*, 23(1): 7–23.

Farnham, D. (1995) Pay, conditions and pay determination of heads and professors in new universities. *Higher Education Review*, 28(1): 20–33.

Farnham, D. and Horton, S. (1993) *Managing the New Public Services*. London: Macmillan.

FEDA (Further Education Development Agency) (1997) *Flagship Management Development Programme Overall Report*. London: FEDA.

FEFC (Further Education Funding Council) (1991) *Funding Guidance 1999–2000*, Circular, 99/07. London: FEFC.

FEFC (Further Education Funding Council) (1998) Staff Statistics, 1995–96 and 1996–97, 1994–95 and 1995–96 retrieved 11 December 1999 from http:// 194.66.249.219/data/staffstatistics.html

FEFC (Further Education Funding Council) (1999) *Funding Guidance 1999–2000*, Circular 99/07. London: FEFC.

Feldman, A. (1991) *Formations of Violence*. Chicago: University of Chicago Press.

Ferguson, K.E. (1994) On bringing more theory, more voices and more politics to the study of organization. *Organization*, 1(1): 81–100.

Fielden, J. and Lockwood, G. (1973) *Planning and Management in Universities: A Study of British Universities*. London: Chatto & Windus.

Fiske, J. (1989) *Reading the Popular*. London: Routledge.

Fiske, J. (1993) *Power Plays, Power Works*. London: Verso.

Fiske, J. (1994) Audiencing, cultural practice and cultural studies, in N. Denzin and Y. Lincoln (eds) *Handbook of Qualitative Analysis*, pp. 189–98. London: Sage.

Fiske, J. (1996a) Opening the hallway: some remarks on the fertility of Stuart Hall's contribution to critical theory, in D. Morley and K. Chen (eds) *Stuart Hall: Critical Dialogues in Cultural Studies*, pp. 212–20. London: Routledge.

Fiske, J. (1996b) Media Matters: Race and Gender in US Politics. Minneapolis, MN: University of Minnesota Press.

Flax, J. (1995) Postmodernism and gender relations in feminist theory, in M. Blair and J. Holland with S. Sheldon (eds) *Identity and Diversity: Gender and the Experience of Education*, pp. 143–60. Clevedon: The Open University.

Flint, C. and Austin, M. (eds) (1994) *Going Further: Essays in Further Education*. Bristol: Staff College and Association for Colleges.

Flynn, N. (1990) *Public Sector Management*. London: Harvester Wheatsheaf.

Fook, N.Y.M. (1994) 'Marketing orientation in professional organizations: the case of further education', unpublished PhD thesis. Nottingham Trent University.

Ford, P., Goodyear, P., Heseltine, R., Lewis, R., Darby, J., Graves, J., Satorius, P., Harwood, D. and King, T. (1996) *Managing Change in Higher Education: A Learning Environment Architecture*. Buckingham: SRHE & Open University Press.

Foucault, M. (1972) *The Archaeology of Knowledge*. London: Routledge.

Foucault, M. (1979) Governmentality. *Ideology and Consciousness*, 6: 5–25.

Foucault, M. (1980) *Power/Knowledge: Selected Interviews and other Writings by Michel Foucault, 1972–7* (trans. C. Gordon). Brighton: Harvester.

Foucault, M. (1982) The subject and power, in H.L. Dreyfus and P. Rabinow (eds) *Michel Foucault: Beyond Structuralism and Hermenuetics*, pp. 208–26. London: Harvester.

Foucault, M. (1983) The subject and power, in H.L. Dreyfus and P. Rabinow (eds) *Michel Foucault: Beyond Structuralism and Hermeneutics*, pp. 208–66. Chicago: Chicago University Press.

Foucault, M. (1984) The order of discourse, in M. Shapiro (ed.) *Language and Politics*, pp. 108–38. Oxford: Blackwell.

Foucault, M. (1990) *The History of Sexuality*, vol. 1. Harmondsworth: Penguin.

Foucault, M. (1991) *Discipline and Punish: The Birth of the Prison*. Harmondsworth: Penguin.

Fox, N.J. (1993) *Postmodernism, Sociology and Health*. Buckingham: Open University Press.

Frain, J. (1993) *The Changing Culture of a College*. London: Falmer Press.

Frank, A.W. (1991) For a sociology of the body: an analytical review, in M. Featherstone, M. Hepworth and B.S. Turner (eds) *The Body: Social Process and Cultural Theory*. London: Sage.

Game, A. (1991) *Undoing the Social: Towards a Deconstructive Sociology.* Buckingham: Open University Press.

Game, A. (1994) Matter out of place: the management of academic work. *Organization*, 1(1): 47–50.

Geetz, C. (1972) Deep play: notes on the Balinese cockfight. *Daedalus*, Winter: 1–37.

Gewirtz, S., Ball, S. and Bowe, R. (1995) *Markets, Choice and Equity in Education.* Buckingham: Open University Press.

Giddens, A. (1979) *Central Problems in Social Theory: Action, Structure and Contradiction in Social Analysis.* London: Macmillan.

Giddens, A. (1990) *The Consequences of Modernity.* Cambridge: Polity.

Gleeson, D. and Shain, F. (1999) Managing ambiguity: between markets and managerialism: a case study of 'middle' managers in further education. *Sociological Review*, 47(3): 461–90.

Gordon, C. (ed.) (1980) *Power/Knowledge: Selected Interviews and Other Writings by Michel Foucault, 1972–1977.* Brighton: Harvester.

Gordon, C. (1991) Governmental rationality: an introduction, in? G. Burchell, C. Gordon and P. Miller (eds) *The Foucault Effect: Studies in Governmentality,* pp. 1–51. Brighton: Harvester.

Gorringe, R. and Toogood, P. (eds) (1994) Changing the culture of a college. *Coombe Lodge Report*, 24(3): 183–277.

Gower, D. and Legge, K. (1996) The meaning of management and the management of meaning, in S. Linstead, R. Grafton-Small and P. Jeffcutt (eds) *Understanding Management,* pp. 34–50. London: Sage.

Grant, B. (1997) Disciplining students: the construction of student subjectivities. *British Journal of Sociology of Education*, 18(1): 101–14.

Gray, H. and Hoy, C. (1989) University development: the balance between research and teaching. *Higher Education Review*, 22(1): 35–46.

Grint, K. (1994) Re-engineering history: social resonances and business process reegineering. *Organization*, 1(1): 179–201.

Hales, C. (1993) *Managing Through Organisations: The Management Process, Forms of Organisations and Work of Managers.* London: Routlege.

Hales, C. and Tamangani, Z. (1998) An investigation of the relationship between organizational structure, managerial role expectations and managers' work activities. *Journal of Management Studies*, 33(6): 731–56.

Halford, S., Savage, M. and Witz, A. (1997) *Gender, Careers and Organisation.* London: Macmillan.

Hall, S. (1981) Notes on deconstructing 'the popular', in R. Samuel (ed.) *People's History and Socialist Theory,* pp. 227–40. London: Routledge & Kegan Paul.

Hall, S. (1993) Thatcherism today, *New Statesman and Society*, 26 November: 14–16.

Hall, S. (1996) Introduction: 'who needs identity?' in S. Hall and P. du Gay (eds) *Questions of Cultural Identity,* pp. 1–17. London: Sage.

Hall, V. (1994) *Further Education in the United Kingdom,* 2nd edn. London: Collins & The Staff College.

Hall, V. (1997) Dusting off the phoenix: gender and educational leadership. *Educational Management and Administration*, 35(3): 309–24.

Halliday, M.A.K. (1985) *An Introduction to Functional Grammar.* London: Arnold.

Halsey, A.H. (1992) *Decline of Donnish Dominion: the British Academic Professions in the Twentieth Century.* Oxford: Clarendon.

Hammer, M. and Champy, J. (1993) Re-engineering the Corporation: A Manifesto for Business Revolution. London: Nicholas Brealey.

Hammond, J. (1999) Judgement of Hammond, J. in Association of University Staff of New Zealand *vs.* The University of Waikato. High Court of New Zealand, Hamilton Registry, 31 March.

Hansard Society for Parliamentary Government (1990) *Report of the Hansard Society Commission on Women at the Top.* London: Hansard Society.

Harper, H. (1997) *Management in Further Education: Theory and Practice.* London: David Fulton Publishers.

Harvey, L. and Knight, P.T. (1996) *Transforming Higher Education.* Buckingham: SRHE & Open University Press.

Harvey, D. (1993) Class relations, social justice and the politics of difference, in M. Keith and S. Pile (eds) *Place and the Politics of Identity,* pp. 41–66. London: Routledge.

Hatch, M.J. (1996) The role of the researcher: an analysis of narrative position in organization theory. *Journal of Management Enquiry,* 5(4): 359–74.

Hearn, J. (1998) Is the critical study of men managers in universities also about women, change and the culture of universities. Paper presented at the 'Winds of Change: Women and the Culture of Universities' conference, University of Technology, Sydney, July.

HEFCE (Higher Education Funding Council for England) (1996) *Circular 15/96: Analysis of 1996 Financial Forecast, September* (available at http://www.niss/ac.uk/education/hefce/pub96/c15_96.html as at 16 July 1997).

HEFCE (Higher Education Funding Council for England) (1998) *Funding Higher Education in England: How the HEFCE Allocates its Funds, Guide 98/67* (available at http://www.niss.ac.uk/education/hefce/pub98/98_67.html as at 26 February 1999).

Henson, S.L. (1995) *No Escape from Judgement: Appraisal and PRP in Higher Education* (occasional paper in organizational analysis no. 2). Portsmouth: University of Portsmouth Department of Business and Management.

Heward, C. (1994) Academic snakes and merit ladders: reconceptualising the 'glass ceiling'. *Gender and Education,* 6(3): 249–62.

Heward, C. and Taylor, P. (1992) Women at the top in higher education: equal opportunities policies in action? *Policy and Politics,* 20(2): 111–21.

Heward, C. and Taylor, P. (1994) Gender and sexuality in successful academic careers. Paper presented to the British Sociological Association conference, University of Central Lancashire, July.

Heward, C., Taylor, P. and Vickers, R. (1997) Gender, race and career success in the academic profession. *Journal of Further and Higher Education,* 21(2): 205–18.

Hodge, R. and Kress, G. (1993) *Language as Ideology,* 2nd edn. London: Routledge.

Hoggett, P. (1996) New modes of control in the public services. *Public Administration,* 74(spring): 9–32.

Hollway, W. (1991) *Work Psychology and Organizational Behaviour.* London: Sage.

Holmer-Nadesen, M. (1996) Organizational identity and space of action. *Organization Studies,* 17(1): 49–81.

Hood, C. (1991) A public management for all seasons? *Public Administration,* 69(spring): 3–19.

House, D. and Watson, D. (1995) Managing change, in D. Warner and E. Crosthwaite (ed.) *Human Resource Management in Higher and Further Education,* pp. 7–19. Buckingham: SRHE & Open University Press.

Hughes, C. (1994) FE: all dressed up, but does it know where to go? in C. Flint and M. Austin (eds) *Going Further: Essays in Further Education.* Bristol: Staff College & Association for Colleges.

Hughes, C., Taylor, P. and Tight, M. (1996) The ever-changing world of further education: a case for research. *Research in Post-Compulsory Education*, 1(1): 7–18.

Humprey, C., Moizer, P. and Owen, D. (1995) Questioning the value of the research selectivity process in British university accounting. *Accouting, Auditing and Accountability Journal*, 8(3): 139–62.

Ibarra-Colado, E. (1996) Excellence at large: power, knowledge and organizational forms in Mexican universities, in S. Clegg and G. Palmer (eds) *The Politics of Management Knowledges*, pp. 99–120. London: Sage.

Isaac-Henry, K., Painter, C. and Barnes, C. (1992) *Management in the Public Sector: Challenge and Change*. London: Chapman & Hall.

Itzin, C. and Newman, J. (eds) (1995) *Gender, Culture and Organizational Change: Putting Theory into Practice*. London: Routledge.

Jackson, B. (1996) Re-engineering the sense of self: the manager and the management guru. *Journal of Management Studies*, 33(5): 571–90.

Jacques, R. (1996) *Manufacturing the Employee: Management Knowledge from the 19th to the 21st Centuries*. London: Sage.

Jenkins, S. (1995) *Accountable to None: the Tory Nationalization of Britain*. Harmondsworth: Penguin.

Jephcote, M. (1996) Principals' response to incorporation: a window on their culture. *Journal of Further and Higher Education*, 20(2): 33–47.

Jermier, J. (1998) Introduction: critical perspectives on organizational control. *Administrative Science Quarterly*, 43: 235–56.

Johnnes, J. and Taylor, J. (1990) *Performance Indicators in Higher Education*. Buckingham: SRHE & Open University Press.

Jones, S. (1997a) Time to introduce the 'my best manager' column, *Times Educational Supplement*, 7 March.

Jones, S. (1997b) In the interests of unity, *Times Educational Supplement*, 2 May.

Kanter, R.M. (1997) *Men and Women of the Corporation*. New York: Basic Books.

Kerfoot, D. and Whitehead, S. (1995) 'And so say all of us': the problematics of masculinity and managerial work. Paper presented at the 'Gender and Life in Organisations' conference, University of Portsmouth Business School, July.

King, C. (ed.) (1993) *Through the Glass Ceiling: Effective Senior Management Development for Women*. Kent: Tudor Business Publications.

King, C. (1995) Making it happen: reflections on a varied career, in M. Slowey (ed.) *Implementing Change from Within Universities and Colleges: 10 Personal Accounts*, pp. 41–9. London: Kogan Page.

King, C. (1997) Through the glass ceiling: networking by women managers in higher education, in H. Eggin (ed.) *Women as Leaders and Managers in Higher Education*, pp. 91–100. Buckingham: SRHE & Open University Press.

King, R. (1994) The institutional compact, in J. Bocock and D. Watson (eds) *Managing the University Curriculum: Making Common Cause*. Buckingham: SRHE & Open University Press.

Knights, D. (1989) Subjectivity, power and the labour process, in D. Knights and H. Willmott (eds) *Labour Process Theory*, pp. 297–335. London: Macmillan.

Knights, D. (1992) Changing spaces: the disruptive impact of a new epistemological location for the study of management. *Academy of Management Review*, 17(3): 514–36.

Knights, D. (1997) Organization theory in the age of deconstruction: dualism, gender and postmodernism revisted. *Organization Studies*, 18(1): 1–19.

Knights, D. and Vurdusakis, T. (1994) Foucault, resistance and all that, in J. Jermier, D. Knights and W. Nord (eds) *Power and Resistance in Organisations*, pp. 167–98. London: Routledge.

Knights, D. and Willmott, H. (1985) Power and identity in theory and practice. *Sociological Review*, 33(1): 22–46.

Knights, D. and Willmott, H. (1989) Power and subjectivity in work. *Sociology*, 23(4): 537–55.

Kogan, M. (1988) Managerialism in higher education, in D. Lawton (ed.) *The Education Reform Act: Choice and Control*. London: Hodder & Stoughton.

Kondo, D. (1990) *Crafting Selves: Power, Gender and Discourses of Identity in a Japanese Workplace*. Chicago: University of Chicago Press.

Laclau, E. and Mouffe, C. (1985) *Hegemony and Socialist Strategy: Towards a Radical Democratic Politics*. London: Verso.

Lander, D. (1996) The campus transgressions of the cook, the poet and the philosopher. Paper presented at the 'International Conference on Semiotics', Amsterdam School of Cultural Analysis, August.

Law, J. (1994a) *Organizing Modernity*. London: Blackwell.

Law, J. (1994b) Organization, narrative and strategy, in J. Hassard and M. Parker (eds) *Towards a New Theory of Organizations*, pp. 248–68. London: Routledge.

Law, J. (1996) The manager and his powers. Paper presented to the Mediaset Convention, Venice, 12 November. Published by the Centre for Social Theory and Technology, Keele University at: http://www.keele.ac.uk/depts/sst/cstt2/pubs-JL1.htm.

Lawrence, B. (1995) *A Guide to College Resource and Financial Management*. London: Falmer Press.

Leonard, P. (1998) Gendering change? Management, masculinity and the dynamics of incorporation. *Gender and Education*, 10(1): 71–84.

Levitt, T. (1976) Management and the 'post-industrial society'. *Public Interest*, 44(summer): 73–4.

Lewin, K. (1951) *Field Theory in Social Science*. New York: Harper & Row.

Linstead, S., Grafton Small, R. and Jeffcutt, P. (eds) (1996) *Understanding Management*. London: Sage.

Lockwood, G. and Davies, J. (1985) *Universities: The Management Challenge*. Windsor: SRHE & NFER-Nelson.

Longhurst, R.J. (1996) Education as a commodity: the political economy of the new further education. *Journal of Further and Higher Education*, 20(2): 49–66.

Lyotard, J.F. (1984) *The Postmodern Condition*. Manchester: Manchester University Press.

McGinty, J. and Fish, J. (1993) *Further Education in the Marketplace*. London: Routledge.

MacInnes, J. (1987) *Thatcherism at Work: Industrial Relations and Economic Change*. Milton Keynes: Open University Press.

McLaren, P. (1995) *Critical Pedagogy and Predatory Culture: Oppositional Politics in a Postmodern Era*. London: Routledge.

Maclure, M. and Stonach, I. (1996) *Undoing Education Research*. Buckingham: Open University Press.

McNay, I. (1988) *The Reality of College Management: Critical Incidents in FHE*. York: Longman & Further Education Unit.

McNay, I. (1994) Amateur managers, *Times Higher Education Supplement*, 9 December: 12.

McNay, I. (1995) From the collegial academy to corporate enterprise: the changing culture of universities, in T. Schuller (ed.) *The Changing University?* pp. 105–15. Buckingham: SRHE & Open University Press.

McNay, I. (1996) Work's committees, in R. Cuthbert (ed.) *Working in Higher Education*, pp. 119–29. Buckingham: SRHE & Open University Press.

McNay, L. (1992) *Foucault and Feminism.* Cambridge: Polity Press.

McVicar, M. (1993) Education, in D. Farnham and S. Horton (eds) *Managing the New Public Services.* London: Macmillan.

Maile, S. (1995) The gendered nature of managerial discourse. *Gender, Work and Organization*, 2(2): 76–88.

Mangham, I. and Pye, A. (1991) *The Doing of Managing.* London: Blackwell.

Mansell, P. (1996) Changing your perspective, *FE Now!*, October (30): 13–15.

Marsden, R. and Townley, B. (1996) The owl of Minerva: reflections on theory in practice, in Clegg *et al.* (eds) *Handbook of Organization Studies*, pp. 659–75. London: Sage.

Meadmore, D., Limerick, B., Thomas, P. and Lucas, H. (1995) Devolving practices: managing the managers. *Journal of Education Policy*, 10(4): 399–411.

Melville, D. (1999) Delivering results. Speech to the FEFC Annual Conference, Birmingham, February 1999, accessed at http://194.66.249.219/news.index.html.

Middlehurst, R. (1993) *Leading Academics.* Buckingham: SRHE & Open University Press.

Middlehurst, R. (1995) Changing leadership in universities, in T. Schuller (ed.) *The Changing University*, pp. 75–92. Buckingham: SRHE & Open University Press.

Middlehurst, R. (1997) Leadership, women and higher education, in H. Eggins (ed.) *Women as Leaders and Managers in Higher Education*, pp. 3–16. Buckingham: SRHE & Open University Press.

Middlehurst, R. and Elton, L. (1992) Leadership and management in higher education. *Studies in Higher Education*, 17(3): 251–64.

Middleton, P. (1993) *The Inward Gaze: Masculinity and Subjectivity in Modern Culture.* London: Routledge.

Midgley, S. (1996) Caught in the middle, *FE Now!*, December (32): 14, available at http://www.niss.ac.uk/hobsons/fe-now/issue32/fe32p14.html as at 1 July 1997.

Miller, H. (1994) Management and change in universities: Australia, Canada and the United Kingdom. *Association of Commonwealth Universities Bulletin of Current Documentation*, 115: 30–4.

Miller, H. (1995a) Academics and their labour process, in C. Smith, D. Knights and H. Willmott (eds) *White-Collar Work: the Non-manual Labour Process*, pp. 109–38. London: Macmillan.

Miller, H. (1995b) *Management of Change in Universities: Universities, State and Economy in Australia, Canada and the United Kingdom.* Buckingham: SRHE & Open University Press.

Miller, H. (1996) Management of the key profession, in R. Fincham (ed.) *New Relationships in the Organized Professions.* Averbury: Aldershot.

Miller, H. and Edwards, T. (1995) Managerialism, markets and the changing character of the academic profession. Paper presented to the SRHE conference 'The changing university', Heriot-Watt University, Edinburgh, December.

Miller, H. and Higson, H. (1996) Secretaries' and administrators' work and social relations. Paper presented at the SRHE conference 'Working in Higher Education: The Staff Experience', Cardiff, December.

Miller, P. and Rose, N. (1990) Governing economic life. *Economy and Society*, 19(1): 1–31.

Miller, P. and Rose, N. (1995) Production, identity and democracy. *Theory and Society*, 24(3): 427–67.

Morley, L. (1994) Glass ceiling or iron cage: women in UK academia. *Gender, Work and Organization,* 1(4): 194–204.

Morley, L. and Walsh, V. (eds) (1995) *Feminist Academics: Creative Agents for Change.* London: Taylor & Francis.

Mumby, D. and Stohl, C. (1991) Power in organization studies: absence and the dialectic of control. *Discourse and Society,* 2(3): 313–32.

Murray, C. (1996) Researching the employment experiences of women academic staff in further education. *Research in Post-Compulsory Education,* 1(2): 253–8.

NAB (National Advisory Board for Public Sector Higher Education) (1987) *Management for a Purpose.* London: NAB.

Nash, I. (1995) Bullies rise up the ranks, *Times Education Supplement,* 22 September: 32.

Nash, I. (1997) Staff take up early retirement carrot, *Times Education Supplement,* 17 January: 29.

National Audit Office (1995) *Managing to be Independent: Management and Financial Control at Colleges in the Further Education Sector* (HC179). London: HMSO.

National Audit Office (1997) *The Further Education Funding Council for England* (HC223). London: HMSO.

National Committee of Inquiry into Higher Education (1997) *Higher Education in the Learning Society* (The 'Dearing Report'). London: HMSO (available at http://www.ncl.ac.uk/ncihe/index.html, as at 17 July 1997).

Newman, J. (1994) The limits of management: gender and the politics of change, in J. Clarke, A. Cochrane and E. McLaughlin (eds) *Managing Social Policy,* pp. 182–209. London: Sage.

Noble, D. (1998) Digital diploma mills: the automation of higher education. *First Monday,* 3(1), accessed at: http://www.firstmonday.dk/issues/issue3_1/noble/index.html.

O'Doherty, D. and Willmott, H. (1998) Recent contributions to the development of labour process analysis. Paper presented at the Annual International Labour Process Conference, Manchester, April.

Ozga, J. (ed.) (1993) *Women in Education Management.* Buckingham: Open University Press.

Page, C. (1997) The facts are black and white, *FE Now!,* 38 June (Available at http://www.niss.ac.uk/hobsons/fe-now/issue38/fe38p29.html, as at 21 July).

Parker, M. and Jary, D. (1995) The McUniversity: organisations, management and academic subjectivity. *Organization,* 2(2): 319–38.

Pateman, C. (1988) *The Sexual Contract.* Cambridge: Polity Press.

Peters, M. (1992) Performance and accountability in 'post-industrial' society: the crisis of British universities. *Studies in Higher Education,* 17(2): 123–39.

Peters, M. (1996a) Cybernetics, cyberspace and the politics of university reform. *Australian Journal of Education,* 40(2): 162–76.

Peters, M. (1996b) *Poststructuralism, Politics and Education.* London: Bergin & Garvey.

Peters, T. (1987) *Thriving on Chaos: A Handbook for a Management Revolution.* London: Macmillan.

Phillips, R. (1994) Growth and diversity: a new era in colleges and universities, in S. Weil (ed.) *Introducing Change from the Top in Universities and Colleges: 10 Personal Accounts,* pp. 169–82. London: Kogan Page.

Pollitt, C. (1990) Doing business in the temple? Manager and quality assurance in the public services. *Public Administration,* 68 (Winter): 435–52.

Pollitt, C. (1992) *Managerialism and the Public Services,* 2nd edn. Oxford: Blackwell.

Pollitt, C. (1993) The struggle for quality. *Policy and Politics,* 21(3): 161–70.

Potter, D. (1993) Potter hits at BBC 'Daleks', *Guardian*, 28 August: 1.

Potter, J. and Wetherell, M. (1987) *Discourse and Social Psychology*. London: Sage.

Potter, J. and Wetherell, M. (1994) Analysing discourse, in A. Bryman and A. Burgess (eds) *Analysing Quailtative Data*, pp. 47–66. London: Routledge.

Power, M. (1996) I audit therefore I am, *Times Higher Education Supplement*, 18 October: x.

Powney, J. (1997) On becoming and being a manager in education, in H. Eggin (ed.) *Women as Leaders and Managers in Higher Education*, pp. 49–62. Buckingham: SRHE & Open University Press.

Pratt, J. (1991) Editorial, managerialism in higher education. *Higher Education Review*, 23(2): 3–8.

Pratt, J. (1996) *The Polytechnic Experiment, 1965–1992*. Buckingham: SRHE & Open University Press.

Pratt, J. and Locke, M. (1994) Maintaining diversity: strategic plans as a basis for funding. *Higher Education Review*, 26(3): 39–50.

Pratt, J. and Silverman, S. (1989) *Responding to Constraint: Policy and Management in Higher Education*. Buckingham: SRHE & Open University Press.

Price, C. (1994) Piloting HE change: a view from the helm, in S. Weil (ed.) *Introducing Change from the Top in Universities and Colleges: 10 Personal Accounts*, pp. 29–40. London: Kogan Page.

Prichard, C. (1995) Doing the business: customers, managers and market discourse among university vice-chancellors. Paper presented to the SRHE annual conference, Heriot-Watt University, December.

Prichard, C. (1996a) Making managers accountable or making managers? The case of a code for management in a higher education institution. *Education Management and Administration*, 24(1): 79–91.

Prichard, C. (1996b) University management: is it men's work? in D. Collinson and J. Hearn (eds) *Men as Managers, Managers as Men: Critical Perspectives on Men, Masculinities and Managements*, pp. 227–38. London: Sage.

Prichard, C. (forthcoming) The body typography of education management, in J. Hassard, R. Holliday and H. Willmott (eds) *The Body and Organization*. London: Sage.

Prichard, C. and Willmott, H. (1997) Just how managed is the McUniversity? *Organization Studies*, 18(2): 287–316.

Prichard, C., Deem, R. and Ozga, J. (1998) Managing further education: is it still men's work too? Paper presented at the 'Gender, work and organizations' conference, UMIST and Manchester Metropolitan University, January.

Putnam, L. (1996) Commentary: situating the author and the text. *Journal of Management Inquiry*, 5(4): 382–6.

Putnam, L., Phillips, N. and Chapman, P. (1996) Metaphors of communication and organization, in Clegg *et al.* (eds) *Handbook of Organization Studies*, pp. 375–408. London: Sage.

Randle, K. and Brady, N. (1997) Further education and the new managerialism. *Journal of Further and Higher Education*, 21(2): 229–39.

Redwood, J. (1994) Call goes out for More Mellow Fellows, *Times Higher Education Supplement*, 4 August: 12.

Reed, M. (1990) The labour process perspective on management organization: a critique and reformulation, in J. Hassard and D. Pym (eds) *The Philosophy of Organizations*, pp. 63–82. London: Routledge.

Reed, M. (1997) In praise of duality and dualism: rethinking agency and structure in organizational analysis. *Organization Studies*, 18(1): 21–42.

Reeves, F. (1995) *The Modernity of Further Education.* Wolverhampton: Bilston College Press.

Ritzer, G. (1992) *The McDonaldization of Society.* Newbury Park, CA: Pine Forge.

Ritzer, G. (1996) McUniversity in the postmodern consumer society. Plenary address to the 'Dilemmas in Mass Higher Education' Confence, Staffordshire University, April.

Robertson, D. (1998) The emerging political economy of higher education. *Studies in Higher Education,* 23(2): 221–8.

Roper, M. (1996) Seduction and succession: circuits of homosocial desire in management, in D. Collinson and J. Hearn (eds) *Men as Managers, Managers as Men: Critical Perspectives on Men, Masculinities and Managements,* pp. 210–26. London: Sage.

Rose, N. (1989) *Governing the Soul: The Shaping of the Private Self.* London: Routledge.

Rose, N. (1996a) Identity, genealogy, history, in S. Hall and P. du Gay (eds) *Questions of Cultural Identity,* pp. 128–50. London: Sage.

Rose, N. (1996b) The death of the social? Re-figuring the territory of government. *Economy and Society,* 25(3): 327–56.

Russell, B. (1997a) Principals to bring budgets in line, *Times Education Supplement,* 21 March: 31.

Russell, B. (1997b) Cuts plunge one in five into debt, *Times Education Supplement,* 13 June.

Russell, B. (1997c) Inspectors attack poor results, *Times Education Supplement,* 18 April: 31.

Russell, B. (1997d) Untrained malady in college management, *Times Education Supplement,* 20 June: 29.

Ryan, D. (1998) The Thatcher government's attack on higher education in historical perspective. *New Left Review,* (227): 3–32.

Ryder, A. (1996) Reform and UK higher education in the enterprise era. *Higher Education Quarterly,* 50(1): 54–70.

Salter, B. and Tapper, T. (1994) *The State and Higher Education.* Essex: Woburn Press.

Scarbrough, H. and Burrell, G. (1996) The axeman cometh: the changing roles and knowledges of middle managers, in S. Clegg and G. Palmer (eds) *The Politics of Management Knowledges,* pp. 173–89. London: Sage.

Schuller, T. (ed.) (1995) *The Changing University.* Buckingham: SRHE & Open University Press.

Scott, P. (1989) Higher education, in D. Kavangh and A. Seldon (eds) *The Thatcher Effect: A Decade of Change,* pp. 198–212. Oxford: Oxford University Press.

Scott, P. (1995) *The Meaning of Mass Higher Education.* Buckingham: SRHE & Open University Press.

Scott, P. and Watson, D. (1994) Managing the curriculum: roles and responsibilities, in J. Bocock and D. Watson (eds) *Managing the University Curriculum: Making Common Cause,* pp. 33–47. Buckingham: SRHE & Open University Press.

Scribbins, K. and Walton, F. (1987) *Staff Appraisal in Further and Higher Education: A Study in Performance Review and Development.* Bristol: Further Education Staff College.

Selway, I. (1995) Stories from the tower: changes in the academic role in a restructured higher education institution. Paper presented at the SRHE annual conference, Heriot-Watt University, Edinburgh, December.

Shattock, M. (1994) *Derby College, Wilmorton: Report of an Enquiry into the Governance and Management of the College.* Coventy: FEFC.

Shore, C. and Roberts, S. (1995) Higher education and the panopticon paradigm: quality assessment as 'disciplinary technology'. *Higher Education Review,* 27(3): 8–17.

Shore, C. and Selwyn, T. (1998) The marketisation of higher education: management, discourse and the politics of performance, in D. Jary and M. Parker (eds) *The New Higher Education*, pp. 153–72. Stafford: Staffordshire University Press.

Shotter, J. (1993) *Conversational Realities: Constructing Life Through Language*. London: Sage.

Shumar, W. (1997) *College for Sale: A Critique of the Commodification of Higher Education*. London: Falmer.

Silverman, D. (1993) *Interpreting Qualitative Data: Methods for Analysing Talk, Texts and Interaction*. London: Sage.

Sinclair, A. (1992) The tyranny of team ideology. *Organisation Studies*, 13(4): 611–26.

Sinclair, J., Ironside, M. and Seifert, R. (1996) Classroom struggle? Market orientated education reforms and their impact on teachers' professional autonomy, labour intensification and resistance. *Work, Employment and Society*, 10(4): 641–61.

Sizer, J. (1988) The management of institutional adaption and change under conditions of financial stringency, in H. Eggin (ed.) *Restructuring Higher Education*, pp. 80–92. Milton Keynes: SRHE & Open University Press.

Smith, D., Bargh, C., Mackay, L. and Scott, P. (1995) Central imperatives and local needs: further education in a centrally driven system. *Higher Education Review*, 28(1): 34–50.

Smyth, J. (1989) Collegiality as a counter discourse to the intrusion of corporate management into higher education. *Journal of Tertiary Educational Administration*, 11(2): 143–55.

Smyth, J. (ed.) (1995) *Academic Work*. Buckingham: SRHE & Open University Press.

Sosteric, M. (1996) Subjectivity and the labour process: a case study in the restaurant industry. *Work, Employment and Society*, 10(2): 297–318.

Staffordshire University (1993) *Annual Review 1991/2*. Stafford: Staffordshire University.

Stainton-Rogers, W. and Stainton-Rogers, R. (1992) *Stories of Childhood: Shifting Agenda of Child Concern*. London: Harvester.

Stewart, J. and Walsh, K. (1992) Change in the management of public services. *Public Administration*, 70(Winter): 499–518.

Stott, C. and Lawson, L. (1997) *Women at the Top in Further Education: FEDA Report 2(2)*. London: FEDA.

Tavares, H. (1996) Classroom management and subjectivities: a genealogy of educational identities. *Educational Theory*, 46(2): 189–201.

Taylor, L. (1994) *The Laurie Taylor guide to Higher Education*. London: Butterworth Heinemann.

Taylor, L. (1998a) *Times Higher Education Supplement*, 3 April: 60.

Taylor, L. (1998b) *Times Higher Education Supplement*, 26 June: 52.

Taylor, L. (1998c) *Times Higher Education Supplement*, 6 March: 56.

Taylor, L. (1998d) *Times Higher Education Supplement*, 1 May: 56.

Taylor, L. (1999) *Times Higher Education Supplement*, 15 January: 60.

Teulings, A.W.M. (1986) Managerial labour processes in organised capitalism: the power of corporate management and the powerlessness of corporate management, in D. Knights and H. Wilmott (eds) *Managing the Labour Process*, pp. 142–65. London: Gower.

Thody, A. (1989) University management observed: a method of studying its unique nature? *Studies in Higher Education*, 14(3): 279–96.

Thomas, H. (1996) Resource allocation in higher education: a cultural perspective. *Research in Post-Compulsory Education*, 1(1): 35–52.

Thomas, H. (1997) Forewarned is forearmed. *Managing HE*, (6), available at http://back.niss.ac.uk/hobsons/mhe/issue6/mhe6p30.html, as at 9 March 1997.

Thomas, R. (1994) Gendered cultures and performance appraisal: the experience of women academics. Paper presented to the British Academy of Management conference, Lancaster University, September.

Thompson, P. (1983) *The Nature of Work: An Introduction to Debates on the Labour Process.* London: Macmillan.

Thompson, P. (1989) Crawling from the wreckage: the labour process and the politics of production, in D. Knights and H. Willmott (eds) *Labour Process Theory*, pp. 95–124. London: Macmillan.

Thompson, P. and Ackrody, S. (1995) All quiet on the workplace front? A critique of recent trends in British industrial sociology. *Sociology*, 29(4): 615–33.

Thompson, P. and McHugh, D. (1990) *Work Organizations* London: Macmillan.

Thompson, P. and McHugh, D. (1995) *Work Organizations*, 2nd edn. London: Macmillan.

Thorne, M. and Cuthbert, R. (1996) Autonomy, bureaucracy and competition: the ABC of control in higher education, in R. Cuthbert (ed.) *Working in Higher Education*, pp. 170–93. Buckingham: SRHE & Open University Press.

Times Higher Education Supplement (1997) Women professors league 1996/7, available at http://www.thes.co.uk/in Statistics Section access on October 14, 1999.

Todd, I. (1995) Strategic management of the further education curriculum, in M. Slowey (ed.) *Implementing Change from Within Universities and Colleges: 10 Personal Accounts*, pp. 125–34. London: Kogan Page.

Touche Ross Management Consultants (1992) *Getting Your College Ready: A Handbook of Guidance.* London: HMSO.

Townley, B. (1993a) Performance appraisal and the emergence of management. *Journal of Management Studies*, 30(2): 222–38.

Townley, B. (1993b) Foucault, power/knowledge, and its relevance for human resource management. *Academy of Management Review*, 18(3): 518–45.

Townley, B. (1994) *Reframing Human Resource Management: Power, Ethics and the Subject at Work.* London: Routledge.

Townley, B. (1997) The institutional logic of performance appraisal. *Organization Studies*, 18(2): 261–80.

Trow, M. (1994) Managerialism and the academic profession: the case of England. *Higher Education Policy*, 7(2): 11–18.

Trowler, P. (1996) Beyond the Robbins Trap: reconceptualising academic responses to change in higher education (or . . . quiet flows the don?). Paper for the 'Dilemmas in Mass Higher Education' conference, Staffordshire University, April.

Trowler, P. (1998) *Academics Responding to Change: New Higher Education Frameworks and Academic Cultures.* Buckingham: SRHE & Open University Press.

Turner, D. and Pratt, J. (1990) Bidding for funds in higher education. *Higher Education Review*, 22(3): 19–33.

Twyman, P. (1985) Management and leadership in further education, in M. Hughes, P. Ribbins and H. Thomas (eds) *Managing Education: The Systems and the Institutions*, pp. 325–42. London: Holt, Rinehart & Winston.

Utley, A. (1994a) Single minded feel the squeeze. *The Times Higher Education Supplement*, 29 April.

Utley, A. (1994b) Opportunity knocks for women managers, *The Times Higher Education Supplement*, 4 October.

Utley, A. (1995) Leeds college overspent £1m. *Times Higher Education Supplement*, 20 October: 1, 3.

Upton, P. (1995) 'Women and management: aspects of gendered power relations in a further education college', unpublished MBA (education) dissertation. University of Leicester.

Usher, R. and Edwards, R. (1994) *Postmodernism and Education: Different Voices, Different Worlds.* London: Routledge.

Utley, A. (1994) Single-minded feel the squeeze, *Times Higher Education Supplement,* 29 April: 6.

Utley, A. (1997) Sector £800 in red, *Times Higher Education Supplement,* 5 December: 1.

van Dijk, T.A. (ed.) (1985) *Handbook of Discourse Analysis, vol. 3: Dialogue and Discourse.* London: Academic Press.

Walker, M. (1997) Women in the academy: ambiguity and complexity in a South African University. *Gender and Education,* 9(3): 365–81.

Walker, M. (1998) Academic identities: women on a South African landscape. *British Journal of Sociology of Education,* 19(3): 335–54.

Ward, L. (1995) Women who surf the gender network, *Times Education Supplement,* 1 December: 25.

Ward, L. (1996) Principals opting for early retirement, *Times Education Supplement,* 18 October: 23.

Ward, R. (1995) Industrial relations strategies and tactics, in D. Warner and E. Crosthwaite (eds) *Human Resource Management in Higher and Further Education,* pp. 152–70. Buckingham: SRHE & Open University Press.

Warner, D. and Crosthwaite, E. (eds) (1995) *Human Resource Management in Higher and Further Education.* Buckingham: SRHE & Open University Press.

Warner, D. and Palfreyman, D. (eds) (1996) *Higher Education Management: The Key Elements.* Buckingham: SRHE & Open University Press.

Watson, T. (1994) *In Search of Management: Culture, Chaos and Control in Managerial Work.* London: Routledge.

Watson, D. and House, D. (1995) Managing change, in D. Warner and E. Crosthwaite (eds) *Human Resource Management in Higher and Further Education.* Buckingham: Open University Press.

Webb, A. (1994) Two tales from a reluctant manager, in S. Weil (ed.) *Introducing Change from the Top in Universities and Colleges: 10 Personal Accounts,* pp. 41–55. London: Kogan Page.

Weedon, C. (1987) *Feminist Practice and Post-structuralist Theory.* Oxford: Blackwell.

Weick, K. (1976) Educational institutions as loosely coupled systems. *Administrative Science Quarterly,* 21(1): 1–19.

Weil, S. (1994) Bringing about cultural change in colleges and universities: the power and potential of story, in S. Weil (ed.) *Introducing Change from the Top in Universities and Colleges: 10 Personal Accounts,* pp. 149–67. London: Kogan Page.

Wendt, R. (1994) Learning to 'walk the talk', a critical tale of the micropolitics of a total quality university. *Management Communication Quarterly,* 8(1): 5–45.

Wetherell, M. and Potter, J. (1992) *Mapping the Language of Racism: Discourse and the Legitimation of Exploitation.* London: Harvester.

Whitehead, S. (1995) Men manager: the gendered/gendering subject. Paper presented to the 'Understanding the Social World' conference, University of Huddersfield, 17–19 July.

Whitehead, S. (1996a) 'Public and private men: masculinities at work in education management', unpublished PhD thesis. Leeds Metropolitan University.

Whitehead, S. (1996b) Men/managers and the shifting discourses of post-compulsory education. *Research in Post-Compulsory Education,* 1(2): 151–68.

Whitehead, S. (1997a) The gendered transition of education management. Paper presented to the 'Gender and Education' international conference 'Transitions 97', University of Warwick, April.

Whitehead, S. (1997b) Identifying the subject at work: arenas of power/resistance in education management. Paper presented to the British Sociological Association annual conference 'Power/Resistance', University of York, April.

Whitley, R. (1989) On the nature of managerial tasks and skills: their distinguishing characteristics and organization. *Journal of Management Studies*, 26(3): 209–23.

Whyte, G. (1994) 'The enterprising college', unpublished PhD thesis. University of Nottingham.

Wild, R. (1994) Barriers to women's promotion in further education. *Journal of Further and Higher Education*, 18(3): 83–98.

Williams, E. (1995) Lipstick and white collars, *Times Higher Education Supplement*, 28 July: 18–19.

Williams, G. (1992) *Changing Patterns of Finance in Higher Education*. Buckingham: SRHE & Open University Press.

Williams, M. and May, T. (1996) *Introduction to the Philosophy of Social Science*. London: UCL Press.

Willmott, H. (1989) Subjectivity and the dialectics of praxis: opening up the core of labour process analysis, in D. Knights and H. Willmott (eds) *Labour Process Theory*, pp. 336–78. London: Macmillan.

Willmott, H. (1993) Strength is ignorance, slavery is freedom: managing culture in modern organizations. *Journal of Management Studies*, 30(4): 515–52.

Willmott, H. (1994) Bringing agency (back) into organizational analysis: responding to the crisis of (post)modernity, in J. Hassard and M. Parker (eds) *Towards a New Theory of Organizations*, pp. 87–130. London: Routledge.

Willmott, H. (1995) Managing the academics: commodification and control in the development of university education in the UK. *Human Relations*, 48(9): 993–1027.

Willmott, H. (1998) Rethinking management and managerial work: capitalisms, control and subjectivity. *Human Relations*, 50(11): 1329–59.

Willocks, L. and Harrow, J. (1992) (eds) *Rediscovering Public Services Management*. London: McGraw-Hill.

Wilson, A. (1994) The management of change in a large civic university, in S. Weil (ed.) *Introducing Change from the Top in Universities and Colleges: 10 Personal Accounts*. London: Kogan Page.

Wilson, T. (1991) The proletarianisation of academic labour. *Industrial Relations Journal*, 22(4): 250–62.

Winter, R. (1995) The university of life plc: the 'industrialisation' of higher education? in J. Smyth (ed.) *Academic Work*, pp. 129–43. Buckingham: SRHE & Open University Press.

Yeatman, A. (1995) The gendered management of equity-oriented change in higher education, in J. Smyth (ed.) *Academic Work*, pp. 195–205. Buckingham: SRHE & Open University Press.

Index

242 *Making Managers in Universities and Colleges*

University/ies, 101
annual reports, 102, 108
as big business, 124–5
as business-like, 104, 126
collegiality, 133
corporate entity, 112
corporate surveillance mechanism, 112
fratriarchies in, 186–7
intensively managed, 102
loosely coupled, 196
management and, 198
management types, 195–6
managers as small business people, 115
man-managed, 189–99
mix of discourses in, 102
new organizational forms, 201
nuclear families and, 190–1
performance, 114
post-1992, 102, 108, 113, 114, 115, 116, 117, 122, 195, 203
power relations and, 102–3
pre-1992, 102, 108, 113–14, 122, 203
production processes in, 104
project teams in, 193
public enterprise, 102
research strategies, 114
resistance to management, 114
service providers, 107
sexism in, 189
staff overloading, 114
as subject positions and, 107
without 'managers', 136
University of Sheffield annual report, 108–13
Urban College, 78–80, 84, 85, 152, 155, 156, 180
gender and management in, 174

van Dijk, T.A., 209
vice-chancellors, 101, 102
access to research sites, 204
as chief executives, 126–7
didacticism and, 126
female, 195
ideological struggle and, 107
labour power and, 105
power relations and, 103
subject positions and, 105
Vickers, R., 172

voice, 211
Vurdusakis, T., 23

Waikato University in New Zealand, 174
Walker, M., 189
Walsh, K., 49, 180
Walton, F., 64
Ward, L., 178
Ward, Roger (former Head College Employers Forum and Association of Colleges), 1, 62, 151
Warner, D., 6, 24, 65, 194
Watson, D., 24, 64, 65, 70, 72, 182
Watson, T., 45, 142, 152, 210
Webb, A., 27
Weedon, C., 172
Weick, K., 196
Weil, S., 25–6
Weiner, G., 195
Wetherell, M., 39, 209
Whitehead, S., 17–20, 29, 79, 171, 177, 178, 190
Whitley, 31, 35
Whyte, G., 7, 68
Williams, G., 54, 55, 58, 60
Williams, M., 11
Willmott, H., xi, 9, 11, 20, 36, 23, 34, 36, 41, 72, 146
Willocks, L., 48
Wilson, Professor Alan (Vice-Chancellor, University of Leeds), 113–14
Wilson, T., 20
Winter, R., 20, 104
Witz, A., 210
wo-managing (universities), 190–6
women
as change agents, 174
outsiders to management, 174
senior posts and, 185
women and management, 173
women managers, 28
see gender
Women Professors League, 185
women's networks, 195
work, 28–9
work organizations
gender and, 172–3
world openness, 36
writing
as practice of bureaucracy, 121

Yeatman, A., 174, 184, 188

The Society for Research into Higher Education

The Society for Research into Higher Education (SRHE) exists to stimulate and coordinate research into all aspects of higher education. It aims to improve the quality of higher education through the encouragement of debate and publication on issues of policy, on the organization and management of higher education institutions, and on the curriculum, teaching and learning methods.

The Society is entirely independent and receives no subsidies, although individual events often receive sponsorship from business or industry. The Society is financed through corporate and individual subscriptions and has members from many parts of the world.

Under the imprint *SRHE & Open University Press*, the Society is a specialist publisher of research, having over 80 titles in print. In addition to *SRHE News*, the Society's newsletter, the Society publishes three journals: *Studies in Higher Education* (three issues a year), *Higher Education Quarterly* and *Research into Higher Education Abstracts* (three issues a year).

The Society runs frequent conferences, consultations, seminars and other events. The annual conference in December is organized at and with a higher education institution. There are a growing number of networks which focus on particular areas of interest, including:

Access	Learning Environment
Assessment	Legal Education
Consultants	Managing Innovation
Curriculum Development	New Technology for Learning
Eastern Europe	Postgraduate Issues
Educational Development Research	Quantitative Studies
FE/HE	Student Development
Funding	Vocational Qualifications
Graduate Employment	

Benefits to members

Individual

- The opportunity to participate in the Society's networks

- Reduced rates for the annual conferences
- Free copies of *Research into Higher Education Abstracts*
- Reduced rates for *Studies in Higher Education*
- Reduced rates for *Higher Education Quarterly*
- Free copy of *Register of Members' Research Interests* – includes valuable reference material on research being pursued by the Society's members
- Free copy of occasional in-house publications, e.g. *The Thirtieth Anniversary Seminars Presented by the Vice-Presidents*
- Free copies of *SRHE News* which informs members of the Society's activities and provides a calendar of events, with additional material provided in regular mailings
- A 35 per cent discount on all SRHE/Open University Press books
- Access to HESA statistics for student members
- The opportunity for you to apply for the annual research grants
- Inclusion of your research in the *Register of Members' Research Interests*

Corporate

- Reduced rates for the annual conferences
- The opportunity for members of the Institution to attend SRHE's network events at reduced rates
- Free copies of *Research into Higher Education Abstracts*
- Free copies of *Studies in Higher Education*
- Free copies of *Register of Members' Research Interests* – includes valuable reference material on research being pursued by the Society's members
- Free copy of occasional in-house publications
- Free copies of *SRHE News*
- A 35 per cent discount on all SRHE/Open University Press books
- Access to HESA statistics for research for students of the Institution
- The opportunity for members of the Institution to submit applications for the Society's research grants
- The opportunity to work with the Society and co-host conferences
- The opportunity to include in the *Register of Members' Research Interest* your Institution's research into aspects of higher education

Membership details: SRHE, 3 Devonshire Street, London W1N 2BA, UK. Tel: 020 7637 2766. Fax: 020 7637 2781. email: srhe@mailbox.ulcc.ac.uk world wide web: http://www.srhe.ac.uk./srhe/ *Catalogue*: SRHE & Open University Press, Celtic Court, 22 Ballmoor, Buckingham MK18 1XW. Tel: 01280 823388. Fax: 01280 823233. email: enquiries@openup.co.uk